TEA
LEA
STR
PHY
HAN
STU

TEACHING AND LEARNING STRATEGIES FOR PHYSICALLY HANDICAPPED STUDENTS

Mary Lynne Calhoun, Ph.D.
Coordinator of Training
Human Development Center
Winthrop College
Rock Hill, South Carolina

and

Margaret F. Hawisher, Ph.D.
Assistant Professor
Department of Special Education
Winthrop College
Rock Hill, South Carolina

University Park Press
Baltimore

UNIVERSITY PARK PRESS
International Publishers in Science, Medicine, and Education
233 East Redwood Street
Baltimore, Maryland 21202

Composed by University Park Press, Typesetting Division.
Manufactured in the United States of America by
Universal Lithographers, Inc., and The Maple Press Company.

Library of Congress Cataloging in Publication Data

Calhoun, Mary Lynne.
Teaching and learning strategies for physically handicapped students.

Bibliography: p.
1. Physically handicapped children — Education. I. Hawisher, Margaret F., joint author. II. Title. [DNLM: 1. Education, Special. 2. Handicapped.
LC4015   C152t]
LC4215.C29   371.9'1   79-12255
ISBN O-8391-1394-3

CONTENTS

PREFACE

This book is for teachers of children with physical disabilities. At this time, more physically handicapped children are going to school than ever before, because of both recent medical advances and newly enacted legislation that requires appropriate educational programming for all handicapped children. There is a strong need for teachers and other school personnel to develop thoughtful, well researched and caring guidelines for establishing new programs and improving existing programs for physically handicapped children and young people. This text is designed to help school personnel as they attempt to meet this need.

The practical issues of setting up a classroom program, finding appropriate assessment techniques, developing teaching materials, and working with other professionals are discussed within the framework of the current research on the educational needs of the physically handicapped population.

Questions are raised for which the answers are still only tentative. Because of the small number of physically handicapped children in schools and because of the great diversity of their educational needs, available research is often inconclusive. Teaching techniques and materials that might be helpful to many physically handicapped children may not be disseminated because of the isolation of individual teachers and programs. It is hoped that this book will make a start in the sharing of ideas. The authors look forward to hearing from educators about other teaching/learning strategies that work well.

In this text we hope to communicate the following professional philosophy:

1. Although it is important for teachers to be aware of the physical limitations of handicapped children, a more crucial concern is how best to teach the child to maximize his/her intellectual potential.
2. The principle of normalization is valued in the education of physically handicapped children: They are more like other children than they are different from them, and they should be served in settings that are as similar to regular education programs as possible.
3. The teacher of physically handicapped students must be creative and flexible — she must be a problem solver.

ACKNOWLEDGMENTS

We are grateful for the support of friends and colleagues in this project. Karen Hambright, a teacher of orthopaedically handicapped students in Union County, S.C., served as research assistant. Special thanks are due to Dan Bright and Joel Nichols for their fine photography and to Paige McDaniel Bridges for her sensitive illustrations. We appreciate the help of the following programs in obtaining photographs:

Human Development Center
    Winthrop College
    Rock Hill, South Carolina
Metro Center
    Charlotte-Mecklenburg Public Schools
    Charlotte, North Carolina
Cerebral Palsy Developmental Center
    Charlotte, North Carolina

The curriculum goals in Chapter 8 are an outgrowth of our consultant work with the Model Vocational OH Project, Richland School District no. 1, Columbia, South Carolina. We are grateful to Barbara Bradford, project director, and Carol Fusco, South Carolina Department of Education consultant to programs for the physically handicapped, for the opportunity to work with this fine project.

Special thanks are given to the students and staff of Condon School, Cincinnati, Ohio, 1968–70, who provided the incentive for the development of this book. They convinced a beginning teacher that, for vocational satisfaction, nothing can match the stimulation and creative struggle of finding effective teaching/learning strategies for severely physically handicapped students.

Our families have faced a creative challenge in guiding us through this project. Their loving support has been extraordinary, and we are grateful to Lawrence and Eliza Calhoun and Tommy, David, Karen, and Hal Hawisher.

TEACHING AND LEARNING STRATEGIES FOR PHYSICALLY HANDICAPPED STUDENTS

1

EDUCATION FOR ALL HANDICAPPED CHILDREN

Figure 1-1. P.L. 94-142, The Education for All Handicapped Children Act, guarantees the availability of special education services to all who need them.

Since the time of the earliest settlements the ideal of education for all American children has been a hallmark of the American dream. As in the case of many ideals, however, the reality has fallen short of the dream.

Until very recently, "education for all children" was interpreted to mean all those children who were able to profit from the regular classroom program. This interpretation effectively excluded from public schools children who were mentally retarded, physically handicapped, or emotionally disturbed. Compulsory attendance laws in many states contained provisions similar to those in the Nevada statutes that provided a child could be excluded from school when "the child's physical or mental condition or attitude is such as to prevent or render inadvisable his attendance at school or his application to study" (Spillane, 1975).

In practical terms, these provisions meant that a child in braces who was unable to walk down the steps to the cafeteria could be excluded from school, as could a child with a spinal cord injury who could not develop bladder control, or a cerebral palsied child who was unable to walk and who had speech and learning problems.

In spite of this flaw in state compulsory attendance laws, some physically handicapped children found excellent educational opportunities available to them in special schools or classes provided by their school districts; others found minimal educational opportunities through two or three hours a week of homebound instruction or private programs established by foundations (such as the Easter Seal Society) or parent groups (Benison, 1976). Many physically handicapped children, however, because of an accident of geography or the nature of their individual handicaps, had been denied any educational opportunity whatsoever.

A major step toward the educational ideal was taken on September 1, 1978, when it became a violation of federal law to deny a free, appropriate, public education to any handicapped child. The Education for All Handicapped Children Act (P.L. 94-142), which was signed into law by President Gerald R. Ford in September, 1975, has four major purposes:

1. To guarantee the availability of special education services to handicapped children and youth
2. To ensure fairness in decision-making about special education services for handicapped children and youth
3. To establish quality control — clear management and auditing requirements for special education at all levels of government
4. To provide financial assistance in the form of federal funds to state and local governments as they provide educational services. (Abeson and Weintraub, 1977)

This important act defines special education as "the specially designed instruction at no cost to parents or guardians, to meet the unique needs of a handicapped child, including classroom instruction, instruction in physical education, home instruction and instruction in hospitals and institutions" (Abeson and Weintraub, 1977). The thrust of this legislation, then, not only mandates that school systems provide services for all handicapped children, but also ensures that those services be of high quality.

The heart of P.L. 94-142 is the requirement of a written individualized educational program (IEP); this program is a written description of the special education and related services aspects of a child's individual education program. The IEP must address itself to the unique needs of a particular child by stating present levels of performance, annual goals, short-term objectives, the related services required, and a method for evaluating progress. The IEP is developed by school personnel involved in assessment and special services; parental participation is encouraged in the development, implementation, and review of the plan.

Thus, the ideal of free education for all children has now been extended to include individually planned programs to meet the needs of the handicapped. For this new ideal, however, reality may once again fall short of the dream. Spillane (1975) points out that the connection between legislation and funding in education is quite simple: "The politicians mandate that the schools do a particular thing and never give enough money so that we can do a decent job." Laws can be written quickly; effective services are not provided as quickly. The new programs mandated by P.L. 94-142 will be expensive; there will sometimes be a lack of trained personnel to provide services; shortcuts may be sought. In addition to fiscal and personnel complexities, some programs may not be of high quality because so little is known about meeting the unique educational needs of the individual children in the particular program.

Physically handicapped children may present the kinds of learning and management problems that make implementation of P.L. 94-142 quite difficult. It is the purpose of this book, then, to facilitate the development of strong, high-quality programs that will meet the unique needs of this group. This chapter describes the physically handicapped school population in general terms. The next chapter focuses on specific handicapping conditions and the special educational needs associated with each. Other chapters discuss techniques for assessing potential and setting educational goals, establishing school programs to provide the "least restrictive environment" for persons with physical handicaps, adaptations and modifications of the school curriculum, a description of interdisciplinary team approaches to provide the needed related services, and issues in advocacy for the physically handicapped.

The requirements of the law are stated throughout the book, and suggestions are made to facilitate compliance with these requirements, always keeping in mind the spirit of the ideal: that every child — in particular, every physically handicapped child — deserves access to an education that is not only free, but also so well planned and executed that physically handicapped children will grow, learn, and develop to the fullest extent of their capabilities.

DEFINING THE POPULATION: CAN WE FIND A LABEL?

Creating a one-phrase label for the children described in this book is no easy matter, and even if it were, there remains the question of whether labeling itself is an inherently detrimental process. There are at least two major difficulties in defining the population with special educational needs due to physical disorders. The first difficulty is that professionals, service agencies, parents, and handicapped persons themselves do not use one term consistently. Among the labels used are these, compiled by Fair (1977):

orthopaedically handicapped
physically disabled
physically handicapped
crippled
crippled and other health impaired (COHI)
physically and other health impaired

This wide variety of labels is generally considered to apply to those persons whose range of motion is restricted or whose stamina is limited to the extent that they require a special education program. The group includes children with crippling conditions or chronic health problems, but does not include those whose primary handicap is visual or auditory impairment (Calovini, 1969). Children with visual and auditory disabilities (blind, visually impaired, deaf, hard-of-hearing, deaf-blind) are usually served in special education programs designed to meet the special needs of these particular groups. Because some children with physical disabilities may also have sensory impairment, however, assessment and curriculum adaptations for visual and auditory impairment are mentioned in this text.

The second major difficulty in labeling is the distinction that is sometimes made between the terms "disability" and "handicap." Although these words are often used interchangeably, some clinicians make an important (although inconsistent) distinction between them, and feel strongly about the desirability of using one term over the other.

A disability, according to Wright (1960), has an objective aspect that can be described by a physician. It is a quantifiable, measureable concept. A handicap, on the other hand, reflects a complex somatopsychological relationship. A handicap is the cumulative result of the obstacles that the disability imposes between the individual and his maximum functional level. Disability is seen as a more desirable term because it makes no inferences about the difficulties the person may encounter; it states the fact of physical impairment.

However, this choice of terminology is not universally accepted. A protest against the use of the term disability has recently been issued by Heisler (1977), herself a psychologist with a handicapping polio residual. Heisler cites the dictionary definition of *handicap:* "any disadvantage or hindrance making success in an undertaking more difficult," while *disable* is defined as "to render physically or mentally incapable of proper or effective action." Because many people with handicaps are effective and capable, and the reality of physical impairment does make many undertakings more difficult, Heisler strongly advocates the use of the term handicap.

Both terms — physically handicapped and physically disabled — are used in this book. The term *physical disability* is used to refer, in Wright's (1960) sense, to the measurable, quantifiable aspects of the medical condition. The term *physical handicap* is the preferred term for use in describing the special needs of this particular population of school-age children with physical disabilities of such significance that special educational measures are necessary to help them develop to their fullest potential.

There are school-age children with physical disabilities who do not meet this definition. A child may have cerebral palsy to such a mild degree that, although there are minor incoordination problems, the child is handling a regular school program comfortably and well. A child may be missing a limb but, using a prosthesis to make the disability unnoticeable, he may handle a regular program, even many sports, with ease.

The focus of this discussion is on children who are handicapped because their physical disability impairs their mobility, coordination, stamina, communication, or learning ability to the extent that school-related goals are indeed much more difficult to accomplish, and they require special educational intervention. Because they are handicapped, these children are eligible for the special services and protection afforded by P.L. 94-142.

This discussion of the appropriate name for this group of people with special needs serves to illustrate the power of words in conveying information about people. The label is a short-hand way of conveying some common characteristics, but it is also possible that the labeling process can have harmful effects. By using the term "handicapped person" we may focus more on "handicap" than on "person," thus limiting expectations and chances for genuine human encounters.

The whole question of using labels in special education has been under considerable fire for many years. Labels such as "handicapped," "disabled," "mentally retarded," and "emotionally disturbed" have been used to obtain financial aid for programs for handicapped children (Blatt, 1972); unfortunately, they also lower teachers' expectations and children's self-esteem (Jones, 1972). A label can quickly convey something of the essence of a person's characteristics or functions, but it can also strip that person of some unique feature (Gallagher, 1972).

Ideally, the label "physically handicapped" would convey the message that a person has some special needs to which the system should address itself. Further, the label could often be put aside to enable the physically handicapped child to be seen first as a child more like other children than different from them.

An important definition of this special population was developed in 1970 by a task force on the preparation of teachers of crippled children, sponsored by the Bureau of Education for the Handicapped, U.S. Office of Education. This definition, using the terms "crippled and other health impaired" (COHI), is as follows:

> The population is composed of those children and adults who as a result of permanent, temporary or intermittent physical or medical disabilities require modifications in curriculum or instructional strategies.
> Frequent separation from family and a lack of adequate parental guidance contribute to secondary emotional problems of the COHI population.
> The child's physical limitations are often the basis of functional deficits. The development of realistic expectation levels requires the identification of additional and unique instructional materials, equipment and strategies for evaluation. (Connor, Wald, and Cohen, 1970)

PHYSICALLY HANDICAPPED CHILDREN: VARIABLES TO CONSIDER

The above definition examines the physically handicapped population in three separate dimensions: 1) a physical definition of the problems; 2) some likely functional problems; and 3) desirable program modifications. To understand the special educational needs of physically handicapped children, each of these elements must be considered; each is discussed here in turn.

Physical Definition of the Problem

Special education has been widely criticized from both within and without the field for what has been seen as an inappropriate adherence to a medical model (Wyatt, 1970). The medical model, as practiced in special education, places emphasis on making a differential diagnosis, identifying the cause of the problem, and grouping together persons with the same disability for similar treatment. This approach has been seen as especially inappropriate for children whose handicapping conditions are most apparent in learning situations, that is, the mentally retarded or the learning disabled. Knowing that a child is mentally retarded because of a genetic disorder or learning disabled because of anoxia at birth provides little help in meeting the educational needs of that child. A psychological or behavioral model that focuses on the particular task to be learned and the individual elements of that task that the child can or cannot accomplish is seen as a much more useful and helpful approach to the solution of educational problems (Wollinsky, 1976).

For physically handicapped children, however, medical information has great utility. This is the most medically oriented of all the categories of special education (Wilson, 1973), and for good reason: the functional problems of these children are directly related to their medical problems.

Certain aspects of the medical diagnosis have particular relevance for educational planning. (In this discussion, some specific handicapping conditions are used as illustration; these conditions are described more fully in Chapter 2.) The medical aspects are as follows:

Prognosis   Is this a stable condition or will it change over time? Will it get better or worse? What variables will influence its progress? Children with temporary orthopaedic handicaps, such as Legg-Perthes disease, will require very different educational planning than that required by children with a stable lifelong handicapping condition such as cerebral palsy. Children with cerebral palsy, in turn, will require different kinds of help than those appropriate to a child with a progressive degenerative condition such as muscular dystrophy.

Symptoms-Description of Condition   The teacher should be aware of exactly what physical limitations are imposed on the child because of the disability. It is important to know if the child may be experiencing pain, as might be the case with juvenile rheumatoid arthritis. It is equally important to know if there are health hazards that mandate special protection or care, as is the case with osteogenesis imperfecta. The teacher should know about medications the child is taking and about allergies or other physical problems that would influence the day-to-day school life. This information provides guidelines for reasonable expectations about a child's participation in learning activities and helps the teacher avoid the extremes of overprotection on the one hand and carelessness or callousness on the other.

Age of Onset The length of time the child has had the handicapping condition has educational relevance; a child who has been paralyzed from birth has had very different experiences than those of children who could move and explore their environment. In a real sense, the child handicapped from birth is "environmentally disadvantaged," and extra effort is needed to compensate for the possible deficit in exploratory experiences. On the other hand, a child who has only recently acquired or developed a physical handicap may be facing really difficult adjustment problems that require special support.

Related Disorders Physical handicaps are often part of syndromes; that is, they are part of a group of symptoms that often occur together. If the teacher is aware of the related disorders that are associated with handicapping conditions, he or she will be more likely to seek help if the possibility of a related problem is noted. An example is the relatively frequent occurrence of hearing impairment in conjunction with athetoid cerebral palsy. If a child with athetoid cerebral palsy is having trouble learning to talk, the teacher might attribute this difficulty to the physical handicap and keep trying the same old techniques. If, however, the teacher is familiar with the possibility of hearing loss, a hearing evaluation might be sought, resulting in more appropriate intervention.

Functional Problems

The heart of the educational process is the facilitation of the development of persons who are able to make thoughtful judgments, relate to others, and function independently in the world. Physically handicapping conditions often become stumbling blocks in this kind of development. The teacher of physically handicapped children must be aware of the functional difficulties faced by the handicapped child and develop strategies for ameliorating or compensating for them. Some of these functional difficulties are as follows:

Intellectual Impairment While many physically handicapped children have intellectual potential in the average or above average ranges, others, particularly those with central nervous system damage, experience the additional handicap of mental retardation or severe learning disabilities. For example, one study of 1003 children with cerebral palsy found 59% to have IQs below 70 — the usual cut-off point in defining mental retardation (Hohman and Freedheim, 1958).

The best possible measurement of intellectual potential should be obtained to assist in educational planning. Each handicapped child has the right to the most *appropriate* education; for some children, that will mean an educational program that emphasizes language, self-care, and social skills rather than academics. It must be noted that conventional intelligence testing is often inappropriate for physically handicapped persons because traditional means of communication (talking and writing) are sometimes impaired. This means that a child may have knowledge and understanding that he or she is not able to communicate, and his score will then be spuriously low. In making a determination of intellectual impairment, it is essential that this kind of misdiagnosis be avoided.

Guidelines for adapting intelligence tests to the special needs of physically handicapped children can be found in Chapter 5.

Communication Skills   The ability to receive and to express language is the core of the learning process. Some physically handicapped children are limited in their language functioning because of motor involvement, hearing impairment, physical anomalies, or central nervous system damage. A functional analysis of the child's ability to receive and express language and the development of a plan to develop communication skills are essential in these cases.

Motor Development   Motor functions involve balance, control, coordination, and inhibition of associated movements (Johnston and Magrab, 1976). These motor functions make possible the gross motor skills of sitting, creeping, crawling, standing, and walking, and the fine motor skills such as reaching, grasping, releasing, writing with a pencil, cutting with scissors, and many more.

Many physically handicapping conditions adversely affect motor development and motor skills. For example, a child with advanced muscular dystrophy may have such limited muscle function that he is practically immobile. A child with athetoid cerebral palsy may be so incoordinated that purposeful hand function seems impossible. A child with an upper limb absence will need to learn special one-handed techniques for the fine motor skills that for most of us are two-handed jobs.

Having accurate knowledge of which motor activities are possible for the child, which are not yet possible but are developing, and which are out of the question, will guide the teacher in making decisions about what skills can be remediated and what skill deficiencies must be compensated for. Physical therapists and occupational therapists can be very helpful in gathering this information. Their roles are discussed more fully in Chapter 9.

Social/Adaptive Behavior   Being courteous, considerate of others, making and keeping friends, feeling good about oneself, being a responsible citizen, and functioning independently in the world are all desirable outcomes of the educational process. The road to maturity and independence is never totally smooth, and physically handicapped children have some special obstacles that other children don't face. Physically handicapped children as a group have fewer appropriate opportunities for independence than others their age: restricted mobility may make environmental explorations quite difficult; concern for a child's comfort and safety may inhibit a parent's willingness to allow explorations. The emotional climate in which the physically handicapped child finds himself may also differ considerably from that of other children. More pain, more hospitalizations, more curiosity and pity from others contribute to this "differentness." Independence is further hampered by difficulty in attaining the motor skills necessary to feed, dress, toilet, and transport oneself.

It should be clear that direct teaching of personal-social-independence skills to physically handicapped children is an integral part of the teacher's job. Consideration of the child's skills in these areas is necessary for effective program planning.

Program Modifications

The final dimension to be considered in good educational planning for physically handicapped children is that of program modification. In order to serve physically handicapped children in the "least restrictive environment," school environments must become less restrictive. Many schools still have architectural barriers that limit the participation of physically handicapped youngsters: doors and bathroom stalls must be wide enough for wheelchairs; slick hallways and steep stairways must be modified with handrails and ramps; and classrooms with rows of desks must have pathways cleared.

In addition to eliminating architectural barriers, the environment can be made less restrictive by modifying the instructional program. Techniques that take into consideration physical and communication limitations, and goals that are directed toward the special problems faced by individual children will make great strides in providing an appropriate education. Many of these techniques require special equipment; all will require a sensitivity to individual differences in learning rate and style. Most of the later chapters of this book provide information that can lead to more effective program modification.

Population Trends

The kinds of physical handicaps found among school children have changed dramatically over the last few years. It is not possible to be comfortable about predicting future trends because the causes of changes in the population are diverse: medical advancement has both decreased and increased the numbers and types of handicaps, and social changes have increased and decreased the number and types of handicaps. There is cause for both weeping and rejoicing.

The following statistics, indicating the number of handicapped children in special schools in England (Tew, 1973), illustrate the changing population trends:

	1964	1968	1970
cerebral palsy	2,451	2,755	2,944
poliomyelitis	674	442	316
spina bifida	566	1,046	1,533

This chart illustrates the significant decrease in crippling conditions resulting from infectious diseases, with polio being the prime example. Poliomyelitis accounted for 14.5% of the physically handicapped school population of America in 1950, 7% in 1960, and less than that today (Outland, 1970). The widespread use of the Salk and Sabin vaccines does not guarantee that there will be no more polio outbreaks, but the chances of an outbreak have been dramatically reduced.

Another infectious disease that can result in physical handicaps is rubella (German measles). This disease is mild in adults, usually causing only 2–3 days of discomfort, but if a woman contracts the disease in the first trimester of pregnancy, the results can be devastating for the fetus. A rubella epidemic in 1964 produced a group of crippled children who were mentally retarded and who had vision and hearing problems (Outland, 1970). A rubella vaccine is now available that makes another such epidemic unlikely.

Medical science then, through the discovery of important vaccines, has greatly limited the incidence of certain handicapping conditions. Medical advances do not always limit the incidence of handicapping conditions in schools; sometimes these advances increase the number of physically handicapped children by making it possible for severely handicapped children to live much longer. A few years ago many severely handicapped children would have died shortly after birth, but recent medical advances now ensure their survival well into their school years.

An example of this trend can be found in the case of spina bifida, a birth defect that is a disorder of the spine and that can cause a protrusion of neural tissue through an opening in the spine (myelomeningocele). A few years ago, few children with this condition survived to school age. Today, the medical advances of surgical techniques in closing the spinal defect as early as the first day of life and antibiotics that reduce the risk of infection have greatly increased the life expectancy of children with spina bifida (Sugar and Ames, 1965). A high percentage of children with this birth defect — possibly as many as two-thirds — are now able to go to school because of advances in medical science.

Social changes have also produced changes in the make-up of the physically handicapped population. The availability of prenatal tests for birth defects (such as amniocentesis) and the loosening of legal and societal restrictions on abortion have reduced the incidence of some genetic disorders. However, while "single cause" diseases are on the decline, other kinds of handicapping conditions (particularly those with multiple causes and complex manifestations) are increasing. The increase in teen-age pregnancies and drug and alcohol abuse has increased the incidence of children born with central nervous system damage (such as cerebral palsy) and multiple birth defects. Also on the increase are crippling conditions resulting from trauma: automobile, motorcycle, and sporting accidents account for many cases of paraplegia and quadriplegia; child abuse accounts for other traumatic injuries. In 1970, for example, the National Safety Council estimated that 50,000 children (over half of whom were under five years of age) were permanently crippled or disabled by accidents (Outland, 1970).

A nationwide survey conducted in 1963-1965 and again in 1971 to measure the prevalence of certain impairments in the United States reflects some of these changes (Wilder, 1975). Table 1-1 reports some results of this survey. In looking at the prevalence of certain impairments of the civilian population not confined to institutions, it can be noted that the incidence of paralysis has decreased, probably due to progress in fighting polio. The prevalence of amputation and other orthopaedic problems has remained essentially unchanged over the 8-year period. The prevalence of speech, visual, and hearing impairments has increased; therefore, the possibility of these related disorders occurring along with other physical disabilities has also increased.

These changes in the population are reflected by the changing educational needs of physically handicapped children in schools. Twenty years ago, classes for the orthopaedically handicapped in special and regular schools were composed primarily of students with "normal" IQs who had sufficient mobility and dexterity to accomplish traditional school work (Magnussen, 1976).

These days, ambulatory students are likely to be integrated into regular programs, and more non-ambulatory, multiply handicapped children find their way into special school programs. A recent survey of teachers of the physically handicapped found that multiple handicaps were often found in the children served, and that the most frequently mentioned secondary handicaps were mental retardation, learning disabilities, visual impairments, hearing impairments, emotional disturbance, and speech problems (Kolstoe, 1977). For many of these severely handicapped children, an attempt to water down a "normal" school program would be inappropriate. Instead, special techniques, a special alertness to progress, and intervention that will facilitate the most normal development possible are needed.

Table 1-1. Prevalence of selected impairments reported in health interviews and number per 1000 persons, by type of impairment: United States, 1971 and July 1963–June 1965

Selected Impairments	1971		July 1963–June 1965	
	Number in thousands	Number per 1000 persons	Number in thousands	Number per 1000 persons
Visual impairments	9596	47.4	5390	28.8
Hearing impairments	14491	71.6	8549	45.7
Speech defects	1934	9.6	1298	6.9
*Paralysis, complete or partial	1392	6.9	1516	8.1
*Absence of major extremities	274	1.4	257	1.4
*Orthopaedic impairments (except paralysis or absence):				
Back or spine	8018	39.6	6486	34.7
Upper extremity & shoulder	2440	12.1	2925	15.6
Lower extremity & hip	7387	36.5	6623	35.4
Other and multiple, N.E.C. of limbs, back, and trunk	1034	5.1	1709	9.1

From Wilder, 1975.

SUMMARY

Physically handicapped children are a small hard-to-define group, hetero-geneous in their educational needs and strengths. The population has shifted in recent years to include more non-ambulatory multihandicapped students, who, as a group, have often been unserved (or underserved) in American public schools. The educational needs of this group have a greater chance of being met because of the recent passage of Public Law 94-142, the Education for All Handicapped Children Act, which guarantees special education services to all handicapped children and youth. To comply with the spirit as well as the letter of the law, teachers must learn new skills, explore new areas of knowledge, and develop sensitivity and creativity to break down the barriers to the fullest possible life for persons with physical handicaps.

LITERATURE CITED

Abeson, A., and Weintraub, F. Understanding the individualized education pro-gram. In: S. Torres (ed.), A Primer on Individualized Education Programs for Handicapped Children.

Benison, S. 1976. An interpretation of the early evolution of care and treatment of crippled children in the United States. Birth Defects 12:103–115.

Blatt, B. 1972. Public policy and the education of children with special needs. Except. Child. 38:537–545.

Calovini, G. 1969. The principal looks at classes for the physically handicapped. The Council for Exceptional Children, Washington, D.C.

Connor, F. P., Wald, J. R., and Cohen, M. J. (eds.) 1970. Professional Preparation for Educators of Crippled Children. Teachers College of Columbia University, New York.

Fair, D. R. 1977. Is mainstreaming really happening with the COHI? DOPHHHJ. 3:35–36.

Gallagher, J. J. 1972. The special education contract system for mildly handicapped children. Except. Child. 38:527–535.

Heisler, V. 1977. On handicaps. Letter to the editor. APA Monitor 8:2.

Hohman, L. B., and Freedheim, D. K. 1958. Further studies on intelligence levels in cerebral palsy children. Am. J. Phys. Med. 37:90–97.

Johnston, R. B., and Magrab, P. R. 1976. Developmental Disorders. University Park Press, Baltimore.

Jones, R. L. 1972. Labels and stigma in special education. Except. Child. 38: 553–564.

Kolstoe, B. J. 1977. Are the multihandicapped our responsibility? DOPHHH J. 3: 14–17.

Magnussen, C. J. Will inclusion of the multihandicapped necessarily cripple DOPHHH? Paper presented at the 54th Annual Convention of the Council for Exceptional Children, Chicago, April, 1976.

Outland, R. W. 1970. Cripples and other health impaired — trends in population, characteristics, and in meeting educational needs. In: F. P. Connor, J. F. Wald, and M. J. Cohen (eds.), Professional Preparation for Educators of Crippled Children. Teachers College of Columbia University, New York.

Spillane, R. R. 1975. Trends of education for the future. Paper presented at the Blythedale Conference on the Child with Long-Term Illness, New York, November, 1975.

Sugar, M., and Ames, M. D. 1965. The child with spina bifida cystica. Rehabil. Lit. 26:362–366.

Tew, B. 1973. SBH: Facts, fallacies, and future. Spec. Educ. 62:26–31.

Wilder, C. S. 1975. Prevalence of selected impairments. Vit. Health Statist. 99: 1–64.

Wilson, M. I. 1973. Children with crippling and health disabilities. In: L. M. Dunn (ed.), Exceptional Children in Schools. Holt, Rinehart, & Winston, Inc., New York.

Wollinsky, G. F. Classification of the physically handicapped: Static phenomenon or evolving process. Paper presented at annual convention of the Council for Exceptional Children, Chicago, April, 1976.

Wright, B. A. 1960. Physical Disability — A Psychological Approach. Harper & Row, New York.

Wyatt, K. E. 1970. One Dickens of a Christmas carol. In: F. P. Connor, J. R. Wald, and M. J. Cohen (eds.), Professional Preparation for Teachers of Crippled Children. Teachers College of Columbia University, New York.

2

THE NATURE OF PHYSICALLY HANDICAPPING CONDITIONS

Figure 2-1. A child with severe spastic cerebral palsy: functional problems can include difficulties with mobility, speech, perception, and learning.

Teachers are often tempted to minimize the importance of knowledge about the medical aspects of physical disabilities. A teacher who regards a handicapped child as more like other children than unlike them, and who focuses on progress and strengths rather than on deficits, might view the study of the medical aspects of a disability as negative and unnecessary. However, while focusing on physical limitations may indeed seem negative, a strong case can be made for the necessity of this study. Not knowing which of the child's limitations are permanent and which are temporary, not recognizing and understanding the pain or other special stresses to which the child is subject, and not being aware of likely related disorders, place the teacher at a serious disadvantage in planning an appropriate educational program. When the basic nature of a physical handicap is understood, it is then possible (and certainly desirable) to think beyond the handicap: to view the child as more like other children than unlike them and to focus on progress and strengths rather than deficits.

Understanding the nature of all the physical disabilities possible in the school-age population is not easy. Rare syndromes, unusual diseases, and multiple congenital anomalies of unknown origin are found among this constantly changing population. Thus, the teacher of physically handicapped children can never be certain that he knows exactly what to expect. The teacher should therefore be encouraged to develop an understanding of the general problems likely to accompany the most common conditions, as well as to develop tools for information-gathering when confronted with conditions never before encountered. Whatever the physical condition, the teacher should explore how the medical aspects affect the child's functional abilities and what programmatic modifications are necessary.

This chapter makes no attempt at an exhaustive description of all possible handicaps; rather, it provides a brief introduction to some of the more prevalent conditions. Mattson (1972) lists the following as the most prevalent long-term physical disabilities in childhood (with percentage of the population under the age 18): epilepsy (1%); cardiac conditions (0.5%); cerebral palsy (0.5%); and orthopaedic illness, such as scoliosis and Legg-Perthes disease (0.5%). Other conditions frequently found in classes for physically handicapped students were identified in an Illinois survey (Calovini, 1969). These include spina bifida and hydrocephalus, muscular dystrophy, and osteogenesis imperfecta. Other conditions described here include amputation, cystic fibrosis, hemophilia, juvenile rheumatoid arthritis, polio, sickle cell anemia, spinal cord injury, and spinal muscular atrophy.

Physically handicapping conditions are sometimes grouped into four major categories (Connor et al., 1970): 1) *neurological involvement,* referring to conditions of the nervous system (brain, spinal cord, and peripheral nerves); 2) *health handicaps,* meaning those conditions that are long-term in nature, can affect stamina, physical growth, and development, and may be life-threatening; 3) *muscular problems,* referring to conditions affecting the health and function of muscles; and 4) *orthopaedic difficulties,* meaning conditions affecting bones and joints.

This chapter describes the sixteen conditions mentioned above within the framework of these four major categories. Each condition is discussed in terms of its medical aspects and their resulting functional problems. (It must be remembered that this introduction is from necessity quite general, and this information should be used as a *starting point* for careful, thoughtful, individualized educational planning for the child with a physically handicapping condition.) The conditions are presented in the following sequence:

1. *neurological involvement*
    cerebral palsy
    epilepsy
    hydrocephalus
    polio
    spina bifida
    spinal cord injury
2. *health handicaps*
    cystic fibrosis
    heart disease
    hemophilia
    sickle cell anemia
3. *muscular problems*
    muscular dystrophy
    spinal muscular atrophy
4. *orthopaedic difficulties*
    amputation
    juvenile rheumatoid arthritis
    Legg-Perthes disease
    osteogenesis imperfecta
    scoliosis

NEUROLOGICAL INVOLVEMENT

Cerebral Palsy

Physical Description   The diagnostic term cerebral palsy means injury to the brain that affects the control of muscles in some way (Apgar and Beck, 1974). How great the injury is and the kind of muscle control that is impaired determine how severely handicapped the affected individual will be. Symptoms range from barely noticeable, only slightly inconvenient muscular incoordination to profound multiple handicaps that severely impair movement and learning. The incidence of cerebral palsy is in the range of 3-6 infants per 1000 born in this country (Apgar and Beck, 1974), making this condition one of the most common crippling disorders of childhood.

The cause of cerebral palsy in a particular individual cannot always be determined. A myriad of prenatal, perinatal, and postnatal causes have been identified, including: prenatal rubella infection, Rh disease, anoxia at birth, childhood diseases (such as encephalitis and meningitis), and physical injury to the brain from a blow or gunshot wound. The diagnosis of cerebral palsy is usually reserved for cases in which the insult occurs before birth, during birth, or in the first few years of life — the time period in which the motor cortex, that area of the brain that controls movement, is still developing and somewhat plastic. Some physicians consider this developmental period to be the first five years of life (Capute, 1975). Eighty-six percent of cases of cerebral palsy are congenital or present at birth, while 14% are acquired later in life (Bleck, 1975a). Cerebral palsy, then, is a handicapping condition that affects the child's development from very early in life. It is a chronic disorder, lifelong in nature, and, although it cannot be cured, it usually does not get progressively worse.

To understand the impact of cerebral palsy on the life of an individual, the diagnostic term cerebral palsy alone is only the barest beginning. At least three sub-categories should be considered in learning how this condition affects a particular child. These classifications are 1) the *type* of muscle problem, 2) the *parts* of the body involved, and 3) the *severity* of the involvement.

The American Academy for Cerebral Palsy lists these types of muscle problems: spasticity, athetosis, rigidity, tremor, atonia, and mixed types (Minear, 1956). The first three are the most prevalent. The following is a description of these muscle problems:

Classification	Description
Spasticity	Tense, inaccurate voluntary movement because of the involuntary contraction of the affected muscles when they are stretched.
Athetosis	Marked incoordination and almost constant motion of the extremities. In contrast to spasticity (in which movement is quite restrained) athetosis produces much writhing movement that is not purposeful, and is difficult to control.
Ataxia	Uncoordinated movement and trouble with balance. The gait of a person with ataxia may be characterized by lunges and lurches, not unlike those of a sailor who has not yet recovered his "land legs."
Rigidity	Continuous muscle tension and stiffness.
Tremor	Involuntary shaking and rhythmic motions.
Atonia	Lack of muscle tone: limpness and flaccidity.

It should be remembered that these problems are not within the muscles themselves; rather, it is the brain's ability to control those muscles that is affected. The major defect of cerebral palsy is disordered tone or muscle control (Johnston and Magrab, 1976).

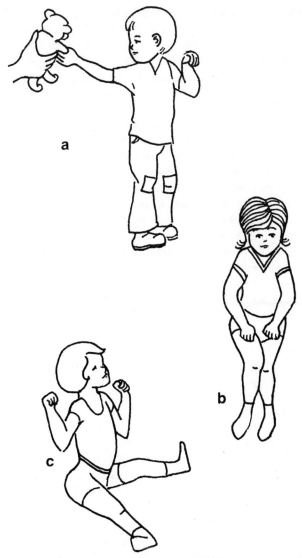

Figure 2-2. Children with cerebral palsy: (a) spastic hemiplegia; (b) spastic quadriplegia; (c) athetosis.

The second major classification criterion of cerebral palsy refers to the parts of the body that are affected by the disorder. (This classification system relates primarily to spasticity because the other types of muscle problems typically affect all extremities [Capute, 1975].) In rare instances spasticity affects only one limb of the body; this is called monoplegia (Figure 2-2a). More commonly the dysfunction is confined to either the right or left side of the body, with both the arm and the leg on the affected side being afflicted; this condition is hemiplegia (Figure 2-2b). Spastic hemiplegia is the most common single diagnostic condition in the cerebral palsied population, accounting for 40% of the total cases (Crothers and Paine, 1959). Quadriplegia refers to dysfunction in all four extremities (Figure 2-2c), although often a person with quadriplegic palsy has difficulty controlling trunk and head muscles as well.

The third classification criterion that should be considered is the severity of the involvement. As has been noted, the severity of the symptoms that fall under the label cerebral palsy varies widely. Some children have such a mild incoordination that it may never be diagnosed as cerebral palsy; others are very slow in their motor development but eventually learn to walk, perhaps with braces and crutches, and develop some control over fine motor movements; still other children may be confined to bed or to a wheelchair, and they may be so stiff that dressing and undressing them is a major undertaking for their caregiver and talking or holding a pencil is impossible for them. The designation of degree (mild, moderate, or severe) is important in determining the prognosis for independence for a child with cerebral palsy. It is important to realize that there is little direct relationship between intelligence and the degree of physical impairment in cerebral palsied persons (Kirk, 1962).

As might be expected in a crippling condition that is the result of injury to the brain, the source of all high-level human behavior, the related disorders in cerebral palsy are many and complicated. In a comparison of the occurrence of secondary disabilities in children with cerebral palsy and in children with other physical handicaps, Love (1970) found that 92% of his sample of cerebral palsied children had secondary disabilities while 74% of otherwise physically handicapped children had these secondary disabilities, which include mental retardation, speech problems, convulsive disorders, hearing impairment, and vision impairment. Capute (1975) and Love (1970) list the relationship of secondary disabilities to the cerebral palsy classifications:

Classification	Related Disorders
Spasticity	convulsive disorders (80%)
	visual disorders (27%)
	speech problems (52%)
	mental retardation — more likely to occur with spasticity than with other types of cerebral palsy
Athetosis	hearing loss (12%)
	visual disorders (20%)
	convulsive disorders (12%)
	speech problems (89%)
Ataxia	speech problems (85%)
	visual problems (29%)

While persons with cerebral palsy are found at all levels of intellectual potential, the chances of being mentally retarded are much greater for persons with cerebral palsy than they are for the population as a whole. While 2%-3% of the population as a whole is mentally retarded, about 50% of cerebral palsied persons function in the mentally retarded range (Apgar and Beck, 1974). Another 15%-20%, although not mentally retarded, do suffer some type of specific learning disability. Speech handicaps are an even more common related disorder. As might be expected in a condition that affects muscle control, speech disorders in persons with cerebral palsy are most commonly related to incoordination of the musculature. Dysarthria (delayed speech) and aphasia are among the most common speech problems. Similarly, incoordination of the musculature is responsible for most visual defects experienced by cerebral palsied persons. Hearing losses are associated with athetoid cerebral palsy, and these two problems often have a single common cause, a prenatal rubella infection or Rh incompatibility. Convulsive disorders are quite common in persons with spastic cerebral palsy but they are rare in athetosis.

Surgical and medical intervention in the treatment of cerebral palsy have not had the curative effect that was once hoped for. Thirty years ago surgery was the prime method of treatment for cerebral palsy; today it it used only in certain situations (Woods, 1975). Surgery may be performed on an older child to correct fixed deformities or to help make minor corrections in gait, or, in rare cases, to promote normal movement in a severely affected younger child whose spasticity in one group of muscles is so severe that mastery of a number of movements is impeded. As a general rule, physical therapy should be tried over a long period of time before surgery is attempted, because, in some cases, therapy can accomplish similar results. Physical therapy is also helpful in preventing such problems as dislocated hips, which limit the chances of independent walking, and contractures, which are deformities resulting from the shortening of muscles in a constant spastic state.

Pharmacological treatment has been tried to help the cerebral palsied child relax, to reduce abnormal muscle tone, and to relieve emotional tension; unfortunately, however, a drug that combines the desirable qualities of a muscle relaxant with an anxiety reducer has not yet been developed (Marks, 1974). Tranquilizers have been used in recent years as muscle relaxants. Temporary use of chlorapromazine, thioridazine, chlordiazepoxide, or diazepam has been useful for some children (Woods, 1975). Some clinicians feel that development of a drug that will help spasticity and athetosis may be just around the corner (Woods, 1975). Another hope for the future, currently in the experimental stage, is the use of electronic pacemakers in the brain to inhibit abnormal movement.

Functional Problems   The preceding long list of symptoms and related disorders should serve as an illustration of the complicated and difficult task with which the cerebral palsied person is faced in trying to develop to his fullest potential. The lack of motor control may make sitting, standing, and walking delayed, difficult, or even impossible. Impaired intellectual potential combined with an unusual environment (for example, confinement to a wheelchair) makes academic learning difficult for many people with cerebral palsy. A cerebral palsied person may have the intelligence and desire to speak but be hampered by speech muscles that refuse to do her bidding. That same person may be spastic-quadriplegic to such a severe degree that the simplest gestures — pointing to a picture or holding a pencil — are out of the question. It is possible to have a good mind locked into a body that does not work well, one of the most distressing and frustrating of human conditions.

Functional problems in learning, speaking, perceiving the environment, moving, and self-care skills are part of the total picture of cerebral palsy. In addition, the emotional problems associated with obvious handicaps and physical limitations must be recognized. It is essential that each child with cerebral palsy be carefully and individually evaluated, because the combination and permutations of levels and types of motor involvement plus the numbers and levels of related disorders are limitless. An individual program planned by persons who know the cerebral palsied child well is essential to maximize that person's potential.

Epilepsy

Physical Description   Epilepsy is the term used to describe a wide variety of disorders that are symptomatic of some abnormality of brain function. Seizures or convulsions are the major symptoms of this disorder. Seizures are the result of excessive electrical discharges in some nerve cells of the brain. This activity causes an alteration of brain function that begins and ends spontaneously (Epilepsy Foundation of America, 1974a). For many epileptics, epilepsy is a "part time" disorder; that is, a high percentage of the person's time is seizure-free, the disorder occurs only occasionally.

The manifestations of convulsive disorders vary considerably. The characteristics of the most familiar types of seizures are described in Table 2-1.

A child who has epilepsy but no other disorder would in all likelihood not require the special help of a program for physically handicapped students. Many children with epilepsy are seizure-free in school. Fifty percent of patients with epilepsy achieve total control of their seizures through medication; 30% achieve partial control through medication (Berg, 1975). Since, however, epilepsy is one manifestation of neurological dysfunction, it is related to others, e.g., cerebral palsy, hydrocephalus, and mental retardation (Denhoff and Robinault, 1960). The population served by the

Table 2-1. Characteristics of the most familiar types of epileptic seizures

Grand mal seizures	Petit mal seizures	Psychomotor seizures
These are major motor seizures that involve an alteration of the function of all brain cells so that the person loses consciousness.	These seizures occur most often in children between the ages of 5 and 10. Like grand mal seizures, they involve a loss of consciousness. Unlike grand mal seizures, they are not easily recognizable because of their very brief duration — 5-10 seconds.	A person having psychomotor seizures appears to have an altered state of consciousness but at the same time is able to carry out complex acts. These acts may be such behaviors as lip-smacking, repetitive hand and arm movements, dressing and undressing, or walking about. The seizure may last from a minute to several hours.
The seizure is characterized by a sudden loss of consciousness and rigidity of the body followed by jerking movements. Inability to control saliva may result in "foaming-at-the-mouth." There may be loss of bowel and bladder control.	A petit mal seizure is characterized by brief episodes of starting and perhaps twitching of the eyelids.	
A grand mal seizure usually lasts less than 2 minutes. Upon regaining consciousness, the person may be disoriented and sleepy.	These seizures may be mistaken for daydreaming. The child may be unaware that he's had a seizure. It is possible to have several hundred petit mal seizures a day.	
Grand mal seizures are sometimes preceded by an aura, a sensory warning (a special smell, sight, or sound) that a seizure is about to occur. An aura may precede the seizure by minutes, hours, or days.		

From Berg, 1975; Haslam, 1975; Epilepsy Foundation of America, 1974a; Epilepsy Foundation of America, 1974b.

Table 2-2. Guidelines for dealing with grand mal seizures

1. Move the child away from potentially dangerous areas and hard, hot, or sharp objects.
2. Do not force anything between the child's teeth.
3. Move the child into a horizontal position. Loosen his collar. Turn the child's head to the side for release of saliva. Place something soft under the head.
4. Keep calm. Remember that you can't stop the seizure; let it run its course.
5. When the child regains consciousness, provide the opportunity for rest.

When does a grand mal seizure require emergency medical intervention?

If the seizure lasts longer than a few minutes, or if the child goes from one seizure to another without regaining consciousness, call the physician for instructions and notify the child's parents.

From Epilepsy Foundation of America, 1974a.

teacher of physically handicapped children includes a high percentage of neurologically impaired children, who are more likely to experience epilepsy than the population as a whole. The teacher of physically handicapped children should be prepared, therefore, to deal with seizures in the classroom, to understand the special needs of children with epilepsy, and to interpret these needs for other teachers. In particular, grand mal seizures warrant special assistance in the classroom. Table 2-2 lists some guidelines for dealing with grand mal seizures.

Functional Problems   The functional problems of physically handicapped children with epilepsy may be a result of an interaction between the seizures and the motor problems that makes learning difficult. In a study of 244 handicapped children with epilepsy, Sillanpaia (1975) looked for a relationship between the degree of the motor handicap and the severity of the epilepsy. The study concluded that the onset of seizures occurs significantly earlier in life in children with motor handicaps and that their seizures are more difficult to control.

A survey of epileptic children attending regular public schools in Great Britain revealed a higher-than-usual incidence of learning and behavior problems (Holdsworth and Whitmore, 1974). Eighty-five children were rated by their teachers and headmasters for general progress, referral to special psychological services, special problems, special aptitudes, school attendance, and frequency of seizures.

One-third of the children rated were making wholly satisfactory progress. Half of the children were functioning at a below-average level in regular classrooms. Reading comprehension was the area of greatest difficulty. One in every six children was seriously behind academically, and one in five presented a behavior problem. The children with behavior problems were more likely to have a school attendance problem than were those children without such problems. The frequency of seizures did not seem to have an effect on educational performance, although the type of seizure did seem to have some bearing. Almost all members of the group who were experiencing major educational problems had grand mal seizures.

It is possible that these learning and behavior problems may be associated with a neurological impairment of which epilepsy is a manifestation. It is also possible that many of these problems are related to psychosocial factors and to the effects of anticonvulsant medication.

The fear of seizures and fear of social rejection because of seizures are problems reported by persons with epilepsy and their families. In regional hearings conducted by the Commission for the Control of Epilepsy and Its Consequences (DHEW, 1977), the following psychosocial needs were articulated:

1. Some individuals with epilepsy said they attempt to live a normal life despite the threat of seizures. Others admitted to withdrawing, from fear of embarrassment, ridicule, or having a seizure mistaken for drunk and disorderly conduct. Some stated that their problems in getting along with others and their fear of rejection made it difficult for them to find work or to function normally in society.
2. Some parents reported that other parents won't allow their children to play with a child who has epilepsy and that children with epilepsy are sometimes ostracized at school. Others told of children being excluded from sports and other recreational activities.
3. Problems seem to be compounded during the teen-age years. The teen-ager with seizures (particularly if they are uncontrolled) may be reluctant to date or to participate in group activities for fear of having a seizure, and he may not be able to drive.

Teachers of children with epilepsy have a responsibility not only to deal with the seizures themselves but also to be aware of the special psychosocial stresses on these children. The teacher should work to include, rather than to exclude, children with epilepsy in as full a school program as possible. She should also educate the other children, parents, and staff about the non-contagious and upsetting but not evil reality of seizures. The Epilepsy Foundation of America has educational materials for both adults and children that are of help in facing these responsibilities.

The recreational needs of children and young people with epilepsy must not go unmet just because of the possibility of seizures. Except for exposure to dangerous heights, unsupervised swimming, or other clearly hazardous activities, ordinary physical and recreational activities should be encouraged and made available.

Other functional problems faced by children with epilepsy may be related to the medication they take to control seizures. In a review of the behavioral effects of antiepileptic drugs, Stores (1975), although he finds many methodological problems with the available research, does find evidence that the medication can, for some persons, exaggerate psychological and/or learning problems. Store's (1975) review finds an often repeated claim that children with epilepsy (including those of at least average intelligence and with good control of seizures) do less well academically than might be expected in view of their basic intellectual ability. It is hypothesized that such children, while perhaps able to rise to the occasion of a formal testing session and perform adequately, may be attentively or motivationally impaired in the classroom as the result of antiepileptic medication.

The optimal dosages and combinations of medications that produce the greatest possible control of seizures while not impairing attention, motivation, learning, and behavior are often difficult to regulate in a growing child. The teacher can actively help to attain the optimal control by carefully observing the child's behavior and by keeping anecdotal records that may help the physician determine if more seizures are occurring or if the medication is causing undesirable side effects. The behaviors that should be noted include:

more activity
less activity
complaints of headache
finger tremor
loss of appetite
drowsiness
increased tension
increased talkativeness
teeth grinding
teeth gnashing
inarticulate speech
frequent stomachache
unexplained lapses of attention

Hydrocephalus

Physical Description   Hydrocephalus is a disability that is associated with myelomeningocele, which is a type of spina bifida discussed later in this chapter. About 90%-95% of children with myelomeningocele have hydrocephalus (Bleck, 1975b), although both conditions can occur individually. In hydrocephalus (literally, "water brain") the cerebrospinal fluid is blocked in the brain. Because the fluid cannot escape from the ventricles in which it is formed, these ventricles expand. This expansion eventually compresses brain cells and causes progressive brain damage, the effects of which can be impaired intelligence, paralysis, convulsive disorders, and visual impairment.

Normally, cerebrospinal fluid is produced continuously at the rate of 3–5 ounces per day (Apgar and Beck, 1974). Most of this fluid is formed within the four ventricles, or small cavities, that lie deep within the brain. The fluid flows from the ventricles out into spaces beneath the base of the brain, down around the spinal cord, and up over the top of the brain, where it is gradually absorbed into the bloodstream. In hydrocephalus, this natural process is impeded by an obstruction in one of the channels. The obstruction can be caused by inflammation, scar tissue, or some kind of malformation.

If the cerebrospinal fluid remains trapped in the ventricles and this condition is unchecked, the progressive results become obvious. To compensate for the increased amount of fluid, the child's skull becomes larger and thinner. Veins may be apparent in the skull, the forehead may bulge, and the eyeballs may be forced downward (producing the "setting sun" effect). Throughout this process, brain cells are being compressed, and progressive brain injury is taking place. In many cases of hydrocephalus however, neurosurgical techniques can halt this process. Surgery involves draining the blocked ventricles and inserting permanent drainage systems called shunts (Figure 2-3). Usually, the sooner the hydrocephalus is corrected, the less brain damage occurs.

The surgery to correct the hydrocephalic condition may have serious complications, including infection and blockage of the tube, both of which can occur soon after surgery, but may also occur in later infancy or childhood. Early signs of these complications are irritability, loss of appetite, vomiting, headache, drowsiness, tense fontanelle, and enlargement of the head (Woods, 1975). Fifty percent of hydrocephalic children require revision of the tube and valve at least once during infancy, while a longer tube may be needed as a replacement after a period of growth.

Functional Problems   Apgar and Beck (1974) report the results of a long-term study of 182 hydrocephalic children who were not treated surgically. Of those children, more than half died in the first years of life. Of the 70 who survived and who were considered to have arrested hydrocephalus, 29 were considered to be of normal intelligence, 21 had below average educational potential, and 20 were moderately or severely mentally retarded. Of these same 70 children, 26 had no physical handicaps, 15 had slight handicaps (such as unsteady gait, balance problems, or impaired vision), and 29 were substantially physically handicapped — blind and/or paralyzed. (It should be noted that, for infants who receive shunt surgery early in life, the 5-year survival rate is at least 80%, and there is a good possibility for normal intellectual and physical development.)

Intellectual impairment and physical disability are possible side effects of hydrocephalus. Tew (1973) points out that the learning problems experienced by children with hydrocephalus are quite complicated, with

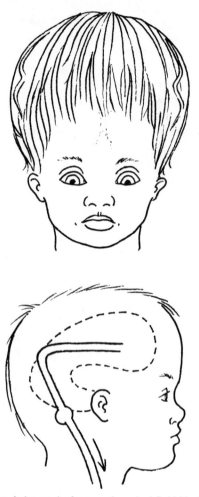

Figure 2-3. Hydrocephalus results from cerebrospinal fluid blocked in the brain.

patterns similar to those of children with learning disabilities. One study investigated the abilities of hydrocephalic children in tactile matching, recognizing visual-spatial relationships, and manual speed. In all these skills, children with hydrocephalus performed at a level below that of a control group. Additional studies of one-year-olds, five-year-olds, and adolescents with hydrocephalus revealed that these children have difficulty with tasks involving eye-hand coordination; therefore, it would seem that motor incoordination and visual perception problems are common for children with hydrocephalus and may make academic achievement difficult.

Language functioning may also be impaired in children with hydro-cephalus. The language of hydrocephalic children has been described as hyperverbal (Fleming, 1968; Swisher and Pinsher, 1971); they may talk excessively, and their speech may lack content. Their production of the syntax of the language is better than their comprehension and expression of the meaning of words. They are able to remember and repeat long strings of words, like people with very high intellectual potential, but they may be unable to derive any meaning from that string of words. This language pattern has been dubbed the "cocktail party chatter syndrome." The language sounds good, is socially appropriate, and indicates alertness, but it may have very little meaning. Although it is unusual for persons to express ideas that are more complicated than they can understand, this is sometimes the case with hydrocephalic children. The fortunate aspect of this unusual language pattern is that it is socially appealing and may make it more likely that other people will respond favorably to the hydrocephalic child. The unfortunate aspect is that it may present a misleading picture of the child's intellectual potential that may make it more difficult for parents and teachers to find and to accept an appropriate educational plan for the child.

Poliomyelitis

Physical Description   Cases of poliomyelitis (polio) are rare in schoolchildren in many parts of the world today due to intensive immunization campaigns. Sporadic cases do occur, however, and major outbreaks are possible if immunization of children in the early months of life becomes less common.

Polio is caused by a viral infection that attacks the large nerve cells of the lower motor neurons in the spinal cord and brainstem (Woods, 1975). After an acute phase of illness (characterized by high fever and painful muscle spasms) varying degrees of neuronal injury exist, ranging from no permanent effect to flaccid paralysis of many muscle groups and even to death (Nelson, 1969). In cases where there is little residual effect, the infection had caused only a swelling of the cells and their supporting tissues. The more serious complications are consequences of cell destruction by the virus (Bleck and Nagel, 1975).

After the acute phase of the illness, the condition is non-progressive, and treatment to increase residual function should begin as soon as possible and should continue for several years. The value of treatment and help has been evidenced by the work of nurses and physical therapists in Kenya (Woods, 1975). They visited isolated villages and treated persons with long-standing after-effects of polio. Crutches, sticks, braces, and raised boots were supplied, deformities were corrected, and independent walking was made possible for many patients.

Figure 2-4. Residual paralysis can be a consequence of poliomyelitis.

Functional Problems   The poliomyelitis virus affects only the neuromuscular system; consequently, intelligence, speech, sensation, and bowel
and bladder functioning are unaffected (Bleck and Nagel, 1975). Most
children with polio after-effects in school programs for the physically
handicapped will have moderate to severe paralysis of the lower limbs and,
at times, the trunk (Figure 2-4). The functional problems will therefore be
in the areas of mobility and independence, but students who have had polio
will probably not have the array of multiple handicaps that can accompany
other kinds of neurological impairment.

Spina Bifida

Physical Description   Spina bifida, a handicapping condition, is a
birth defect in the bony structure of the spinal column, through which some
part of the spinal cord has slipped out to form a cyst or lump on the back.
The developing backbone of every fetus remains open until about the 12th
week of pregnancy. In spina bifida, one or more of the individual vertebrae
fail for some unknown reason to close completely, leaving a defect in the
spine. The words spina bifida literally mean "cleft spine" (National Institute of Neurological Disease and Stroke, 1972).

This defect has three major forms: the slightest form is called spina
bifida occulta, in which one or more of the vertebrae is not completely
formed, but there is no deformity or misplacement of the spinal cord, and
functional problems are minimal or nonexistent. It is most unlikely that a

child with spina bifida occulta would need the special help of a program for physically handicapped children.

In the more serious forms of spina bifida, a sac (perhaps as small as a nut or as large as a grapefruit) protrudes from the backbone (Figure 2-5). At birth this sac may be covered with skin, or nerve tissue may be exposed. When the sac contains some of the coverings (or meninges) of the spinal cord, but no actual nerve materials, the defect is called a meningocele. Because a meningocele contains no neural elements, it is unlikely that the child would be paralyzed, although muscle weakness and incoordination from the point of the lesion downward would not be unusual. This child would require surgery to eliminate the mass on the back, but a good recovery and no further difficulties should be expected, and the child with a meningocele would also be unlikely to need special educational help.

In the most severe form of spina bifida much special help is needed. In this form the sac is called a myelomeningocele, and contains not only some of the spinal cord coverings, but part of the spinal cord itself as well. Spinal fluid may leak out. The lesion, then, significantly interrupts the nerve pathways that connect the brain with peripheral parts of the body, and the consequences for the child are quite serious. Among them are flaccid paralysis and muscle weakness in the back and legs below the lesion, insensitivity of the skin below the myelomeningocele, and a lack of bowel and bladder control (Tew, 1973). Hydrocephalus, discussed above, is a related disorder that can impair perceptual and cognitive functioning.

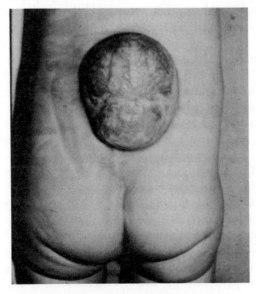

Figure 2-5. Myelomeningocele — an outpouching of the spinal cord.

The immediate medical problem is to surgically close the spinal open-ing, often within the first 24-48 hours of life, in order to reduce the risk of life-threatening infection. It is unlikely, however, that the major nerves in the area of the defect will ever function normally, and therefore the conse-quences of this birth defect are lifelong.

The outlook for children with myelomeningocele is improving, how-ever. Apgar and Beck (1974) report on a long-term study of children with this condition who were followed by a Nashville, Tennessee hospital. In 1962, a progress evaluation was made of 39 children with this condition who had been born at the hospital within the last few years. Twenty-six children had died in the first years of life, 11 had IQs below 80, and two were doing school work appropriate to their age. A more recent study of 50 children born in the same hospital revealed 30 still living by their first birthday, 17 of whom had normal intelligence.

Functional Problems   Children with myelomeningocele are deli-cate, have often had complex neurosurgery, and have many obstacles that must be overcome to enable them to function as independently as possible in society.

The learning capacity of children with spina bifida is influenced by three variables — the type of lesion, the sex of the child, and the severity of hydrocephalus, if present (Tew, 1973). While there is no direct relationship between the severity of the lesion and the IQ, there is a correlation. A child with a meningocele is likely to have an IQ in the average range, the average intellectual capacity of a child with a myelomeningocele is generally in the low average-to-educable mentally retarded range, and a child who has a le-sion close to the head (an encephalocele) is likely to be profoundly mentally retarded.

The sex of the child influences learning because spina bifida is more frequent in females than it is in males, and it has greater effect on intelli-gence in females. The third variable is the degree of hydrocephalus that is present. Children with myelomeningocele and no hydrocephalus have a mean IQ of 100, the average for the population as a whole. The IQ de-creases if hydrocephalus is present, dropping further as the hydrocephalus becomes more progressive. Thus, it is certainly possible for a child with spina bifida to function in the average to above-average intellectual range, but certain aspects of the condition can impair intellectual functioning.

The functional problems of children with myelomeningocele are more pervasive than learning problems alone. The child may have varying degrees of paralysis or weakness below the point of the lesion. He may be able to learn to walk only with the help of braces and crutches (Figure 2-6). Below the lesion, there may be a loss of sensory function causing the child to be insensitive to pain or temperature. This insensitivity not only interferes with learning, but also is a health hazard to the child. The lack of urinary

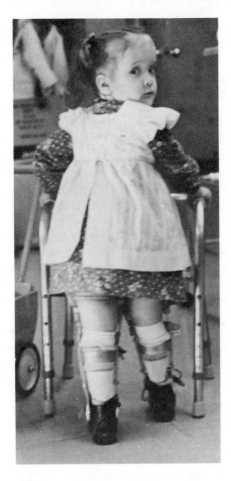

Figure 2-6. A child with a myelomeningocele needs devices like braces, crutches, or walkers for independent walking.

and bowel control presents serious medical management problems as well as complicated social and self-care requirements. The neurological problem of spina bifida requires specialized attention from medical, social, and educational professionals in order to ensure effective treatment and service.

Spinal Cord Injuries

Physical Description   The spinal cord is a cable of millions of tiny nerve fibers and cells encircled by a bony tube. The nerve fibers and cells transmit sensory information from the peripheral nerves to the brain and send motor information from the brain back to the muscles and skin. The nerve fibers of the spinal cord influence voluntary movement, communicate sensation (such as heat, cold, pain, and pressure), and control bowel, bladder, and sexual function.

Injury to the spinal cord can result in paralysis, the loss of voluntary movement. Paralysis may occur below the site of the injury. If the injury occurs at or below the waist, the paralysis is called paraplegia. If the injury occurs at a higher level, quadriplegia may be the consequence. Damage to neural fibers is not always complete; therefore, resulting paralysis also may not be complete. The prognosis for an individual with a spinal cord injury cannot be ascertained for about two months after the injury occurs. During this time, the spinal cord may be in shock and any paralysis present may not be permanent. In the case of a severed (or transected) cord, however, paralysis and loss of sensation will be complete and permanent (Travis, 1976).

Loss of sensation is equally as serious as paralysis. Pain and pressure provide an important warning to the body that something is amiss. Without this warning system, the complications of infection and injury can be quite serious. Pressure sores and bladder infections are two serious and possibly life-threatening situations against which the injured person must guard.

Spinal cord injuries occur most frequently among those given to risk-taking (Travis, 1976). While the injuries can occur to anyone of any age or sex, they happen most frequently to adolescent boys and young men. Automobile accidents, surfing and diving accidents, and gunshot wounds are major causes.

Functional Problems   The physical problems of paralysis and loss of sensation are best dealt with in a rehabilitation hospital. A strenuous program for weeks or months may be necessary to help the individual function at an optimal level. The rehabilitation program will include physical therapy for strengthening arm and shoulder muscles, stretching exercises for the hamstring muscles (so that the injured person can sit with his legs outstretched to dress himself), and the selection of assistive devices (such as electric wheelchairs) to foster independence.

The person with a spinal cord injury will be taught to check his body twice a day for reddening that might indicate the beginning of a pressure sore and to shift his weight at least every two hours to minimize the possibility of developing these open, infected wounds. Since bowel and bladder control will be lost, instruction in a bowel program, using scheduling and suppositories, and catheter care will be provided to prevent genitourinary problems.

A guide to the understanding and carrying-out of these important routines is provided in a booklet, *A Primer for Paraplegics and Quadriplegics.* It can be ordered from:

Institute of Physical Medicine and Rehabilitation
New York Medical Center
400 E. 34th Street
New York, NY

As might be expected in a condition as serious as spinal cord injury, the problems of emotional adjustment are as great as the physical problems. Caywood (1974), a quadriplegic as a result of an automobile accident, describes his feelings of despair at his initial complete dependency on others, his reluctance to deal with long-term vocational and home management issues because of his unwillingness to accept the permanence of paralysis, and the difficulties his friends and family had in dealing with him because of their feelings of guilt, pity, or sorrow. A sense of grief at the loss of independence and strength is a strong initial reaction to spinal cord injury. Serious depression may be a consequence of this permanent handicapping condition.

HEALTH HANDICAPS

Cystic Fibrosis

Physical Description   Cystic fibrosis is a disease that involves the whole body, producing an abnormality of mucus secretions. Normally, the body's mucus works like an extremely light oil that helps to transport the body's chemicals and to keep the lungs clean by carrying out germs and dust particles. In the cystic fibrosis child, however, the mucus is more like a thick glue that clogs, rather than cleans, air passages. When the mucus clogs bronchial tubes, it provides a breeding ground for bacteria, making the child especially susceptible to respiratory infections (Munn, 1977). The major consequences of cystic fibrosis are chronic pulmonary disease, pancreatic deficiency, and a high concentration of sweat electrolytes (*Clinical Aspects of Cystic Fibrosis,* 1976).

Years ago, few children with cystic fibrosis could expect to survive beyond six years of age. The mortality rate 20 years ago was 75% in the first three years of life (Crozier, 1974). Today, thanks to advances in medical treatment, this gloomy figure has fallen to less than 0.5%. The mean survival age is now 15 years, and some patients with cystic fibrosis are surviving to adulthood (*Clinical Aspects of Cystic Fibrosis,* 1976). Factors that have contributed to the decline of early death rates include:

1.   early diagnosis before chest changes are irreversible,
2.   individualized treatment, and
3.   antibiotics (Crozier, 1974).

There is now hope for the continued lengthening of the average lifespan and an increasing possibility of a normal existence for cystic fibrosis children.

Cystic fibrosis is the most common lethal hereditary disease. It is present in approximately one of every 1500–2000 Caucasians born alive. It is inherited through a recessive gene. There is currently no test to identify carriers who do not manifest symptoms (*Clinical Aspects of Cystic Fibrosis,* 1974).

Inhalation treatments, using a mist tent, and postural drainage are ways to ease the breathing of a child with cystic fibrosis. Postural drainage is a technique that involves tilting the patient in several different positions three times a day and patting him over certain areas of the lungs to help loosen the thick mucus. Physical therapists can teach parents the exercises to perform at home (Munn, 1977).

Cystic fibrosis may also affect the digestive system by blocking the natural flow of enzymes from the pancreas, therefore a controlled diet and a pancreatic supplement are usually prescribed.

Cystic fibrosis may affect the appearance of the afflicted child. He may be somewhat barrel-chested because he has to pull harder to draw a breath, and his stomach may protrude somewhat because of the pancreatic difficulties. The fingers and toes may be clubbed because the blood is insufficiently aerated, inhibiting growth of the extremities. Sexual maturation may be delayed (Munn, 1977).

Functional Problems   The child with cystic fibrosis will not need special placement in a class for physically handicapped students. Most children with the disease handle regular classroom placement well. However, because absences due to respiratory infections may be frequent and extended, the child may benefit from supportive tutoring by a special teacher. The special education teacher may be of help to the classroom teacher in understanding certain aspects of the condition (Munn, 1977):

1. The child with cystic fibrosis should not suppress his coughing; the cough is not contagious, and is a helpful defense against the clogged mucus. The child should know that he can leave the room whenever the coughing becomes severe or he needs to go to the bathroom or take medication.
2. The child may eat a lot, and this should not be discouraged. The teacher should be aware of any special dietary restrictions.
3. It is generally best to minimize the child's "differentness" and not to single him out because of the disease. Questions from other children regarding special routines should be played down, and responses should indicate that certain routines must be followed for the maintenance of this child's good health.

In a condition like cystic fibrosis, the patient is not the only person affected. Families with cystic fibrosis children face financial and psychological stress. While many medical expenses may be covered by private insurance and the Crippled Children's Service, medication may cost as much as $125 a month. Therapy equipment, drugs, and clinic, laboratory, and physician's fees can run as high as $5000 a year (Munn, 1977). In addition to financial worries, families must deal with the life-threatening nature of the disease and be constantly on guard against breathing problems and respiratory infections. The hereditary nature of the disease may engender guilt as well as sorrow. Families of children with cystic fibrosis are often overtired, overextended, and emotionally drained. The teacher must be a support to the family by making the child's school routine as normal and pleasant as possible, by expressing a willingness to follow the family's direction in establishing that routine, and by helping the child maintain progress in classwork when absences occur.

Heart Disease

Physical Description   The normal heart is a hollow organ, divided into four chambers through which blood is pumped with the aid of a series of valves that open and close to allow for its flow. Dark blood (low in oxygen) approaches the heart through the veins and enters the right atrium, or upper chamber. This chamber in turn empties into the right ventricle, or lower chamber. The right ventricle drives the blood through the pulmonary artery and valves to the lungs, where it receives oxygen and takes on a bright red color. This blood then returns to the heart through the left atrium. The left ventricle pumps the oxygenated blood out of the aortic valve into general circulation (American Heart Association, 1971). This complicated process is essential to life, because the blood carries life-sustaining oxygen to all parts of the body.

However, structural defects in the heart and the great blood vessel leading to and from it can seriously hinder this process. Approximately 1% of all babies are born with some kind of heart defect (Apgar and Beck, 1974). Congenital heart defects originate in the first 3 months of embryonic development, the time when the heart is being formed. There are several known causes of congenital heart disease: chromosomal aberrations (such as Down's Syndrome), a maternal rubella (German measles) infection in the first trimester of pregnancy, and certain hereditary conditions. In most individual cases, however, the specific cause is unknown (Myers, 1975).

The symptoms of heart disease in children include shortness of breath, limited exercise tolerance, and cyanosis — a bluish appearance caused by the circulation of deoxygenated blood — a condition that is not dangerous in itself.

There are 35 types of congenital heart disease, of which at least 20 are amenable to surgical correction (Apgar and Beck, 1974). However, heart disease is still a major cause of death in early infancy. Surgically correctable conditions often necessitate waiting until the child has reached a certain size or improved state of general health before operating. The child's growth, stamina, and general sense of well-being may be quite limited during this time of waiting.

Functional Problems   A child who is recovering from surgery may have a convalescent period of weeks or even months. Homebound or hospital instruction should therefore begin as soon as is deemed appropriate by the physician.

A child in school who is recovering from surgery or who has a heart disease that is not yet correctable may need shorter school days, restricted activity, special rest periods, or a special diet. Stress and fatigue should be avoided.

The good news for many children is that open heart surgery may completely correct the handicapping condition and make all activities possible. The teacher should consult with the child's parents and physicians on a periodic basis to determine appropriate levels of activity at school.

Hemophilia

Physical Description   Hemophilia (the "bleeder's disease") is a hereditary disorder of the blood clotting process caused by a deficiency in one or more of the ten blood plasma proteins necessary for normal clotting (Henderson, M., 1977). The severity of the disease can vary. A mildly affected person might bruise more easily than most people or bleed slightly more from a cut or scrape, but would not be greatly hampered in day-to-day living. The most severely affected person could bleed so profusely from minor injuries that ordinarily benign situations, such as a pulled tooth or a minor bump, could be life-threatening to him.

Hemophilia is genetically transmitted from mother to son in the sex-linked recessive pattern. The most common types of the disorder are Hemophilia A and Hemophilia B, which account for 85%-90% of all cases and occur only in males (Henderson, M., 1977). There are rare instances of girls with other types of this disorder.

Hemophilia is marked by bleeding episodes that are characterized by severe pain and immobilization. The most dangerous aspect of this disorder, the possibility of internal bleeding, can result in orthopaedic problems from bleeding into the joints and life-threatening danger to vital organs.

These internal bleeding episodes are sometimes triggered by what seem to be relatively minor accidents; at other times there is no known precipitating physical cause. Researchers have noted that emotional excitement or anxiety can trigger bleeding episodes (Lamb, 1977).

The treatment for hemophilia has involved intraveneous transfusions of the blood plasma factor in which the person is deficient whenever a bleeding episode occurs. A recent, much more effective development is the availability of a highly concentrated form of the clotting factor (Henderson, M., 1977).

Functional Problems   As has been noted, the acutely painful and dangerous bleeding episodes may have chronic effects. Repeated bleeding into the ankles, knees, elbows, and other joints can result in soreness, stiffness, and permanent crippling. Physical therapy can decrease the danger of permanently impaired mobility through exercise and bracing.

The psychological implications of hemophilia are enormous. Two periods of special stress for the hemophiliac child and his family have been noted: the preschool and early school years, and the teen-age and young adult years (Henderson, D. B., 1977). In the preschool and early school years (about the ages four to eight) the child begins to experience limitations as a result of this condition. Vigorous games and exploratory activities, such an important part of this time of life, are often discouraged or forbidden, and the hemophiliac child experiences more hospitalizations than most children his age, another kind of loneliness and isolation.

The adolescent with hemophilia faces all the usual growing-up and peer-pressure difficulties of this age, with the added complication of a serious chronic disorder. The young person with hemophilia may rebel against the lifelong restrictions he has experienced by participating in risky physical activities or indulging in alcohol or drugs that may react adversely with his medication. The needs of the young hemophiliac include much emotional support and guidance at this special time.

Sickle Cell Anemia

Physical Description   Sickle cell anemia is the result of a gene mutation that occurred centuries ago, possibly as a protective device against malaria, in Africa and the Mediterranean countries, areas of high malarial incidence (Murray, 1976). At this time, however, sickle cell disease can be said to have no beneficial qualities. Normal red blood cells are round and flat; a person with sickle cell disease has red cells that are converted to a rigid sickle shape. Persons with sickle cell disease face serious health problems: anemia; pain crises (the result of sickle cells jamming blood vessels and depriving tissue of needed blood); and, depending on the area of the body involved in a pain crisis, permanent and serious effects — crippled bones, heart disease, and stroke (Scott, 1976). The course of the disease includes alternate periods of remission and periods of crisis that involve serious pain and health hazards. The life expectancy of a person with sickle cell anemia is shortened. Most children with the disease now reach adulthood; many adults with the condition are crippled as a result of repeated crises. The crisis is typically self-limiting; that is, it will run its course, and in a period of time, no matter what medical intervention is tried, it will end. Medication can, however, relieve pain to some extent and decrease the possibility of dangerous blood clots. The disease can cripple an organ, region, or system in the body (Gaston, 1976).

Good medical management is essential to the well-being of a child with sickle-cell anemia, whether he is in crisis or in remission. Gaston (1976) suggests these guidelines for helping a child in remission:

1. Keep a watchful eye on the child. Possible complications, such as eye problems and growth difficulties, can be ameliorated if caught early.
2. Provide good general pediatric care. Because pain crises in children are often precipitated by infection, immunizations, regular check-ups, and attention to good nutrition are important steps in decreasing the incidence of crisis.
3. Be educated. Parents, teachers, and the children themselves need to know the nature of the disease and what circumstances might precipitate a crisis (infection, fever, or dehydration).
4. Give support for the psychosocial aspects of the illness. A chronic disease that causes obvious discomfort and pain in children is a tremendously stressful situation for a family.

Sickle cell disease is genetically transmitted. To have the disease, one must inherit the sickle gene from both parents. The disease occurs more often in Blacks than in other groups. In the United States, one out of every 600 Blacks has the disease (approximately 50,000 persons in all).

One out of every ten Blacks in this country is a carrier. Carriers have one recessive sickle gene but no symptoms of the disease (Murray, 1976). Carriers are said to have the sickle cell trait, which is a healthy state in which an individual inherits the gene for sickle hemoglobin from one parent and the gene for normal hemoglobin from the other. Rarely are problems associated with the sickle cell trait. Screening programs are available to help determine whether a person has the trait.

At the present time there is no cure for sickle cell disease.

Functional Problems   Neither mental retardation nor specific learning disabilities are associated with sickle cell anemia. The educational problems faced by children with this condition are similar to those of children with other kinds of chronic illness. A child with sickle cell anemia will have more hospitalizations and longer periods of convalescence than most children of the same age. School absenteeism will be higher, and special arrangements must be made to help a child progress academically. Close coordination between school and home or hospital instruction is necessary. Like other chronic illnesses, this disease increases the likelihood of psychosocial distress: parents and children must deal with the severe but intermittent pain, the conflict between wanting to overprotect and to allow as much independence as possible, and the knowledge that the disease is life-threatening.

Some special problems associated with sickle cell disease include growth problems (the child may be small for her age and puberty may be delayed) and urological complications (necessitating frequent trips to the bathroom and possibly increasing the incidence of bed-wetting). These problems do not enhance a child's self-confidence, nor do they make the special stresses of adolescence any easier.

Other functional problems may be due to the long-term effects of sickle cell crises. A child who has experienced heart failure or stroke resulting from a sickling crisis may have residual effects that resemble cerebral palsy. Crises that affect bones and joints may lead to a crippling condition that will permanently restrict mobility. One particularly difficult aspect of this condition is the necessity of accepting the knowledge that other sickling crises may occur at any time.

MUSCULAR PROBLEMS

Muscular Dystrophy

Physical Description   The diagnostic term muscular dystrophy refers to several genetic disorders that are grouped together because they all involve progressive, long-term damage to the muscles supporting the skeleton. These conditions involve increasing muscle weakness and crippling as the affected muscles contract and lose their ability to function.

The most common type of muscular dystrophy in school-age children is pseudohypertrophic or Duchenne type muscular dystrophy (Muscular Dystrophy Associations of America, 1975b). The distinctive characteristic of this type is the enlargement (pseudohypertrophy) of the calf muscles caused by the increased deposits of fat that take the place of the wasting muscle tissue. The progressive deterioration caused by this disease is rapid, with no remission. Death may occur within 10 to 15 years of onset — the time when the symptoms first appear.

Pseudohypertrophic muscular dystrophy is inherited in the sex-linked recessive pattern, which means that the disease is transmitted through the mother and predominantly affects male children. There are sporadic cases of affected girls, probably due to gene mutation as opposed to a clear-cut inheritance pattern. Even though the disease is genetic, the symptoms are usually not apparent until the ages between 2 and 6. The early signs are awkward and clumsy behavior, a tiptoeing walk, and "Gower's sign," a diagnostic clue involving the child's difficulty in rising from the floor. The child handles this difficulty by "walking" up his lower limbs with his hands (Figure 2-7). A complete physical examination is needed for a definite diagnosis, and should include enzyme tests to detect muscle waste, a muscle biopsy, and an electromyogram, which is similar to an electrocardiogram except that small needle electrodes are placed in suspected muscle groups — dystrophic muscles give characteristic readings of somewhat reduced voltage.

The disease is predictable in terms of what muscle groups are affected. Muscles of the pelvic girdle, the foot, and the thigh are affected first, with shoulder and elbow involvement a few years later. Eventually, hand, face,

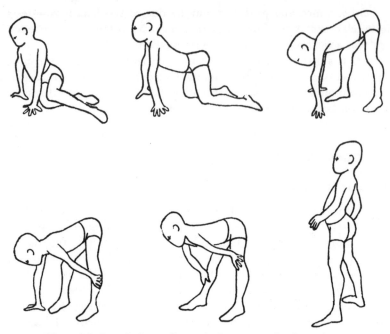

Figure 2-7. Gower's sign: a diagnostic clue to muscular dystrophy.

and neck muscles are involved, with death usually occurring in the late teens due to heart failure or lung infection.

Functional Problems   This brief description of what happens to muscle groups as muscular dystrophy progresses does little to communicate the awesome difficulties faced by a young person with this disease. Its progressive nature means that the child loses power gradually: at one time he could run, now he can walk only with the help of braces and crutches; at one time he could get around on his own, now he is confined to a wheelchair with little power in his arms, shoulders, and hands; once he was in a regular school, now he is confined to bed and every activity of daily living is a major production requiring the help of others. The physical needs and emotional difficulties of a person experiencing this deterioration are enormous.

In addition to physical and emotional problems, the child with muscular dystrophy may have a somewhat difficult time learning in school. While persons with muscular dystrophy can be found at all intellectual levels, psychometric studies indicate that the average IQ of persons with the Duchenne type is in the 80s, the slow learner range, while approximately one-third of those studied had IQs below 80, the borderline or educable mentally handicapped range (Zellweger and Hanson, 1967). Most persons with muscular dystrophy, then, could function academically in regular school programs, but they may have more of a struggle in learning than most children.

What can be done to help? Good medical care and physical therapy are needed to meet the physical needs of children with muscular dystrophy. While medical intervention cannot arrest the process of deterioration or restore muscles that have wasted away, treatment can reduce the side effects of the crippling process. For example, physical therapy may delay the onset of contractures. Because respiratory diseases are particularly hazardous to persons with muscular dystrophy, regular medical attention to these problems is essential. Obesity may become a problem as the child grows older and less active; regular medical care can help avoid this difficulty. Orthopaedic devices, such as walkers, crutches, braces, orthopaedic shoes, wheelchairs, hospital beds, and hydraulic lifts, may be needed. The Muscular Dystrophy Association of America can help provide this equipment and these services (Muscular Dystrophy Associations of America, 1975b).

The special adjustment problems of persons with muscular dystrophy and their families cannot be taken lightly, nor are they easily solved. Patient and family counseling may be helpful, and the teacher of physically handicapped children should be aware of good counselors in the community who can help. It is suggested that questions about the disease be answered truthfully but optimistically — let the child know that some of his muscles don't work as well as they used to, but that scientists are working hard to find a cure, and that the disease is nobody's fault — neither the child nor his parents did anything "bad" to make it happen. The parents should be advised by the physician about the genetic nature of the disease — female children in the family may be carriers. The family should be given guidance and support in receiving respite care and outside help for the day-to-day physical demands of caring for a seriously handicapped child. The child or youth with muscular dystrophy will need support in dealing with his feelings of dependency, lack of privacy, aggression, and hostility, for which the only outlet is verbal abuse. A teacher can be of special help in encouraging a young person to seize the moment and to learn, to grow, and to contribute to the greatest possible extent of his ability.

Ideally, the child with muscular dystrophy will stay in regular school programs for as long as possible. As he grows larger and weaker, special programs for the physically handicapped may be needed. Homebound instruction is the least desirable alternative because the isolation that is often a part of that educational option can exacerbate the loneliness, dependency, and anger that the young person may be experiencing. Camping and recreation programs for the physically handicapped are highly recommended. It is sometimes difficult to recognize the value of school for a person whose future is anything but bright, but the opportunities for friendships, personal growth, and support that are available in a good educational setting cannot be matched.

Spinal Muscular Atrophy

Physical Description   Spinal muscular atrophy (part of the group of disorders called muscular dystrophy) involves the progressive degeneration of motor nerve cells. The cause of the disease is a genetic defect, and the inheritance pattern is recessive; thus, it can strike children of either sex, and, because the recessive pattern requires a gene from each parent for expression, there may be no previous family history of the disease.

There are two major classifications of spinal muscular atrophy — Werdnig-Hoffman Disease and Kugelberg-Welander Disease — and the prognosis is highly variable depending on the classification. Werdnig-Hoffman Disease is a severe, rapidly progressive disorder, beginning very early in life (sometimes before birth), and characterized by a generalized atrophy and weakness of the muscles. The earlier the onset, the graver the prognosis. Death usually occurs before school age (Muscular Dystrophy Association, 1970).

Kugelberg-Welander Disease, the second classification of spinal muscular atrophy, is also a progressive neuromuscular disorder but its progression is slower and the outlook more hopeful. The prognosis can range from a chronic, minimally disabling weakness to moderate disability. The symptoms become apparent in childhood or early adolescence, but persons with this disease may live a normal lifespan and be able to walk for as long as 20 years after the onset of symptoms. The early signs are atrophy and weakness in the leg muscles; later, the muscles of the shoulder girdle, upper arms, and neck are affected, and the patient may have frequent falls and a waddling gait (Muscular Dystrophy Association, 1975).

Functional Problems   The intelligence of persons with spinal muscular atrophy follows the normal distribution. An educational program must address itself to providing a challenging academic program while taking into account the diminished motor skills. The child with spinal muscular atrophy may have difficulty in sitting, walking, or climbing stairs. Weakness in hands and wrists may require special educational adaptation. Early physical therapy is important to prevent some of the side effects of the disease (such as contractures).

ORTHOPAEDIC PROBLEMS

Amputation

Physical Description   Limb absence or limb deficiency can be congenital or acquired through accident or illness. Limb absence is described with regard to the site and level of the absence, and the person's functional capacities are greatly dependent on both the number of limbs that are absent and the level (above or below a major joint like an elbow or knee) at which the absence occurs. In recent years many cases of congenital limb absence have been attributed to the drug Thalidomide, which was proclaimed a "wonder drug" in 1957 but was later found to cause serious birth defects when taken by pregnant women (Wallace, 1976).

Nelson (1969) provides this vocabulary for congenital amputation:

1. amelia — absence of limb
2. hemimelia — defects of distal parts of extremities, such as absence of forearm and hand
3. phocomelia — great reduction in the size of the proximal (near the trunk) segments of the limb, resulting in an approach of the distal parts toward the trunk (there is sometimes a flipper-like appearance to the existing part of the limb). (See Figure 2-8.)

Functional Problems   Persons with limb absence face a wide range of functional problems. A person with a unilateral below-the-knee amputation may be fitted with a prosthetic device and have little difficulty leading an active life. Bilateral above-the-knee amputations usually require the use of a wheelchair. A person missing both arms above the elbow will require much compensatory help and face many difficulties in those activities of

Figure 2-8. The absence of most of the arm is called phocomelia.

daily living that depend heavily on the use of the arms and hands. Artificial limbs can be of varying degrees of help to many persons with limb absence.

Acquired amputation — the loss of a limb due to an accident or a disease (like cancer) — brings with it some special emotional difficulties. The person may experience "phantom limb," the sensation of pain or other feeling in the absent limb, possibly due to exposed nerves in the stump. Persons with acquired amputation may go through a time of mourning, a grieving for the missing limb that is not unlike the grief experienced at the death of someone close. Young people with acquired amputation need help in tackling life from a newly defined perspective. The teacher and counselor can be of special help in developing that perspective.

Juvenile Rheumatoid Arthritis

Physical Description   Juvenile rheumatoid arthritis is a clinical syndrome similar to rheumatoid arthritis in adults, an inflammatory disease with an unknown cause. Juvenile rheumatoid arthritis strikes very young children, girls more often than boys. It may begin as early as six months of age, but the peak incidence of onset occurs between the ages of 2–4 and 8–11 (Travis, 1976). In addition to joint inflammation, 5%–10% of children with this disease experience spiking fever, skin rash, lethargy, and irritability. Most children, however, experience less severe systemic problems and are troubled mainly by swelling and tenderness in the joints (Boone, Baldwin, and Levine, 1974).

Calabro and Marchesana (1967) state that there is no way of forecasting what will happen to any individual child in the early stages of juvenile rheumatoid arthritis. The disease progression stops in about two-thirds of affected children by the age of 10. About one-half can expect disease activity for an average of three years; the others will experience disease activity of an unknown and unpredictable duration. The disease alternates activity with periods of remission, during which the child is symptom-free. Active phases may involve great pain and stiffness.

Involvement of various joints creates problems of function. Travis (1976) notes that wrist involvement is a troublesome and restrictive problem in children. The disease can cause permanent, destructive bone changes. Involved hands can lose muscle strength, grip, and mobility. Hip involvement can impair walking; shoulder and neck involvement can limit motion.

Inflammation of the eyes, a serious complication of juvenile rheumatoid arthritis (Boone et al., 1974), can lead to glaucoma and/or cataracts. Children who rub their eyes or have red or light-sensitive eyes should be seen by an ophthamologist right away.

Treatment for juvenile rheumatoid arthritis involves antiinflammatory drugs (large doses of aspirin are particularly effective), physical therapy to prevent or correct deformities, and, simply, waiting for spontaneous remission or improvement.

Functional Problems   The pain and stiffness of juvenile rheumatoid arthritis may influence school attendance, after-school activity, and physical endurance. Climbing stairs or walking for any considerable distance may not be possible during active phases of the disease. Permanent deformities may greatly restrict mobility. During periods of flare-up the child may experience morning stiffness, fatigue, and joint pain. These difficulties may produce temporary changes in personality: the child may be cranky, demanding, and hostile during this difficult time.

Legg-Perthes Disease

Physical Description   Legg-Perthes disease, a temporary orthopaedic problem that strikes young children between the ages of 4-8, involves the destruction of the growth center of the hip end of the thigh bone (Silberstein, 1975). The cause of this condition is unknown; it may be due to trauma, strain, or some as yet unidentified hereditary factor. The ratio of boys to girls with the disease is approximately 4 to 1 (Bleck and Nagel, 1975). This condition causes the blood supply to the head of the thigh bone to be cut off and, without treatment, leads to permanent crippling. However, treatment is available to lay down new bone, a process that takes 2-3 years. Three major methods of treatment are used, all of which involve protection of the hip joint while the natural repair process is going on. Until a few years ago, children with this disease were maintained in traction, usually in a hospital, until their x-rays indicated that enough healing had taken place to permit weight bearing on their hips, usually necessitating 6-8 months of bed rest. An alternative form of treatment that has recently been gaining favor is an ambulatory treatment program in which the child is placed in a cast or brace that holds the legs far apart; this approach allows the child to walk early in the treatment. The third treatment program involves surgically enclosing the head of the thigh bone; this requires a body cast for 6-8 weeks, followed by 4-6 weeks of physical therapy (Silberstein, 1975). Whatever course of treatment is chosen, it is likely that the child will not have a chronic disability, so this is indeed a temporary handicap.

Functional Problems   The diagnosis and treatment of Legg-Perthes disease will result in a radical change in a young child's lifestyle. The child may be experiencing little pain and leading a very active life when the diagnosis is made. Whatever the treatment plan decided upon, the child will be effectively immobilized for a period of a few weeks to several months. If he receives ambulatory treatment, he may be able to continue in his regular class; other treatment approaches will involve periods of hospitalization. It is important that the child receive emotional support in handling these major changes. It is also important that the child receive adequate academic instruction to enable him to rejoin his peers as an equal when the treatment is completed. The child with Legg-Perthes disease will experience no impairment of cognitive or hand functioning and thus should be able to continue to progress academically without many modifications in the educational plan.

Osteogenesis Imperfecta

Physical Description   Osteogenesis imperfecta is sometimes called "brittle bone disease." It is characterized by defective development in the quantity and quality of bone: the bones do not grow normally in length and thickness and, because they are so brittle, they are easily broken. The skull bones are soft, the limbs are small and may be bowed due to repetitive fractures that don't heal properly, and the spine may be curved. A bone defect in the inner ear may cause deafness (Bleck and Nagel, 1975). Surgery and bracing will alleviate some of the symptoms until the condition stabilizes as the child grows older.

Functional Problems   The intellectual range of children with osteogenesis imperfecta is normal, and intellectual growth should be maximized in the educational setting. Physical education and other strenuous activities are not possible and, in the early years when the child is susceptible to breaks and fractures, he must live in a protective environment. For this reason, special programs for the physically handicapped may be desirable. If a hearing loss has been diagnosed, consultation with a teacher of the hearing impaired will also be required.

Scoliosis

Physical Description   Scoliosis is a lateral curvature of the spine that occurs most often in adolescent girls (Nelson, 1969). These young people have one shoulder blade higher than the other and one shoulder or hip higher than the other. Pain is not usually a problem with this condition; the danger is an increased deformity that can interfere with walking and breathing. In most cases of scoliosis the cause is unknown.

Scoliosis is a temporary orthopaedic handicap that has an excellent prognosis for complete recovery (Silberstein, 1975). Treatment depends on the extent of the curve and the rate of progression. Mild curves may need no treatment, moderate curves are usually treated with a Milwaukee brace (see Figure 2-9), and severe curves may require surgical correction, which consists of inserting steel rods along the spine to straighten the vertebral column.

Functional Problems   The treatment of scoliosis involves restricted mobility and great cooperation from the patient. The Milwaukee brace, which is used to position the spine correctly until growth is complete, is worn for an average of two years. The brace is noticeable and restrictive; for example, patients are not able to sit while wearing the brace. It is worn day and night, with only short breaks for bathing and exercising (Bleck and Nagel, 1975).

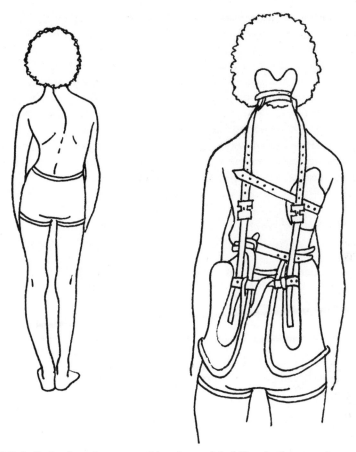

Figure 2-9. Scoliosis, a lateral curvature of the spine, and the Milwaukee brace, used to correct moderate curves.

In the case of surgical treatment, a body cast is worn six months post-operatively and, for some of this time, the young person is required to remain flat on her back.

The teacher should help the student keep up with schoolwork during periods of hospitalization and immobilization and should encourage the student as she tries to find the strength to be different from her adolescent peers by wearing a brace and by doing exercises for her long-term benefit.

SUMMARY

The teacher of physically handicapped children must develop an understanding of the medical aspects of handicapping conditions in order to plan the best possible educational program for the individual child. Major medical issues that could influence educational strategies include whether the child is taking medication that could influence behavior and learning, the degree of pain or restriction of mobility the child may be experiencing, and the prevalence and type of related disorders. Knowledge of medical aspects leads to an understanding of functional problems: the ways in which the handicapping condition makes moving, talking, learning, and getting along with others more difficult. The most common physically handicapping conditions in the school-age population are described briefly here. The teacher should use this information as a starting point in recognizing and understanding the special needs of an individual child.

LITERATURE CITED

American Heart Association. 1970. If Your Child Has a Congenital Heart Defect. New York.

Apgar, V., and Beck, J. 1974. Is My Baby All Right? Pocket Books, New York.

Berg, B. O. 1975. Convulsive Disorders. In: E. E. Bleck and D. A. Nagel (eds.), Physically Handicapped Children — A Medical Atlas for Teachers. Grune and Stratton, New York.

Bleck, E. E. 1975a. Cerebral Palsy. In: E. E. Bleck and D. A. Nagel (eds.), Physically Handicapped Children — A Medical Atlas for Teachers. Grune and Stratton, New York.

Bleck, E. E. 1975b. Myelomeningocele. In: E. E. Bleck and D. A. Nagel (eds.), Physically Handicapped Children — A Medical Atlas for Teachers. Grune and Stratton, New York.

Bleck, E. E., and Nagel, D. A. (eds.), 1975. Physically Handicapped Children — A Medical Atlas for Teachers. Grune and Stratton, New York.

Boone, J. E., Baldwin, J., and Levine, C. 1974. Juvenile rheumatoid arthritis. In: H. W. Bain (ed.), The Pediatric Clinics of North America. W. B. Saunders Company, Philadelphia.

Calabro, J. J., and Marchesana, J. 1967. Current concepts in juvenile rheumatoid arthritis. Med. Intel. 277:696.

Calovini, G. 1969. The principal looks at classes for the physically handicapped. The Council for Exceptional Children, Washington, D.C.

Capute, A. J. 1975. Cerebral palsy and associated dysfunction. In: R. H. A. Haslam and P. J. Valletutti (eds.), Medical Problems in the Classroom. University Park Press, Baltimore.

Caywood, T. 1974. A quadriplegia man looks at treatment. J. Rehabil. 22-25.

Clinical aspects of cystic fibrosis. 1976. J. Pediatr. 9:712-713.

Connor, F. P., Wald, J. R., and Cohen, M. J. (eds.). 1970. Professional Preparation for Educators of Crippled Children. Teachers College of Columbia University, New York.

Crothers, B., and Paine, R. S. 1959. The Natural History of Cerebral Palsy. Harvard University Press, Cambridge, Mass.

Crozier, D. N. 1974. Cystic fibrosis: a not-so-fatal disease. In: H. W. Bain (ed.), The Pediatric Clinics of North America. W. B. Saunders Company, Philadelphia.

Denhoff, E., and Robinault, I. 1960. Cerebral Palsy and Related Disorders. McGraw-Hill Book Company, New York.

Epilepsy Foundation of America. 1974a. Epilepsy School Alert. Washington, D.C.

Epilepsy Foundation of America. 1974b. Facts and Figures on the Epilepsies and Other Neurological Dysfunctions. Washington, D.C.

Fleming, C. P. 1968. The verbal behavior of hydrocephalic children. Dev. Med. Child Neurol. 10 (suppl.):14–16, 74–81.

Gaston, M. 1976. Management of children with SCA between crises. In: Perspectives on Sickle Cell Anemia. Urban Publishing Company, Atlanta.

Haslam, R. H. A. 1975. Teacher awareness of some common pediatric neurological disorders. In: R. H. A. Haslam and P. J. Valletutti (eds.), Medical Problems in the Classroom. University Park Press, Baltimore.

Henderson, D. B. 1977. Clinical presentations and problems in dealing with hemophilia. Paper presented at the Symposium on Psychological Approaches to Hemophilia: The Medical-Psychological Interface. American Psychological Association. August, San Francisco.

Henderson, M. B. 1977. A study of self concept and disease variables in hemophilia. Paper presented at the Symposium on Psychological Approaches to Hemophilia: The Medical-Psychological Interface. American Psychological Association. August, San Francisco.

Holdsworth, L., and Whitmore, K. 1974. A study of children with epilepsy attending ordinary schools. Dev. Med. Child Neurol. 16:746–758.

Johnston, R. B., and Magrab, P. R. 1976. Developmental Disorders. University Park Press, Baltimore.

Kirk, S. A. 1962. Educating Exceptional Children. Houghton Mifflin Company, Boston.

Lamb, W. 1977. Therapeutic intervention with parents of hemophiliacs: review and suggestions. Paper presented at the Symposium on Psychological Approaches to Hemophilia: The Medical-Psychological Interface. American Psychological Association. August, San Francisco.

Love, N. W. 1970. The relative occurrence of secondary disabilities in children with cerebral palsy and other primary physical handicaps. Except. Child. 37:301–302.

Marks, N. C. 1974. Cerebral Palsied and Learning Disabled Children. Charles C Thomas Publisher, Springfield, Ill.

Mattson, A. 1972. Long-term physical illness in childhood: a challenge to psychosocial adaptation. Pediatr. 5:801–809.

Minear, W. L. 1956. A classification of cerebral palsy. Pediatr. 18:841–852.

Munn, V. C. 1977. The C/F child comes to school. Learning 6:38–40.

Murray, R. F. 1976. Genetic counseling in sickle cell anemia and related hemoglobinopathies. In: Perspectives on Sickle Cell Anemia. Urban Publishing Company, Atlanta.

Muscular Dystrophy Associations of America. 1970. Werdnig-Hoffman Disease or Infantile Spinal Muscular Atrophy. New York.

Muscular Dystrophy Associations of America. 1975a. Kugelberg-Welander Disease or Progressive Spinal Muscular Atrophy. New York.

Muscular Dystrophy Association of America. 1975b. Patient and Community Services Program. New York.

Myers, B. A. 1975. The child with a chronic illness. In: R. H. A. Haslam and P. J. Valletutti (eds.), Medical Problems in the Classroom. University Park Press, Baltimore.

National Institute of Neurological Disease and Stroke. 1972. Spina Bifida — A Birth Defect. Baltimore.

Nelson, W. E. (ed.). 1969. Textbook of Pediatrics. W. B. Saunders Company, Philadelphia.

Scott, R. B. 1976. Treatment of the crisis in SCA. In: Perspectives on Sickle Cell Anemia. Urban Publishing Company, Atlanta.

Silberstein, C. E. 1975. Orthopedic problems in the classroom. In: R. H. A. Haslam and P. J. Valletutti (eds.), Medical Problems in the Classroom. University Park Press, Baltimore.

Sillanpaia, M. 1975. The significance of motor handicap in the prognosis of childhood epilepsy. Dev. Med. Child Neurol. 17:52-57.

Stores, G. 1975. Behavioral effects of anti-epileptic drugs. Dev. Med. Child Neurol. 17:647-658.

Swisher, L. P., and Pinsher, B. J. 1971. The language characteristics of hyperverbal hydrocephalic children. Dev. Med. Child Neurol. 15:746-755.

Tew, B. 1973. SBH: facts, fallacies, and future. Spec. Educ. 62:26-31.

Travis, G. 1976. Chronic Illness in Children. Stanford University Press, Stanford, CA.

U.S. Department of Health, Education, and Welfare. 1977. Plan for Nationwide Action on Epilepsy. DHEW Publication No. (NIH) 78-2 76.

Wallace, M. 1976. Thalidomide — how one family turned a curse into a blessing. The Charlotte Observer, September 26, Charlotte, NC.

Woods, G. E. 1975. The Handicapped Child: Assessment and Management. Blackwell Scientific Publications, Great Britain.

Zellweger, H., and Hanson, J. W. 1967. Psychometric studies in muscular dystrophy Type 3A (Duchenne). Dev. Med. Child Neurol. 9:576-581.

3

PSYCHOLOGICAL
ASPECTS OF
PHYSICAL DISABILITY

Figure 3-1. It is important to look beyond the physical handicap and to explore other consequences of a disability: social and psychological development may need special attention.

Psychological adjustment can be defined as an individual's ability to adapt to his environment, to meet changing conditions, to perceive social cues, and to get along well with others (Calhoun, Selby, and King, 1976). A physically handicapped child may face special difficulties in psychological adjustment because of the nature of his disability and the responses of others to him. This chapter explores research related to the psychological adjustment of young physically handicapped people, as well as possible hazards to psychological development and effective approaches to facilitate adjustment. The families of handicapped children may also have special difficulties in adjustment; their needs are also discussed.

53

PSYCHOLOGICAL ADJUSTMENT OF
YOUNG PHYSICALLY HANDICAPPED PEOPLE

There is a commonly held (although erroneous) concept of a neat, single effect of disability. Richardson (1969) points out that a physical disability such as cerebral palsy may involve sensory as well as motor handicaps, psychological as well as academic distress. It is important to look beyond the physical aspects and explore the other consequences of a disability. The available research seems to indicate that children and young people with physical handicaps have a more difficult time with psychological adjustment than do non-handicapped people.

The total school-age population of the Isle of Wight — more than 11,000 children — was evaluated for psychological disorders as part of a British National Health survey (Graham and Rutter, 1968). This study found the rate of psychiatric disorders in the general population of children to be 6.8%. These disorders were nearly twice as common (11.5%) among children with chronic illnesses not involving the central nervous system. An even more dramatic increase was found when physically handicapped children with central nervous system involvement were examined. Over one-third (34.3%) of these children showed psychiatric disorders.

Studies in the United States support the British findings that chronic illness is psychologically stressful for children. Cytryn, Moore, and Robinson (1973) studied a group of 29 children with cystic fibrosis and found that 12 were well-adjusted, 4 were severely disturbed, having such problems as infantile relationships with their mother, aggression, hostility, and anxiety, and 13 showed mild to moderate degrees of disturbance. Similar emotional difficulties have been found in children with heart disease, kidney disorders, and diabetes (Calhoun, Selby, and King, 1976).

Based on a review of data from the United Kingdom National Survey of Health and Development, the Isle of Wight study, and Rochester, N.Y. Studies, Pless (1976) estimates that children with chronic disorders experience significant delays in their psychological development at a rate 15%-20% higher than the rate of occurrence of these delays among comparable healthy children.

HAZARDS TO PSYCHOLOGICAL ADJUSTMENT

Physically handicapped children have more difficulty with psychological adjustment than do the non-handicapped for reasons that are related both to the physical disability itself and to the way in which others view the disability. Although research in this area is limited, some possible explanations for these problems in adjustment have been suggested. (At this point in the state of our knowledge these explanations must be considered hypotheses and they must be subjected to further and more rigorous research.)

Hazards Related to the Disabling Condition

Abnormal Motor Development   A child's orientation in time and space, his appreciation of the physical environment, and his equilibrium, posture, and ability to maintain a stance against gravity depend heavily on neuromuscular development (Blumberg, 1975). During the early childhood years, the non-handicapped youngster achieves increasing physical independence as the maturation of his nervous system allows for balance, coordination, and the ability to ambulate, to explore, and to learn.

The child whose brain was damaged before or during birth may suffer from abnormal motor development, varying according to the area and extent of the damage. This abnormal motor development will interfere with normal growth, exploration, independence, and learning.

Some consequences of abnormal motor development have been suggested by Blumberg (1975): 1) the primitive reflexes may persist beyond the time when they would normally disappear; 2) a child with damage to the cerebellum will have balance difficulties as well as primitive postural and righting reflexes; 3) difficulties in locomotion will result, as may feelings of both psychological and physical insecurity. Children with athetoid cerebral palsy are overresponsive to stimuli: they are constantly struggling to control their involuntary gross movements and to avoid stimuli from other persons. As a consequence of their attempts to cope with their abnormal motor development, these children may resist forming close relationships with others.

The Nature of Chronic Illness   Even when the handicapped child is surrounded by loving, supportive people and the best possible medical care is available, some hazards to personal adjustment are inherent in the nature of chronic illnesses (such as congenital heart disease, juvenile rheumatoid arthritis, muscular dystrophy, and others). Steinhauer, Mushin, and Rae-Grant (1974) suggest these general hazards:

1. separation from parents for hospitalization and treatment (see Chapter 4 for more information concerning the hospitalized child)
2. pain
3. dependency
4. medication that can affect alertness and behavior
5. physical restriction, sensory impairment, and isolation
6. threat or fear of death

These unpleasant feelings and situations often seem mysterious to the child, and children, like their parents, will seek explanations for their illnesses. The explanations the children arrive at depend on their stage of cognitive development. Fairly young children are likely to attribute their illness to magical causes or they may believe that their condition is the result of what they have done or thought or that they are sick because they are bad

(Calhoun, Selby, and King, 1976). Mattson (1972) suggests that young children up to the age of ten attribute illness to recent family happenings. In older children, knowledge of the hereditary nature of certain diseases can cause a special stress.

Special chronic syndromes may have their own special stress factors (Mattson, 1972). For example, a child with epilepsy may fear a loss of consciousness, children with cystic fibrosis may fear suffocation, and a child with heart disease may have a hard time understanding the restrictions that are placed on his activity.

Brain Damage   As previously noted, survey research indicates that the incidence of psychological problems is much higher in brain-injured children than in other chronically ill youngsters (Graham and Rutter, 1968). Among the problems noted in brain-injured children and young people are temper outbursts, hyperactivity, and "catastrophic reactions" — emotional and physical overreactions inappropriate to the situation (Freeman, 1970). Shaffer (1973) suggests that the most likely explanations for these difficulties is that brain injury in some children may result in a deficiency of social perception that distorts patterns of interaction. The brain injury may cause what Johnson and Myklebust (1967) have called "social learning disability" or "social imperception." A person with a social learning disability may be insensitive to the moods or feelings of others, may not pick up cues from the environment about appropriate ways to behave, and, as a consequence, may be constantly doing or saying the wrong thing.

The possibility of social imperception in physically handicapped persons was explored by Seguin (1975). He compared handicapped and healthy children based on the content, organization, and amount of verbal response of the children's personality descriptions (social perceptions) of self, of others, and of how the children thought others would describe them. Twenty-eight physically handicapped children, ages 9–16 years, were matched in sex, age, and IQ with 28 non-handicapped children.

Significant differences in social perception were found in the responses of the 9–13-year-olds. The handicapped children's responses were particularly devoid of statements of mutual interaction, social factors, and indications of knowledge and interpersonal networks. In general, physically handicapped children responded with fewer words, less variability in the amount of verbal responses, and an inferior ability to describe and to organize personality information.

Hazards Related to How Others View the Disability

Atypical Responses of Parents   A dramatic example of how a handicapping condition can disturb a parent-child relationship is reported by Freedman, Fox-Kalenda, and Brown (1976). In careful studies of mother-child interaction with an infant who had multiple handicaps as a result of a prenatal rubella infection, the researchers noted that the baby's posture made cuddling difficult. In addition to being both visually and hearing impaired, the baby was ill much of the time and was hard to feed. His mother had to feed him every 3 hours around the clock for many weeks. Her most obvious response to the obligations of caring for this child with many special needs was fatigue, and her manner in caring for him was perfunctory.

Mothers may be puzzled by a baby's trouble with sucking and swallowing, they may be disturbed by rigid posturing that does not encourage cuddling, and they may be unhappy when the early smiling and cooing responses of most babies are not forthcoming (Battle, 1974). The differences in the handicapped infant's responsiveness may set up a pattern in which the parents' responsiveness to the baby is distorted. The child therefore begins life not only with the special problems inherent in his handicapping condition, but with the additional difficulty of experiencing parental responses that are different from those experienced by most babies.

Dependency   During the first year of life, society does not expect an infant to cooperate, to be altruistic, or to demonstrate independence in self-care skills (Battle, 1974). The physically handicapped child may be treated like an infant (because in some respects he *is* like an infant) for much longer than is appropriate. Shere (1971), in a study conducted in Israel, revealed that mothers of severely handicapped children overlooked the important role of providing the child with appropriate toys for cognitive development. Children who had outgrown the infancy phase cognitively but who were still as helpless as young infants physically either were not provided with toys or other objects for play or, if toys were in the room, were not placed where they could easily reach the objects. This finding was consistent for both "distant" mothers and mothers who were lovingly involved in the care of their children.

The understandable temptation to treat handicapped children as infants and to overprotect a child with significant health or developmental problems may hinder the child's acquisition of the necessary skills and attitudes for independent living. A study of adults with osteogenesis imperfecta found that the greatest problems in adjustment seemed to be a high degree of dependency on others and strong feelings of social alienation (Kiely, Sterne, and Witkop, 1976).

Reactions of Others   The feelings and reactions of non-handicapped people toward those with physical handicaps may interfere with the development of personal relationships between handicapped and non-handicapped persons. Kriegel (1969), a professor who was crippled by polio as a child, states that others' reactions to the reality of his disability denied his individuality. Because of his braces and crutches, Kriegel (1969) reports feeling that non-handicapped people pigeon-holed him into categories: sometimes he was categorized as a holy innocent; at other times, he was categorized as an incompetent. In neither case was he considered a unique human being — he was handicapped. Kriegel (1969) reserves his harshest words for the professionals whose job it was to "rehabilitate" him. They seemed not only to imply that he should be grateful for whatever existence he could scrape together, but also to require gratitude from him for the work they were doing. Seeing only one aspect of a person — seeing only a disability — can eliminate the opportunity for real friendship. The discomfort and subsequent artificiality of normal people in their dealings with the handicapped are detrimental to the psychological adjustment of the handicapped, because only genuine human interaction leads to healthy social growth.

Another potentially harmful reaction of others — the non-handicapped — is the hesitation to confront handicapped people with the usual consequences of unacceptable behavior (Freeman, 1970). Others may not criticize or express anger toward a handicapped person in situations in which non-handicapped persons would be forced to deal with unpleasant reactions. The result of this different treatment is that handicapped people do not have the same opportunity to receive accurate, spontaneous feedback from other people, who instead feel they must be especially considerate or careful of their feelings (Richardson, 1969).

Aids to the Psychological Adjustment

The preceding discussion may leave the impression that a physical disability automatically leads to psychological distress and problems. This is emphatically not the case. Even if it is true, as Pless (1976) suggests, that 15%-20% of chronically ill children experience psychological problems, that still leaves a sizeable majority — over 80% — of handicapped people who are psychologically well-adjusted. Mattson (1972) points out that many studies of long-term childhood disorders reveal a surprisingly adequate psychosocial adaptation of children who were followed to young adulthood. The factors that may facilitate psychological adjustment are discussed below.

Adjustment to Disability "To embrace one's braces and crutches would be an act of the grotesque," says Kriegel (1969), "but to permit one's humanity to be defined by others because of those braces and crutches is even more grotesque." Although no one could argue that a physical disability is desirable, many clinicians and handicapped persons have made the case that accepting that disability *is* desirable. One task for the physically handicapped person that seems to facilitate psychological adjustment is to accept the reality of the disability and then to move on from there to define one's humanity in broader terms.

Acceptance of a disability has been defined by Wright (1960) as a series of value changes, including:

1. the enlargement of the scope of one's values so that those aspects of life not closed to a handicapped person are enhanced
2. the subordination of values in those situations where the importance of that value has been overrated (i.e., the importance of a physically perfect and beautiful body)
3. the containment of the effects of a disability: the reality of a physical disability does not have to restrict a person's capacity to love and to be loved and to contribute to mankind

Wright (1960) maintains that the acceptance of a disability not only "frees the person of devaluation" because of the disability, but also allows that person to seek satisfaction in those activities that befit his/her own characteristics as a unique individual rather than those of an idealized normal standard.

An *Acceptance of Disability Scale,* based on Wright's concept, was developed by Linkowski and Dunn (1974) and used in studies on physically handicapped college students. The researchers reported a significant correlation between acceptance of a disability and both self-esteem and satisfaction with social relationships. Further research using this scale was conducted with 72 teen-agers with oral-facial clefts (Starr and Heiserman, 1977). Significant differences were found between the group with extremely favorable self-concepts and the group with low self-concepts in terms of the acceptance of a disability: once again, the acceptance of the disability was related to positive psychological adjustment.

The problems associated with physical impairment still exist for those who accept their disability, but their acceptance frees them to go on with the business of living. Robert Louis Stevenson, a victim of pulmonary tuberculosis, once wrote, "Life is not a matter of holding good cards but of playing a poor hand well" (Mattson, 1972).

Appropriate Education and Other Activities   Although research indicates that the acceptance of a disability leads to better psychological adjustment, there is, as of yet, no clear evidence of what specific factors facilitate that acceptance. Some research indicates that appropriate education and other meaningful activities contribute to acceptance of, and adjustment to, a disability.

Battle (1974) asserts that a combination of special class help and regular classroom placement is the ideal situation for many physically handicapped children. The disabled child needs the opportunity to have normal models and to interact with the non-handicapped because they are the people with whom the handicapped will be in contact for most of their lives. On the other hand, special class placement has the advantage of providing the handicapped child with role models who are themselves handicapped and who have made a successful adjustment. In addition, the environment of a special class may be structured in such a way that the child can compete more successfully in an academic situation.

Clearly, research concerning the ideal placement for physically handicapped children as a group has not produced definite answers. For example, a British comparison of students in residential special schools for physically handicapped children with students in day treatment programs found no significant differences with regard to self-concept and social adjustment (Bishop, 1977). An integrated preschool experience — with multiply handicapped and nonhandicapped children in the same classroom — did increase the social skills and social participation of the handicapped children (Kushman, 1976). (Because of the great diversity in the physically handicapped population, it is difficult to isolate these variables that influence ideal school placement [Jones, 1974]. Chapter 5 offers a discussion of the variables that should be considered.)

In addition to good school programs, other activities have been helpful in promoting good psychological adjustment. High on the list are sports and other recreational activities. A study of the physical and mental reactions of physically handicapped children during and after horseback riding lessons found that, in addition to the pleasure derived, the mobility, motivation, and courage of the physically handicapped students had increased (Rosenthal, 1978). In another study, handicapped college students showed a significant improvement in skill, self-concept, and self-acceptance after participation in a bowling program (Ankenbrand, 1973). Mattson (1972) suggests that the well-adjusted physically handicapped child finds satisfaction in a variety of compensatory motor activities and intellectual pursuits.

Good Explanations   As has been noted previously, many chronically ill children raise questions about their disabilities and often have magical explanations for them (Calhoun, Selby, and King, 1976). Even young children (ages 6–10) who are fatally ill seem to have some fear and understanding of impending death, and express great anxiety, although they do not talk directly about death itself (Spinetta, 1974). Physicians who care for chronically ill young people have noted that adolescents with such problems as cystic fibrosis or cerebral palsy sometimes realize suddenly in a flash of insight and for the first time that they have a major problem that will not be outgrown (Green, 1976).

Clinicians working with handicapped children suggest that clear and honest information about the nature of the disorder, and preparation for what the eventual consequences of the condition will be, are essential for the development of trust and for psychological adjustment (Steinhauer, Mushin, and Rae-Grant, 1974). The child's understanding of the nature of his condition and his feelings about it should be explored. Open communication, support, and encouragement are the watchwords for professionals who deal with physically handicapped children.

Deal with Health as Well as Illness   In reviewing work with children in a cancer ward, Lucas (1977) found that some of the children and their families and staff were prepared for death, but not for life. Of all children that enter cancer centers for treatment, 50% will be considered cured — "cured" meaning they will experience a continuous and complete remission for an indefinite period of time (Van Eys, 1977). In other words, children who have what is commonly considered a fatal illness might live rather than die. The patients, therefore, need help in preparing for the possibility of a future as well as for death. Lucas (1977) states that normal growth and development must be emphasized in working with seriously ill children.

This observation can be extended to all handicapped children as a group. The effects of a disability should not be allowed to spread to the extent that every other aspect of life is colored. Helping children understand that many of the challenges and problems they face are part of all human growth and development, and are not unique to handicapped people, will foster psychological adjustment.

FAMILIES WITH HANDICAPPED CHILDREN

Young handicapped people do not face their special hazards to psychological adjustment alone; their families face these difficulties also. To best meet the emotional needs of these young people, therefore, the teacher must be aware of any special stress their families might be facing. The teacher's role in helping the families of her students should be that of an empathetic listener who is able to refer the family to supportive counselors when professional help seems appropriate, and to provide clear information about the child's needs and progress.

It is important that teachers be aware of at least the two most important differences between themselves and parents in their shared concern for the child: 1) teachers have *chosen* to work with handicapped people, while parents did not make a voluntary choice, and 2) teachers can leave their responsibility in the evenings and on weekends, while parents never can. The more difficult job, then, is obviously that of the parent.

The special needs of these families begin when the handicapping condition is diagnosed, which may be at the time of birth or at some later time. Wright (1976) lists six stages of adjustment experienced by parents at the time of diagnosis of a handicap: shock, denial, guilt and anger, shame and martyrdom, depression, and recovery. The period described as *shock* is the parents' attempt to avoid the news: "There must be a mistake." "There was a mix-up with the babies." "There is an error in diagnosis." Shock shortly gives way to *denial,* which may take many forms: the parents may shop from doctor to doctor seeking a new diagnosis, they may find activities outside of the home to fill their days, or they may work with the child to remediate the problem. Parents express *guilt and anger* by blaming someone, perhaps one another, or themselves: "If only I hadn't had the flu." "It's a punishment for a sin." Obviously, this period is extremely dangerous to the stability of the family unit, because anger and guilt are debilitating emotions. The parents' feelings of *shame and martyrdom* are fed by our society's love of perfection and the social judgments of parenting skills as measured by the child's successes. *Depression* comes and goes throughout all of these stages. According to Wright (1976), when parents realize that there will be no cure but that there is hope, they have reached a period of *recovery.* Recovery is characterized by the parents' acceptance of the child and the limitations imposed by the handicap. During recovery parents will engage in reordering (called *reconstruction* by Wright) and a reorientation of their lives, represented by the focusing of their energies toward positive actions.

It is possible for people to hate being the parents of a physically handicapped child. They may fantasize about the death of the child and then smother these "unnatural" desires with a show of unreasonable concern over the child's health and safety (Hamilton, 1977).

Parental anguish is evidenced by the statistical demonstration of higher-than-expected divorce rates, desertion of the family, usually by fathers, and psychiatric hospitalization of one or both parents (Calhoun, 1976).

The impact of having a handicapped child in the home is not felt only by the parents: all family members are affected. The non-handicapped siblings are often expected to assume more responsibility and independence than is warranted (Shere, 1955). The physical care responsibilities for the child may fall heavily upon the sisters (Grossman, 1972). (It should also be noted that the birth of a handicapped child inhibits parental desires for another child [Holt, 1958].) A younger brother or sister may be expected to behave in a very responsible way before he or she is developmentally ready for such responsibility (Calhoun, 1976).

Social class affiliation also influences the family's reactions to the handicapped child. Calhoun's (1976) review of social class status and family reactions to handicapped children suggests that upper-class families recognize the need to help a child with an obvious physical handicap more easily than they recognize the need to help the child who has no external deformity, but who is mentally retarded. This family has more adjustment problems because dreams of success must be discarded for more realistic goals. Conversely, lower-class families with limited incomes face a greater adjustment with a physically handicapped child, who needs expensive medical attention and therapy, than they do with a mentally retarded child. Calhoun continues that the more obvious and severe the physical handicap, the more easily the upper-class family adjusts to the circumstances.

There is evidence to suggest that the sex of the handicapped child also influences the family's reaction. Parental expectations are higher for males than for females. This fact was demonstrated in Farber, Jenne, and Torgo's (1960) study, which reported that mothers express greater emotional distress if the handicapped child is a boy.

Periods of Family Crisis

The birth of a handicapped child constitutes a crisis in the family unit. As the family works through the emotional stages outlined by Wright (1977) and enters the period of reconstruction and reorientation, the crisis subsides and gives way to positively directed action and decision-making. Other crises include the times when institutionalization is considered, the time when the educational plans must be made, adolescence, and early adulthood.

The second major period of crisis will occur if the child's handicap is severe enough to warrant the consideration of institutionalization. The current emphasis in public health planning is on deinstitutionalization and the development of more community-based programs. However, in spite of this shift of emphasis, there are families with special needs who must consider residential treatment centers. Institutionalization is a viable option for the family whose child's handicap is so severe that special technology is required for life support. The necessity of twenty-four hour nursing care beyond the first three years of life may also suggest the need for institutionalization. For the family of limited income, a state-supported agency may be able to provide the medical care and educational program most beneficial to the child. Lastly, the family may feel that the presence of the handicapped child interferes with the dynamics of the family unit to such an extent that the majority of the family members will be healthier emotionally if the child is removed from the home.

Not all families are willing to consider the possibility of institutionalization. Calhoun (1976) suggests that the decision to place a child in an institution is usually made when the family is undergoing additional kinds of stress, including financial pressures, marital problems, or child-affiliated problems, such as toilet-training difficulty, effects of growth, puberty, or the necessity of constant nursing care.

Wolf and Whitehead's (1975) study indicates that the decision to institutionalize a handicapped child is also influenced by the child's sex and the marital relationship of the parents. A child who requires a great deal of physical care is more likely to be placed away from the home (Mercer, 1966). Fatheringham, Skelton, and Hoddinott (1971) report that children who are disruptive at home and at school are apt to be institutionalized.

There is evidence that keeping a severely handicapped child in the home may present many problems for the family. In Tizard's (1964) study dealing with families of mentally retarded children, the data gathered indicate that families who retained their children in the home experienced more adjustment problems than did those families whose children were placed in institutions. The quality of living of those families with handicapped children in the home was also affected, no doubt as a result of financial expenditures related to the handicapping condition, the demands of care to meet the needs of the child, and, to some degree, the period of withdrawal referred to by Wright (1976). (It should be noted that Tizard's work was conducted before the advent of many community-based programs, the availability of which might have influenced the results.)

Families of handicapped children facing the decision of whether to institutionalize exhibit emotional stress reactions similar to those reactions described by Wright (1976) following the diagnosis of the handicapping condition: guilt, shame, depression, and, when the decision has been made, recovery.

The third period of crisis is encountered when educational plans are made. The teacher who meets with the family at this time should carefully explain the educational program as it relates to the special needs of the individual child. Conferences and conversations should be relaxed and not hurried. The family should be provided with written statements pertaining to the educational program to allow for specific reference later as family members gather and compare information prior to decision-making.

"What do you think we should do?" is asked frequently. The role of the teacher, however, is not to tell the parent what to do; she is a responsive listener and provider of information. She should itemize and describe those components of the educational program that she perceives as beneficial for their child and, further, she should discuss any additional areas of need for which her program may be unable to provide.

Since the 1975 passage of the Education for All Handicapped Children Act (Public Law 94-142), the teacher is not the only educator to speak with the family. Institutions and public schools provide diagnostic and evaluative services for the family and recommend the specific educational placement that the committee of educators feels is most appropriate for the individual handicapped child. The parent may accept the recommendations of the committee or disagree with their decision and seek additional information, evaluation, and guidance.

The fourth anticipated crisis period corresponds to the onset of puberty. Adolescence is a time of change in the young person; physical changes, attitude changes, and changes in the relationships between parents and child. For the non-handicapped, adolescence represents a period of growing autonomy and independence. Obviously, the handicapped youth experiences frustration and unhappiness to a greater degree during this period than he did previously, because his growing need for independence may be denied. The developmentally disabled teen-ager presents a somewhat different picture from that of the normal youngster. The normal child has an assigned sex role accompanied by the appropriate urges, and he or she is socialized through contact with others in the neighborhood, at school, and at social gatherings. In this manner, the non-handicapped child is given the opportunity to develop a healthy self-image as a male or female. The physically handicapped youth leads a much more sheltered life. In some instances, he must depend on others to provide his basic self-care. Often the handicapped person is supervised closely, allowing little or no opportunity for free interactions with his peers. The stifling of desirable, normal peer relationships and unsupervised experiences with peers limits the opportunities for the development of autonomy, independence, and value systems.

The issue of adolescent sexuality is a frequent source of parental discomfort under the best of circumstances. The young person who uninhibitedly demonstrates an increasing interest in sexual activity can increase the family's stress.

Sex education in this country is often dichotomous. On one hand, professional psychologists and counselors recommend open communication between parents and their children, acknowledging the normalcy and naturalness of sexual interests and activities in an honest, understanding manner. On the other hand, many parents have great difficulty dealing with the subject of sex for a variety of reasons.

It may be assumed that the handicapped youngster will have questions, doubts, and fears regarding sex, his sexuality, and his potential for independence. At this time, the family is best served by a renewed concentration of support and assistance. The teacher who is well acquainted with the handicapped youngster will be best able to recognize the symptoms of tension and stress and to offer helpful and informative suggestions to the family. Professional counseling may be recommended by the teacher for the handicapped individual and/or his family. Chapters 8 and 10 offer some suggestions for family living education for physically handicapped persons.

The family faces another major period of turmoil when planning for the child's adult life. The concerns about continuing care after the death of the parents and the post-school endeavors of the handicapped require major decisions that must be faced.

Parents who have sacrificed to keep a severely handicapped child at home in a sheltered, loving environment will find it very difficult to face the likelihood that the child will have to be institutionalized after their death. Siblings may be asked to promise to provide for the handicapped member in their own homes in order to avoid the alternative of institutionalization.

Provisions for the continuation of appropriate care and treatment will be of concern, both emotionally and financially. Parents generally seek information regarding public funds, trusts, and insurance policies to provide monies for care of the handicapped person until his death.

For those physically handicapped persons who are capable of some degree of independent living, the post-school years will necessitate planning and decision-making. The family will need to investigate possibilities for employment, vocational training, recreation, and leisure time activities.

Throughout the periods of crisis, the family will consult with many different professionals and agencies in search of answers and services. Gorham (1975) recommends that the teacher suggest to the parents that they keep records of the information and data gathered to provide for a comparison of information or a source of reference in the future. Gorham would tell the parent: "You are the primary helper, monitor, coordinator, observer, record keeper and decision maker for your child. Insist that you be treated as such" (Gorham, 1975).

The educator can serve the family by providing information regarding available community and state resources, parent action groups, and state and national organizations that provide literature and support for the handicapped and their families.

However, in addition to sharing information of a professional nature with the family, the teacher should find moments in which to share information of a nurturing nature. The teacher should acknowledge the positive endeavors of the home that may be extensions of the educational or treatment program (e.g., infant stimulation) and the establishment of family unit practices that promote the independence of the handicapped member. The teacher should point out the progress that is being made, even those ever-so-small increments of learning, in order to keep the parents informed, not only of the progress being made, but also of the interest and concern of others for this family member.

SUMMARY

Physically handicapped children and their families face special psychological hazards. Although research indicates that there is a greater incidence of psychological problems among the handicapped, these problems are not inevitable, and many handicapped people lead remarkably well-adjusted lives. The teacher's role in facilitating psychological adjustment includes fostering acceptance of the disability, providing appropriate educational and recreational opportunities, and focusing on the health and normal growth and development of the child, rather than overemphasizing the disability. The teacher should be aware of the stress that the families of handicapped children endure and provide good information and concerned support to these special people.

LITERATURE CITED

Ankenbrand, L. J. 1973. The self concept of students physically handicapped and non-handicapped related to participation in an individual sport. Dissert. Abstr. Internat. 34:1115.

Battle, C. U. 1974. Disruptions in the socialization of a young severely handicapped child. Rehabil. Lit. 35:130-140.

Bishop, E. S. 1977. Self-concept, social adjustment and family relations: A comparison of physically handicapped adolescents in day and residential special schools in Great Britain. Dissert. Abstr. Internat. 37:5824.

Blumberg, M. L. 1975. Psychodynamics of the young handicapped person. Am. J. Psychother. 29:466-467.

Calhoun, L. G., Selby, J. W., and King, H. S. 1976. Dealing With Crisis. Prentice-Hall, Inc., Englewood Cliffs, N.J.

Calhoun, M. L. 1976. The handicapped child. In: L. G. Calhoun, J. W. Shelby, and H. E. King, Dealing With Crisis. Prentice-Hall, Englewood Cliffs, N.J.

Cytryn, L., Moore, P. V. P., and Robinson, M. S. 1973. Psychological adjustment of children with cystic fibrosis. In: E. J. Anthony and C. Koupernik (eds.), The Child in His Family, Vol. 2. John Wiley & Sons, Inc., Toronto, Canada.

Farber, B., Jenne, W. C., and Torgo, R. 1960. Family Crisis and the Decision to Institutionalize the Retarded Child. Council for Exceptional Children, NEA Research Monograph Series, A-1.

Fatheringham, J. B., Skelton, M., and Hoddinott, B. A. 1971. The Retarded Child and His Family: The Effects of Home and Institution. The Ontario Institute for Studies in Education, Toronto, Canada.

Freedman, D. A., Fox-Kalenda, B. J., and Brown, S. L. 1970. A multihandicapped rubella baby: the first 18 months. J. Am. Acad. Child Psychiatry. 9:298-317.

Freeman, R. D. 1970. Psychiatric problems in adolescents with cerebral palsy. Dev. Med. Child Neurol. 12:64.

Gorham, K. A. 1975. A lost generation of parents. Except. Child. 41:8, 521-525.

Graham, P., and Rutter, M. 1968. Organic brain dysfunction and child psychiatric disorder. Br. Med. J. 3:695.

Green, M. 1976. The management of children with chronic disease. Proc. Inst. Med. Chicago. 31:51-54, 80.

Grossman, F. K. 1972. Brothers and Sisters of Retarded Children. Syracuse University Press, Syracuse, New York.

Hamilton, J. 1977. The dark child. Except. Parent 7:3, 31-32.

Holt, J. 1958. The influence of retarded child on family limitation. J. Ment. Defic. 2:28-36.

Johnson, D. J., and Myklebust, H. R. 1972. Learning Disabilities. Grune and Stratton, New York.

Jones, R. L. 1974. Correlates of orthopedically disabled school children's school achievement and interpersonal relationships. Rehabil. Lit. 35:272-274, 288.

Kiely, L., Sterne, R., and Witkip, C. J. 1976. Psychosocial factors in low-incidence genetic disease. Soc. Work Health Care 1:409-420.

Kriegel, L. 1969. Uncle Tom and Tiny Tim: some reflections on the cripple as negro. Am. Scholar. 38:412-430.

Kushman, K. M. 1976. A comparison of the effects of integrated and non-integrated preschool experience on degrees of social participation among able-bodied and multiply physically handicapped children. Dissert. Abstr. Internat. 36:5996.

Linkowski, D. C., and Dunn, M. A. 1974. Self-concept and acceptance of disability. Rehabil. Counsel. Bull. 17:28-32.

Lucas, R. H. 1977. Children with cancer: denying death or denying life? Paper presented at the 85th annual convention of the American Psychological Association, August, San Francisco.

Mattson, A. 1972. Long-term physical illness in childhood: A challenge to psychosocial adaptation. Pediatr. 5:801-809.

Mercer, J. R. 1966. Patterns of family crisis related to reacceptance of the retardate. Am. J. Ment. Defic. 71:19-31.

Pless, I. F. 1976. Individual and family needs in the health care of children with developmental disorders. Birth Defects. 12:91-102.

Richardson, S. A. 1969. The effect of physical disability on the socialization of a child. In: P. A. Goslin (ed.), Handbook of Socialization Theory and Research. Rand McNally, Chicago.

Rosenthal, S. R. 1978. Risk exercise and the physically handicapped. Rehabil. Lit. 36:144-149.

Shaffer, D. 1973. Psychiatric aspects of brain injury in childhood: A review. Dev. Med. Child Neurol. 15:211-220.

Shere, E. S. 1971. Patterns of child rearing in cerebral palsy: Effects upon the child's cognitive development. Pediatr. Digest 28.

Shere, M. D. 1955. Socioemotional factors in families with one twin with cerebral palsy. Except. Child. 22:197, 206-208.

Spinetta, J. J. 1974. The dying child's awareness of death. Psychol. Bull. 4:256-260.

Starr, P., and Heiserman, K. 1977. Acceptance of disability by teenagers with oral-facial clefts. Rehabil. Counsel. Bull. 198-201.

Steinhauer, P. D., Mushin, D. N., and Rae-Grant, Q. 1974. Psychological aspects of chronic illness. Pediatr. Clin. North Am. 21:825-840.

Tizard, J. 1964. Community Services for the Mentally Handicapped. Oxford University Press, London.

Van Eys, J., 1977. The outlook for the child with cancer. J. School Health, Special Issue: Cancer in School Age Children, March, 165-169.

Wolf, L. C., and Whitehead, P. C. 1975. The decision to institutionalize retarded children; comparison of individually matched groups. Ment. Retard. 13:3-7.

Wright, B. A. 1960. Physical Disability — A Psychological Approach. Harper and Row, New York.

Wright, L. 1976. The theoretical and research base for a program of early stimulation care and training of premature infants. In: J. Hellmuth (ed.), The Exceptional Infant, Vol. 2. Brunner/Mazel, New York.

4

SPECIAL NEEDS GROUPS

Figure 4-1. Infant stimulation programs are designed to ameliorate the consequences of a disabling condition: education begins early!

Although all physically handicapped persons have special needs, there are, within the parameters of the handicapped population, several subgroups of persons with certain special programming needs in common, all of which are beyond the scope of typical school programs for 6- to 18-year-olds. These subgroups are distinguished not by medical diagnosis of disability, but by their age or the severity of the handicapping condition. This chapter deals with the physically handicapped infant, the hospitalized child, the severely/profoundly handicapped, and the post-school-age handicapped person.

INFANTS

The time from conception to birth is a nine-month period of phenomenal growth. The development of the fetus is fraught with potential problems and yet, miraculously, the great majority of infants are healthy and intact at birth. The physically handicapped infant, however, has an impairment that may have originated during gestation.

In the first three months of fetal life, the brain and body structures are formed. Physical handicaps originating during this period might affect the heart, limbs, oral structure, spinal neural complex, or the brain itself. The second three months of gestation are a period of growth of the nerve cells; the third trimester (the last three months of gestation) is the period during which the fetus "completes" the growth process.

Development of the brain is not completed until the infant is approximately two years of age. During this post-natal period, the cerebellum, the glial cells, and the nerve cell connections are growing rapidly. The cerebellum is that part of the brain that is associated with muscle coordination. The glial cells provide insulating material for the nerve cells to ensure swift, efficient nerve transmissions. The first two years of life are critical to the continuing physical growth of the child.

As might be expected, the fetus injured during the prenatal (in utero) period is often the most severely damaged child. One-half of the children in institutions for the severely and profoundly handicapped are victims of pre-natal injuries (Haring, Hayden, and Beck, 1976). It is also during the pre-natal period that chromosomal and brain aberrations related to drugs and virus infections occur. Infant size at birth (not connected with prematurity) is affected during the second trimester, the period in which the cells should multiply. The precarious experience of birth itself (the perinatal stage) can result in infants who are handicapped because of oxygen deprivation, metabolic malfunctions, and direct trauma to the nerve cells (Haring, Hayden, and Beck, 1976).

Once an infant is identified as being handicapped, there is the realization that crucial early learning experiences will be hampered. White (1975) states that his own studies and those of others "have clearly indicated that the experiences of those first years are more important than we had previously thought. In their simple everyday activities, infants and toddlers form the foundations of all later development."

The nature-nurture controversy, the search to determine whether biological inheritance is more, less, or equally as significant as environmental stimuli and experiences in their influence on the growing infant, remains unsolved. Research has determined that social behaviors, physical growth, cognitive abilities, and language development are greatly affected by environmental influences (Hayden and McGinness, 1977). The handicapped infant may be faced with both an abnormal "nature" — an inefficient central nervous system — and an abnormal "nurturing" environment.

It is significant to note that a handicap of one sensory system can produce handicaps of another system (Hayden and McGinness, 1977). This detrimental contagion may be spread as a result of unsatisfactory interactions between the infant and caregiver. For example, the deaf infant of four months vocalizes but soon stops because of lack of feedback. The mother may then feel rejected and frustrated by a non-responsive or highly irritable infant and therefore reduce the amount of loving, stimulating encouragement she would otherwise give. Or, the fear of hurting or mishandling a malformed infant may cause the mother such distress that the only times the infant and parent are together are during feeding and cleaning activities. These examples illustrate conditions that can lead to a lack of the sensory stimulation that is so vital for infant learning.

Early Intervention

There are two major target populations of most infant intervention programs. The first are those babies who are called "high risk" because of social disadvantage or compromising medical situations. They are not expected to develop normally unless special procedures are introduced into their early environment. Without special help, these infants might function as if they were handicapped in future years. The other target population includes those children with "established risk" — a diagnosed handicap, such as cerebral palsy or spina bifida. For these children, the purpose of early intervention is to help them function at the top of whatever range is possible for them (Mira, 1977).

Early intervention is vital for the physically handicapped infant. Traditionally, educational programs have been initiated at the age of 5 or 6. It is now recognized that intervention programs are more successful if begun much earlier, while the development of the infant more closely approximates the norm. Early intervention with the severely/profoundly handicapped infant is seen by Bricker and Iacino (1977) as a positive action with the following objectives:

1. to prevent the development of associated problems (e.g., the development of contractures in the spastic child due to lack of proper exercise and positioning)
2. to minimize the acquisition of unwanted behaviors (e.g., self-mutilation and self-stimulation)
3. to provide desperately needed support for the parents and families of these children

Wright's (1971) study supported the merits of early intervention with the premature infant. Stimulation by handling, rocking, music, and color was accompanied by gains in the experimental group as compared to the control group infants. Scarr-Salapatek and Williams (1973) studied the effects of early intervention with premature infants born to disadvantaged mothers. Rapid gains were observed in the experimental group following hospital nursery introduction of rocking, holding, and language bombardment during the babies' feedings. The follow-up intervention incorporated in the home was accomplished by a social worker, who offered advice to the mother on toy selection and use and health care services and taught the mother how to provide enriching learning experiences for the infant.

Early Stimulation

Early stimulation is the major focus of infant intervention programs. It is from the environment that the normal infant gathers the information that serves as a basis for additional information gathering; he learns. Through movement, sensory perceptions, and interactions with the people in his life, concomitant with the continuing maturation process, the infant prepares to walk and to talk and to develop other skills that will in turn provide untold opportunities for learning.

The high-risk infant, however, may not be capable of gathering information in an incidental fashion as does his normal peer. In order to maximize the high-risk infant's opportunity to learn, infant stimulation programs prepare the environment to accentuate the stimuli to which the child is exposed. Information that the infant is to absorb is presented in an exaggerated fashion, or more frequently than might be usual. For example, it is not unusual for an infant of 6 months to be exposed to a game of peek-a-boo. This little game, played for years by infants and their caregivers, is recognized as a cognitive experience termed "object permanence." In an infant stimulation program, peek-a-boo would be explained as an important experience for the child and the caregivers would deliberately play this game with the infant. The game would be "taught" to the child using a task analysis approach, perhaps beginning with the establishment of eye contact.

Other prevalent activities in infant stimulation programs include visual, auditory, kinesthetic, and tactile experiences, the object of which is the stimulation of the sensory modalities in order to heighten the infants' awareness and knowledge of the environment. The curricular materials for eye focusing and coordination, eye-hand coordination, hand-hearing coordination, grabbing, pulling, and cognitive reasoning are readily available: mobiles, rattles, plastic containers, shaped objects, fuzzy, soft, and hard textured objects, and human voices are fundamental materials.

The Severely Handicapped Infant

The severely handicapped infant requires additional professional support in order to accomplish the objectives of an early stimulation program. To assist the severely handicapped infant in meeting the objectives of the early stimulation program, it may be necessary to create special methods or to construct special apparatus. The infant with little strength in his arms, for instance, will need to be positioned so that he can see his hands. The infant who cannot kick her feet or wave her hands about will need to be physically manipulated in order to discover these sensations. It may be necessary to use passive exercise techniques if the child is unable to move her body sufficiently to give muscles an opportunity to grow stronger.

Waiting four or five years before beginning to work with a severely handicapped child misses the opportunity to deal with the developmental problems when they are the least complex (Bricker and Iacino, 1977). However, a major concern of educators who work with these infants at very early ages is the selection of intervention activities and the establishment of meaningful, relevant goals.

Several suggestions are offered to facilitate the selection of appropriate strategies. The rationale suggested by Bricker and Iacino (1977) blends developmental learning theory and behavioral learning approaches:

1. The infant generally comes equipped with a series of reflexive responses. Through subsequent interaction with the environment, the infant modifies his basic reflexive behavior into successively more complex levels of development.
2. Behavioral development seems to follow a developmental hierarchy that is consistent for most children.
3. For those children who are not born with the necessary reflexive behavior, or who do not subsequently acquire more complex behavior, the environment must be arranged or structured to facilitate the acquisition of important responses (Bricker and Iacino, 1977).

Robinson (1976) recommends that two questions be asked of every objective before it is included in the curriculum:

1. Does this behavior that I am teaching this child give him (or build toward) additional control over his physical environment?
2. Does this behavior that I am teaching this child give him (or build toward) additional control over his social environment? If "yes" cannot be the response to one or both of these questions, there is no justification for the inclusion of the objective under consideration (Robinson, 1976).

A special caution is directed to the teachers of these handicapped infants: When evaluating the infants' capabilities, the teacher must recognize the emphasis placed on mature responses in many assessment instruments. Kagan (1970) suggests that too much emphasis has been placed on motoric responses as precursors of cognitive abilities. The inability to perform a task may be due to physical disability rather than a lack of intellectual ability.

The child's mind must not be wasted because it is housed in a handicapped body.

An Interdisciplinary Approach

An interdisciplinary approach is preferred for the education of the handicapped infant because the needs of these babies cannot be met by the educator alone. An interdisciplinary approach consists of interaction among and input from many fields concerned with the development of children. Genetic as well as environmental factors must be considered for proper educational programming. The child with a developmental disorder, regardless of the diagnosis, rarely has a single problem that requires the service of only one professional. The parents, the pediatrician, and the teacher are the key people in the initial phase of identifying disabilities, but a wide range of professional support is usually required for definitive diagnosis and treatment planning. Disciplines that have expertise to offer in the treatment planning include social work, medicine, genetics, physical and occupational therapy, psychology, special education, audiology, speech and language therapy, nutrition, dentistry, and nursing (Johnston and Magrab, 1976). (See Chapter 9 for a further discussion of the interdisciplinary process.)

The infant may be seen by an interdisciplinary agency for an hour or so a day or for as little as one day a week. Because the infant's primary caregivers and educators will be the parents, they must thoroughly understand and accept the treatment program to ensure that treatment will be continued in the home as a daily routine.

The procedures used to assess the infant's skills follow the clinical teaching model: identification of acquired skills, selection of areas for development and stimulation, delineation of strategies and techniques to be used in the stimulation, implementation of these strategies and techniques, and re-evaluation of acquired skills to determine if the tasks have been learned or acquired. This overview of assessment procedures and selection of behaviors to be taught is misleading in its simplicity.

Because the severely/profoundly handicapped infant has so many areas in need of attention, it is necessary to establish priorities. In addition, because many persons may be involved in the interaction with the parent or caregiver, there is a real need for consistency of approach, just as there is a need for an established teaching methodology that is honored by all who work with the infant.

The goals of early intervention should be the establishment and refinement of well-developed rationales, carefully trained staff members, suitable developmental curricula, and useful evaluation methods (Bricker and Iacino, 1977).

THE HOSPITALIZED CHILD

It is necessary for some children to spend time in a hospital setting. The frequency and duration of stays will be directly related to the individual child's particular physical disability or chronic illness. The long-ago stigma of the hospital as a "house of death" has been eradicated; still, the hospital is not perceived as a desirable or pleasant place to visit. Adult patients feel fear and distress at the unfamiliar aspects of the hospital routine, even though they may have had numerous hospital experiences and trust the physician and nursing staff. The child, who has less trust in the staff and a greater fear of the unknown, could find the hospital experience filled with real trauma.

The reactions of children to the hospital experience vary according to the treatment as it relates to their handicapping condition. Bergman (1965) reports that the orthopaedic patient is more accepting of treatment because of the highly visible nature of his disability. Traction pulleys, body casts, and braces provide a stark and uncompromising manifestation of the child's situation. In contrast, Bergman states that the young cardiac patient has difficulty understanding the workings of the heart; this shadowy understanding creates fantasy and mysterious unknowns.

The hospitalized child has all the same emotions as the healthy child; the repeatedly hospitalized child experiences these same emotions, with the additional factors of stress and pain, which heighten his need for reassurance, attention, and support.

The child who is exposed to repeated hospitalizations does not develop confidence because of the experience and familiarity: Bergman (1965) states that the previous experiences produce heightened anxiety and insecurity.

Drawings by second-grade hospitalized children emphasize familiar objects (food, televisions, and telephones); however, the general theme of these drawings is a loss of independence (Jones and Wakeley, 1974). The preschool-age child may perceive hospitalization as a punishment for wrong thoughts or deeds; the school-age child may worry about what is happening at home and at school while he is not there (Solnet, 1975).

The recent advances in the technology of early identification, intervention, and treatment have produced a larger number of hospitalized children. The orthopaedically handicapped child may have prolonged periods of hospitalization, while the child handicapped by chronic illness may have numerous hospitalization periods of varying lengths.

A very small part of the hospitalized child's day is actually devoted to medical needs and treatments. The larger portion of his day might be spent in idleness or in daydreaming, neither of which is beneficial to his emotional health. The inactive child is likely to develop feelings of loneliness, rejection, isolation, and fear.

Hospital Educational Programming

Teachers of hospitalized children must keep in mind the schedule of treatments and medical care for their students as well as their emotional needs. The hospital will have established policies and procedures that must be followed for the benefit of all the patients.

The instructional program is determined by the onset of the illness or disability and the length of time required for care and treatment. The teaching may be conducted by a teacher of the home-bound, by hospital-school closed circuit television, or by a hospital-based teacher.

Depending upon the duration of the child's stay in the hospital, the educational goals may include remedial or developmental instruction. In the hospital, the educational goals often include a therapeutic component: an attempt is made to help the child understand the medical treatment and to encourage the child to become an active participant in the rehabilitation process. Involvement in learning tasks and completion of homework assignments keep the child's mind occupied in a positive direction: he has something to think about other than his disability. As with all educational undertakings, the student should be exposed to meaningful, relevant learning experiences appropriate to his individual learning needs.

In-service programs for those hospital personnel who are in contact with the handicapped child give the teacher an opportunity to share his academic accomplishments. It is sometimes necessary to remind some of the busy technicians and physicians of the worries that fill a child's empty moments.

SEVERELY HANDICAPPED INDIVIDUALS

In the past, severely disabled persons were isolated early in life. Physicians and other professionals often urged the family to place these handicapped family members in private or public institutions. The families were often counseled that the handicapped member would receive better care in a residential setting, while at the same time the family would be able to continue a normal life without the encumberances imposed by the care demands of severe handicapping conditions.

Regardless of placement, the needs of this group have been neglected in the past. Few centers or residential care agencies provided total educational programs for these persons. There is, however, evidence of greater neglect in the treatment programs of many severely handicapped persons who were kept at home, often receiving little or no professional services.

In recent years, concern for the welfare of the severely handicapped has surfaced, and good attempts are being made to reach these persons. Well-trained and keenly interested people are searching for techniques, technologies, and strategies to assist the educator in the effort to maximize each individual's potential.

The U.S. Office of Education, Department of Health, Education, and Welfare, provides the following definition of this particular group of handicapped persons:

> "Severely Handicapped Children" are those who, because of the intensity of their physical, mental or emotional problems, or a combination of such problems, need educational, social, psychological and medical services beyond those which are traditionally offered by regular and special educational programs, in order to maximize their full potential for useful and meaningful participation in society and for self-fulfillment.
>
> a. The term includes those children who are classified as seriously emotionally disturbed (including children who are schizophrenic or autistic), profoundly and severely mentally retarded and those with two or more serious handicapping conditions, such as the mentally retarded, the blind, and the cerebral palsied child.
>
> b. "Severely handicapped children" 1) may possess severe language and/or perceptual-cognitive deprivations, and evidence abnormal behaviors such as i) failure to respond to pronounced social stimuli, ii) self-mutiliation, iii) self-stimulation, iv) manifestations of intense and prolonged temper tantrums, and v) the absence of rudimentary forms of verbal control, and 2) may also have extremely fragile physiological conditions. (Sontag, 1977)

Thomas (1976) defines the severely and profoundly handicapped as being small for their age and demonstrating their most severe handicaps in the areas of motor response, physical ability, and language. They may have frequent seizures, stiff limbs and muscles, and establish little or no eye contact (Thomas, 1976).

Haring, Nietupski, and Hamre-Nietupski (1976, as cited in Sontag, 1977) suggest a dynamic and educationally relevant definition: "the level of resources necessary to produce acceptable educational progress, on accepted curricula, toward independent functioning, greatly exceeds the level of resources provided in regular education."

As has already been mentioned, the severely and profoundly handicapped have previously been either isolated in the home or placed at very early ages in residential facilities for life-time care. With the passage of Public Law 94-142 in 1975, special educators intensified efforts to find methods and techniques that are effective in training programs for these people. Because of "the complexities of multiple handicaps, the needs for prosthetic aid, the necessity of evaluation adjustments, facility modifications, curriculum revisions and the interdisciplinary training requirements of parents, teachers, para-professionals and ancillary personnel over and above the traditional list of staff, the severely and profoundly handicapped indeed challenge the concept of zero reject." (Thomas, 1976)

In 1974 a parent-professional group — The American Association for the Education of the Severely/Profoundly Handicapped (AAESPH) — was formed in an attempt to improve education for these individuals and foster public awareness and understanding. The goals established for the AAESPH are:

1. to serve as an advocate organization for the development and implementation of comprehensive, high-quality educational services
2. to facilitate parent involvement in program services for these handicapped persons
3. to serve as an advocate of relevant pre- and in-service teacher-training programs; to develop specialized doctoral level teacher training and research
4. to disseminate instructional programs and information (Harmon and Haring, 1976).

High-Quality Educational Services

The primary difficulty in the education of the severely/profoundly handicapped is a result of the diverse clinical problems they present. The degree of mental retardation, the degree of restricted communication, and the degree of impaired motor ability, all of varying proportions, require services that are the epitome of individualization. Not only must educational programs be determined for each person through specialized evaluation techniques, but adaptive innovative devices and technology are necessary to prepare the student and the environment for the learning experience.

Evaluation procedures for the severely/profoundly handicapped must utilize behavioral data. The norm-referenced instrument (in which a child is compared to a population of his own age) is of little or no value when seeking to determine the appropriate educational program. By definition, a severely handicapped child is functioning well below the level of most children his age (the norm). Bigge and O'Donnell (1976) recommend descriptive and precise observation, defining descriptive as "a process which is continuous and free-floating within the natural environment. It is an ongoing part of every teaching day and every interaction with a handicapped child." Precise observation "must grow out of descriptive observation. It is exactly what the term implies: highly precise, not only with regard to that which is being observed, but also to the conditions under which it is being observed and the changes which occur as a deliberate part of that observation" (Bigge and O'Donnell, 1976). Descriptive evaluation can be recorded by the ward attendant, parent, therapist, and educator. These persons can also conduct the precise observation, although this requires specialized techniques and prior training.

The teacher of severely handicapped persons should be concerned with ongoing evaluation of the educational experience. Accurate records of the strategies and techniques used and student progress are essential for several reasons. First, the teacher will be reporting to a supervisor. Second, the unique needs of each student will engender creative ideas, some of which will prove successful and should be shared with other educators. Third, the teacher must be able to recognize the student's progress. Often progress is slow and each small step should be noticed and celebrated by the student and the teacher.

The type of measurement approach to be used in any program must depend upon the individual pupil's response characteristics as well as the nature of each task. Severely and profoundly handicapped persons learn so slowly that care must be taken to ensure an effective measure of performance so that pupils can progress in the most expeditious manner possible toward long-range goals (Haring, 1977).

Measurement techniques recommended by Haring (1977) include checklists, percentages of correct and incorrect responses, and the number of trials to criterion. The teacher will have more valuable decision-making information if frequency (how often), latency (time elapsed between stimulus and response), and duration (length of time of the measured behavior) are included in the measurement process (Haring, 1977).

Because there is no one preferred way to measure the learning of this handicapped population, perhaps the best procedure in any case is to decide first which measure will give the best picture of performance (effectiveness) and a good approximation of that ideal picture while still being fairly easy to implement (economics or feasibility). This will yield an *efficiency* answer. Given all considerations, such an answer is sometimes the best one possible (Haring, 1977).

Educational Programs

Programs should evolve along an ascending developmental hierarchy, beginning with the lowest-level skill acquired. It is necessary to prepare both the student and the environment prior to teaching. The prerequisite adaptations depend on the individual student's needs and abilities.

At this time, there is no precise formula for developing a curriculum, nor is it possible to suggest which of the existing curricula is the most viable. Williams and Gotts (1977) suggest these steps for consideration in the development of a curriculum:

1. Analyze the student's present and future life spaces (home, vocational, recreational). Attempt to identify which skills the student will need to function in these life spaces.
2. Examine available curricula critically to determine if they will teach the skills you have identified.
3. Select the curriculum that most closely matches the student's needs.
4. Adapt the curriculum to your needs.
5. Devise methods for involving parents and members of the community in the development, implementation, and evaluation of the curriculum.
6. Delegate and coordinate the specific teaching responsibilities.

Task analysis is the most appropriate technique for identifying the necessary adaptations of a curriculum. Some practitioners suggest that teachers of severely handicapped students are rarely able to use commercially available or normal child development sequences without adapting them substantially. It is essential also that teachers possess the skills required for task analysis so that, in practical situations, they can adapt available sequences or create new sequences to fit the developmental functioning levels and needs of their students (Williams and Gotts, 1977).

Socialization skills are a prerequisite to learning; for example: "Does the student watch a person move directly in his line of vision?" (Cooperative Educational Service Agency, 1976). There will be severely/profoundly handicapped persons who are unable to meet this first criterion without instruction. The *Portage Guide to Early Education* provides sequential developmental teaching and testing lessons that may be appropriate for this group.

Behavioral Characteristics Progression (Vort Corporation, 1973) items are selected because they are observable behaviors and cover skill development from early childhood through adulthood. Examples of the dressing skills selected from 48 different behaviors are:

1. cooperates passively when being dressed
4. identifies own clothing
13. pulls pants up from knees to waist
48. selects clothing for different occasions and locations

A cognitive approach to learning based on Piagetian theory is provided by Uzgiris and Hunt (1975). The cognitive sequences may not precisely specify observable behaviors; thus, there is a possibility of varying interpretation among those evaluating the student's progress (Williams and Gotts, 1977). Stephens (1977) recommends that the teacher remember the following tenets of cognitive development: 1) knowledge of a person's present level of cognitive development is a prerequisite to individualized planning, and 2) the teacher may provide the opportunity to learn or experience for the student who has to do the learning or experiencing.

Daily living skills are a major component of the educational program for the severely/profoundly handicapped. Those severely handicapped persons capable of learning daily activity skills will need direct, carefully planned instruction for independent living and vocational activities. The *Life Experience Program* (Office of the Santa Clara County Superintendent of Schools, 1975) illustrates a task-analytic curriculum appropriate for the handicapped student preparing for independent living. Evaluations and activities are presented for mental and physical development and for enhancing self-esteem. Programming guidelines are presented for the various skills necessary for independence: household skills and community and leisure time activities.

A task-analytic approach to the development of eye-hand coordination and language and motor skills is the format for the educational program described by Popovich (1977). Her book, *A Prescriptive Behavioral Checklist for the Severely and Profoundly Retarded*, provides a thorough guide with methods and materials clearly identified.

There is no magic about the implementation of educational treatments and programs for these children, provided that the administrator of these services knows what is to be done, how frequently and for what duration the skill is to be taught, and the supportive rationale for the activity. Parent and/or therapist will find the attainment of each small increment of learning much more rewarding if each increment is perceived as a stepping stone to the development of more advanced skills.

Parent Involvement in Programming

Throughout the special education system there is an attempt to involve parents in the programming decisions for their children. Parent approval is mandated by Public Law 94-142 in order that the child receive special educational services regardless of handicapping conditions. However, no other special education program solicits parent involvement in the actual program activities as vigorously as the program that deals with the severely/profoundly handicapped.

Parent involvement is sought because 1) the handicap may be emotionally devastating to the family, and their involvement in a therapeutic/educational process can provide an avenue for easing their feelings of helplessness and uselessness, and 2) the therapeutic/educational process is slow, and manpower shortages often make the desired frequency and intensity of treatments impossible without volunteer help from parents.

Thomas (1976) reports that parents often are reluctant to share the child's care with educators. If the parents have been the only caregivers for a child isolated in the home, they may resent the intrusion of an outsider who claims to know what is best for the child. To alleviate the parents' fears, Thomas advocates learning from the parents the child's likes, dislikes, habits, and skills. By recognizing that the parents do know the child better than anyone else, and by suggesting activities, rather than asserting a professional authority, the educator will gain the parents' confidence.

Dissemination of Information

Dissemination of information regarding researched techniques and practices for the education and treatment of the severely/profoundly handicapped is necessary to advance the field of knowledge in this relatively new educational endeavor. Communication through professional journals is an effective mode, although the delay in publication sometimes impedes the advancement of techniques. The isolation of residential centers scattered throughout the world also compounds the difficulty of sharing information and often produces a duplication of effort. An example of this redundancy is observable in the area of technological devices to assist the handicapped learner. Copeland's preface (1974) comments on this problem: "The authors come from various countries where often they have worked in isolation without knowledge of similar developments elsewhere in the world. Hence the reader will detect that there is a duplication of effort."

Because communication of educational successes is of extreme importance, the teacher should be in touch with others and share their efforts. Involvement in professional organizations and association with others in the field serves as a stimulating experience for educators of the severely/profoundly handicapped.

The dissemination of reports, research, and public and private endeavors is made available through journals and microfiche available at all libraries through inter-library loans. Information-sharing programs are being developed in each state and the teacher is encouraged to visit local agencies to share experiences with others and be inspired and educated by their successes. Appendix A provides the addresses of some agencies interested in sharing such information.

HANDICAPPED PERSONS IN THE POST-SCHOOL YEARS

Attending school and sharing experiences with a group of peers is a protected life. The handicapped person is protected, not from rejection, because that will happen, and not from failure and frustration, because they will happen, too, but in the sense that the people in the school become used to seeing him and demonstrate a consistency in their manner of responding to him. The physically handicapped may not have many novel experiences with rejection, curiosity, and avoidance until "coming of age," when the time arrives to seek independence from family and school. Thus, the years of therapy, counseling, education, and vocational preparation are directed toward one goal: the preparation of the handicapped individual for a rewarding life of contribution to the world of work and meaningful interaction with others.

Acceptance into the Community

The handicapped adult faces a prejudiced society. From Captain Hook, to the beanstalk giant, to the patched-eye bad guy, we have been taught that deformity connotes evil. Advertisements try to convince us that youth, beauty, and sex appeal are the matrix of a good life (Betts, 1977). There are some changes being made in this attitude due to a concerted effort to educate the public at an awareness level. Reserved parking spaces, ramps, walkways and railings, bumper stickers, and TV spot commercials evidence the subtle approach being used to cause a societal attitude change.

Another attempt to provoke change is less subtle. The Rehabilitation Act of 1973 prohibits discrimination against the handicapped. This law, which became effective June 1, 1977, applies to any institution that receives Health, Education, and Welfare funds, and prohibits employers from refusing to hire qualified, capable persons because of a disability or disease.

A militant atmosphere is created by frustrated handicapped persons who, as outspoken critics of the society that prefers to ignore them, picket and publicly demonstrate for the implementation of the Rehabilitation Act. "The fact that they are speaking out about injustice indicates that the therapy (process) has been successful. Rehabilitation therapy has sought to make them independent and part of the mainstream of life — and part of the mainstream of life nowadays is that you speak up and be heard from" (Betts, 1977).

Acceptance into the World of Work

In spite of the "work ethic" in America, which prizes the worker and downgrades the non-productive citizen, the capable handicapped person is not always able to find employment. Nathanson (1977) addresses the myths that prevail in the business world and that slow compliance with the laws that prevent discrimination against the handicapped in hiring practices. DuPont's analysis of safety records indicate that 96% of the employees with disabilities rated average or better when compared with the general work force in job performance. It also determined that few disabled workers needed special work arrangements (Nathanson, 1977).

Nathanson's review of the DuPont study provides evidence that business should consider the facts and discard the "old wives tales" that the disabled employee will raise insurance rates, lower productivity, increase absenteeism because of illness, and necessitate expensive equipment and facility changes.

With the increasing employment of the disabled, vocational rehabilitation has developed into a major national social commitment (Leviton and Faggart, 1977). The vocational rehabilitation program serves those physically or mentally handicapped persons who are limited in their work opportunities and who are apt to benefit from the services provided. The program serves a wide range of clients, from the most severely disabled to those with minor work limitations. Sheltered workshops for the severely disabled are one component of this system.

The convenience of speaking in generalities must be avoided when examining the world of work for the disabled. The disabled population is comprised of persons with many different disabilities. The type of disability and its secondary effects (if any) must be considered. For example: while arthritis alone might not present an employment liability, if it is accompanied by high blood pressure it might seriously limit the person's opportunities.

Many persons with physical disabilities are independent in their job search and in handling job requirements; others need the support of vocational counselors.

For many handicapped persons, work opportunities have declined with technological advances and the increase in urban living and job competition with the non-handicapped, e.g., youth, women, and, in some cases, illegal immigrants. To locate an appropriate employment situation for a handicapped person, the handicapping condition, work experience, demographic characteristic, and personal attributes of the individual must be considered (Levitan and Faggart, 1977). The word "work" connotes employment in exchange for pay. However, for some handicapped persons for whom employment is unattainable, "work" means participating in their environment with as much independence as possible.

Severely handicapped people might find work in sheltered workshops, rehabilitation centers, and institutions. Sheltered workshop programs provide long-term employment in a competitive job market (Conley, 1972). The workshop tasks are usually arranged so that one or two basic operations are covered at each work station (Nelson, 1971). Before vocational counselors help clients select a suitable position, the worker will have a skills level evaluation that will be matched to a job-skills analysis. The application of task analysis to occupational chores provides a hierarchy of skills necessary for the successful completion of the assignment. The following task ladder provides a sample analysis of an occupational chore:

> Task Analysis of Washing Dishes
> A. Preliminary Sorting
>   Silverware
>   Glassware
>   Types of Dishes
>   Bread and Butter Plates
>   Saucers
>   Dinner Plates
>   Bowls
>   Cups
>   Pots and Pans
> B. Racking
> C. Measuring of Detergent
> D. Starting Machine
> From: *A Task Analysis Approach to Prevocational and Vocational Training for the Handicapped* (Duquesne University, 1975).

Today's labor market calls for the intensive preparation of handicapped persons in order to ensure steady employment. Thoroughness of preparation is reported by the Chicago Goodwill Rehabilitation Center, which serves clients 16–60 years of age, with a median client age of 38. This agency describes the employment preparation process as including vocational eval-

uation, vocational orientation and exploration, counseling, and psychological therapy. These steps are followed by work adjustment training, remedial education as necessary, work and vocational education, job seeking
skills, job placement services, residential adjustment counseling, and residential services.

In addition to those talents related to guidance and instruction of
work-related skills, the instructor of post-school training for the handicapped will also need interpersonal skills to coordinate the efforts of many helping professionals. This teacher will work closely with agency and service personnel and members of the business community.

Recreation

The physically handicapped adult needs to play as well as to work. Recreation serves to stimulate, refresh, entertain, and enrich our lives while providing a satisfactory and positive use of leisure time.

Although many hobbies and interests can be pursued in the home, socialization and recreation with other people is a stimulating and enjoyable
experience. Recognition of the need to be with others is demonstrated by
the increased cooperation of community service agencies. Betts (1977)
states that the community itself benefits along with the handicapped person
as a result of his being in society and out in the community: "We, who are
not handicapped, try to ignore the fact pain and suffering exist. Well, let
me tell you that these people have gone through an extremely hard time. As
a result, they are very likely to be extraordinary as to what they can contribute to the people around them."

In many communities recreation opportunities for handicapped people are not readily available. Goldman (1975) advocates a community service system that is legally able to provide or purchase services for eligible
persons within a given geopolitical area. Such a system would prevent competitive and conflicting agency efforts. Through such community agency
consortiums the problems of staffing, programming, and transportation
can be eliminated, enabling the handicapped to locate socialization opportunities (Bigge and O'Donnell, 1977).

Service agencies (i.e., Jaycees, Women's Clubs, and Rotary Clubs), action groups (i.e., PTA's, Boy Scouts, and Rainbow Girls), and interest
groups (i.e., senior citizens, religious groups, and auxiliaries) can be asked
to provide transportation to program facilities (swimming pools, parks,
YMCA's, YWCA's, theaters, and gymnasiums) in order to greatly expand
the opportunities for the handicapped. An example of community effort is
the Knoxville Zoological Park in Tennessee, which is adapting its facilities
to be fully accessible to the handicapped. Steps have been replaced by
ramps, drinking fountains and pay phones have been lowered, braille maps

have been installed, and taped messages guide visitors (*Parks and Recreation*, 1977).

Day activity and social development centers for severely handicapped persons eighteen and over are very much needed in this period of deinstitutionalization. In many cases Title XVI funds are available to such centers for the social rehabilitation of individuals receiving Supplemental Security Income. Several existing programs combine private and governmental funding to provide recreational opportunities for local handicapped citizens. The Los Angeles Recreation and Parks Department provides programs for handicapped persons of all ages five days a week. A Washington, D.C. program funded by the Kennedy Foundation and Civitans International has an enrollment of 3,500 persons between the ages of 3 and 60 and operates 6 days a week, year round. This program has three nine-week summer camps. Philadelphia provides a recreation program throughout the year in which 750 people participate weekly (Adams, 1977).

Camping for the handicapped has grown in popularity and the scope of these programs is similar to the camping opportunities for the non-handicapped population. The camps' activities vary in settings, activities, and program length, as well as in terms of therapeutic goals. Many camping programs offer a purely recreational outlet based on the philosophy that camping is therapeutic for everyone (Report of the Committee on Camping for the Handicapped, 1974). Supportive research for the camping experience is provided by Holden (1960), who demonstrated that camping experiences led to an improved body image for physically handicapped children. Kinzie (1958) reported improved peer relationships and self-care skills among the physically handicapped as a result of camping.

The sports, hobbies, and recreational opportunities selected can be therapeutic as well as pleasurable. A few examples are provided based on the work of Adams (1977):

Disease Category	Recreational Implication
Spina bifida	Activities selected should develop strength in shoulders and arms. Wheelchair activities (relays, ball games, archery, table tennis, weight lifting, and swimming) are appropriate.
Scoliosis	The use of a Milwaukee brace will be somewhat inhibiting; however, the client should be encouraged to increase activity while wearing the brace. To assist balance movements, choose activities such as volleyball, tennis, ice and roller skating, crafts, bowling, and bicycling. Swimming is also encouraged with the brace removed.

| Muscular dystrophy | Active motion and exercise should be started early. Recreation activities prevent atrophy; calorie intake should be reduced. Sports must be those that do not call for strength, such as riflery, billiards, and shuffleboard. Musical instruments, typing, and piano playing are appropriate hobby interests. |
| Cerebral palsy | Competitive sports are not recommended because excitement and tension are contraindicated. The degree of motor disability will determine the recreational activities. Some water activities are helpful with supportive wings and floats to eliminate any fear. |

The use of recreational facilities gives physically handicapped persons an opportunity for advisable and helpful socialization and therapy. The cooperative efforts of both public and private agencies and organizations under a coordinating director will facilitate the location of wanted and/or needed programs. The educator with a background in recreation as either a physical education teacher or recreational therapist will be able to recommend those recreational activities that are pleasurable and therapeutic.

Independent Living Arrangements

For those physically handicapped persons who have the inclination and ability to assume an independent or semi-dependent place in the community, cloistered placement can be a dehumanizing experience. The stated goal of educational programs is to enable the individual to attain the greatest degree of independence possible. In many instances the natural extension of classroom learning for the physically handicapped is the provision of simulated or actual independent living facilities. A continuum of such services begins with home and family living courses introduced in a classroom setting and extends to "house living" in a residential community. The following examples are typical of the stages of independence that may be acquired.

Will (1975) describes a curriculum guide from the Home and Family Living Laboratory, which serves retarded teenagers and adults. Next door to the school is a house that serves as a laboratory setting for the practice of independent living skills. Topics of study include: living in a neighborhood, money and the consumer, personal needs within the family, interior home care, home maintenance, emergencies, and leisure time activities.

Whitten Village, South Carolina, provides apartment living experiences for clients who are preparing to move into the community. The apartments on the campus of this residential treatment center are renovated dormitories. The clients share a bedroom with a roommate and a kitchen and living room with four others. They are responsible for the cooking and the cleaning of their apartment under the supervision of a housemother. These apartment dwellers are employed in the nearby communities and, with the exception of supervision and counseling that is available when it is wanted or needed, they lead independent, contributing lives.

The half-way house program is similar to those described above except that the house is located in the residential community away from institutional protection or isolation. Cherington and Dybwad (1974) describe the experiences faced by handicapped citizens in their quest for a home in a residential area. (For further information on independent living, see Chapter 10.)

SUMMARY

Within the physically handicapped population are subgroups with very special needs: infants, preschool-age and hospitalized children, the severely/profoundly handicapped, and post-school-age persons. Because of increased awareness and understanding of these special needs, schools and community agencies are now extending activity opportunities and assistance to these persons. However, because of a lack of tradition of prior service, much remains to be discovered about effective helping strategies. The teacher of these physically handicapped individuals has a responsibility to be innovative in teaching, careful in the monitoring of progress, and generous in sharing the results of successful experiences with others.

LITERATURE CITED

Adams, R. 1977. Program implications for children with orthopaedic and related impairments. In: Physical Education and Recreation for Impaired, Disabled and Handicapped Individuals: Past, Present and Future. American Alliance for Health, Physical Education, and Recreation. Washington, D.C.

Bergman, T. 1965. *Children in the Hospital.* International Universities Press, New York.

Betts, H. B. 1977. Latest on helping the handicapped "We have come a long way." U.S. News and World Report, Inc., January 31, 61-63.

Bigge, J. L., and O'Donnell, P. A. 1976. Teaching Individuals with Physical and Multiple Disabilities. Charles E. Merrill Publishing Company, Columbus, Ohio.

Bricker, P. D., and Iacino, R. 1977. Early intervention with severely/profoundly handicapped children. In: E. Sontag (ed.), Educational Programming for the Severely and Profoundly Handicapped. Council for Exceptional Children, Mental Retardation Division, Reston, Va.

Cherington, C., and Dybwad, G. (eds.). 1974. New Neighbors: the Retarded Citizen in Quest of a Home. President's Committee on Mental Retardation (ERIC Document Reproduction Service No. ED 165670), Washington, D.C.

Conley, R. 1972. The Economics of Mental Retardation. Johns Hopkins Press, Baltimore.

Cooperative Educational Service Agency (#12). 1976. Portage Guide to Early Education. Portage, Wisc.

Copeland, K. (ed.). 1974. Aids for the Severely Handicapped. Grune and Stratton, New York.

Duquesne University, School of Education. 1975. A Task Analysis Approach to Prevocational Training for the Handicapped. Duquesne University, Pittsburgh.

Goldman, E. R. 1975. A state model for community services. Ment. Retard. 13:5, 33–36.

Haring, N. G. 1977. Measurement and evaluation procedures for programming with the severely and profoundly handicapped. In: E. Sontag (ed.), Educational Programming for the Severely/Profoundly Handicapped. The Council for Exceptional Children, Mental Retardation Division, Reston, Va.

Haring, N. G., Hayden, A. H., and Beck, G. R. 1976. General principles and guidelines in "programming" for severely handicapped children and young adults. Focus on Exceptional Children, April, 1–15.

Haring, N. G., Nietupski, J., and Hamre-Nietupski, S. 1976. Guidelines for effective intervention with the severely handicapped: Toward independent functioning. Unpublished manuscript, University of Washington, Seattle. In: E. Sontag (ed.), Educational Programming for the Severely and Profoundly Handicapped. The Council for Exceptional Children, Mental Retardation Division, Reston, Va.

Harmon, E., and Haring, N. G. 1976. Meet AAESPH. Educ. Train. Ment. Retard. 11:2, 101–105.

Hayden, A. H., and McGinness, G. D. 1977. Basis for early intervention. In: E. Sontag (ed.), Educational Programming for the Severely/Profoundly Handicapped. The Council for Exceptional Children, Mental Retardation Division, Reston, Va.

Holden, R. 1960. Changes in body imagery of physically handicapped children due to summer camping experiences. Unpublished doctoral dissertation (abstr.), Boston University, Boston.

Johnston, R. B., and Magrab, P. R. 1976. Developmental Disorders: Assessment, Treatment, Education. University Park Press, Baltimore.

Jones, L., and Wakely, C. 1974. "Tell me about your picture." Imprint 21:1, 20–22.

Kagan, J. 1970. Attention and psychological change in the young child. Science 170:826–832.

Kinzie, S. M. 1958. Parental assessment of change in handicapped children resulting from a camping experience. Unpublished masters thesis (abstr.), University of Toronto, School of Social Work, Toronto.

Levitan, S. A., and Faggart, R. 1977. Employment problems of disabled persons. Monthly Labor Review March, 3–12.

McDowell, F. B., and Sontag, E. 1977. The severely and profoundly handicapped as catalysts for change. In: E. Sontag (ed.), Educational Programming for the Severely/Profoundly Handicapped. The Council for Exceptional Children, Mental Retardation Division, Reston, Va.

Mira, M. 1977. Tracking the motor behavior of multihandicapped infants. Ment. Retard. 15:32–37.

Nathanson, R. B. 1977. The disabled employee: separating myth from fact. Harvard Business Review May-June, 6–8.

National Therapeutic Recreation Society. 1974. Report of the Committee on Camping for the Handicapped. Washington, D.C.

Nelson, N. 1971. Workshops for the Handicapped in the United States. Charles C Thomas Publisher, Springfield, Ill.

Office of the Santa Clara County Superintendent of Schools. 1975. Life Experience Program. Santa Clara, California.

Parks and Recreation. 1977. Mobilizing for a Barrier-Free Zoo. Knoxville, Tn.

Popovich, D. 1977. A Prescriptive Behavioral Checklist for the Severely and Profoundly Retarded. University Park Press, Baltimore.

Robinson, D. C. 1976. Application of Piagetian sensorimotor concepts to assessment
and curriculum for severely handicapped children. AAESPH Rev. 1:8.

Scarr-Salapatek, S., and Williams, M. L. 1973. The effects of early stimulation on
low birth weight infants. Child Dev. 44:94–101.

Schilder, P., and Weschler, D. 1934. The attitude of children toward death. J. Gen.
Pediatr. 45:406–451.

Solnit, A. 1975. Reaction of school-aged children to hospitalization. Paper presented at the 10th annual Conference of the Association for the Care of Children
in Hospitals, Boston.

Sontag, E. (ed.). 1977. Educational Programming for the Severely/Profoundly
Handicapped. The Council for Exceptional Children, Mental Retardation Division, Reston, Va.

Stephens, B. 1977. A Piagetian approach to curriculum development for the severely, profoundly, and multiply handicapped. In: E. Sontag (ed.), Educational
Programming for the Severely/Profoundly Handicapped. The Council for Exceptional Children, Mental Retardation Division, Reston, Va.

Thomas, M. A. 1976. We turned the corner and started doing more: implementing
programs for the severely and profoundly handicapped — conversations with Jean
Carvin and Richard Sherr. Educ. Training Ment. Retard. 11:1, 83–92.

Tizard, J. 1976. Community Services for the Mentally Handicapped. Oxford University Press, London.

Uzgiris, I. C., and Hunt, J. McV. 1975. Assessment in Infancy. University of Illinois
Press, Chicago.

Vort Corporation. 1973. Behavioral Characteristics Progression. Palo Alto, Calif.

White, B. L. 1975. The First Three Years of Life. Prentice Hall, Englewood Cliffs,
N.J.

Will, P. (ed.). 1975. Home and Family Living Laboratory Curriculum Guide.
(ERIC Document Reproduction Service No. ED 112599)

Williams, W., and Gotts, E. A. 1977. Selected consideration on developing curriculum for severely handicapped students. In: E. Sontag (ed.), Educational Programming for the Severely/Profoundly Handicapped. The Council for Exceptional Children, Mental Retardation Division, Reston, Va.

Wright, L. 1971. The theoretical and research base for a program of early stimulation, care and training of premature infants. In: J. Hellmuth (ed.), The Exceptional Infant, Vol. 2. Brunner/Mazel, New York.

5

THE LEAST
RESTRICTIVE
ENVIRONMENT

Figure 5-1. Building modifications, such as ramps, open doors to education for physically handicapped students.

All handicapped children are entitled to a free, appropriate education in the "least restrictive environment" (P.L. 94–142). This important legal phrase has at least three implications:

1. Handicapped children should be served in learning environments that are as similar to those of their non-handicapped peers as possible. For handicapped children who are able to learn the same things at the same rate as non-handicapped children, isolation in a special school or class is considered restrictive; a regular school placement is the "least restrictive environment."

2. Handicapped children should be served in the learning environments that best meet their special needs. For some handicapped children, this best learning environment is not a regular classroom. A severely multiply handicapped child is often best served in a small special class with intensive one-to-one learning experiences and therapy; for this child, a regular classroom is "restrictive" because in such an environment he is able to learn very little.

3. Placement in the "least restrictive environment" cannot be made without safeguards for the rights of the child and his family. The safeguards established by law include:

    a. The placement decision must be made by a committee of at least three educators and approved by the parents or guardians of the student.

    b. This committee must also delineate the student's educational plan, including stated educational goals for the student, which serves as a guide for teacher planning — this document is the Individual Educational Plan (IEP) discussed further in Chapter 8.

    c. The student's progress must be evaluated at least once a year, and the evaluation must be followed by a subsequent revision of the educational goals.

    d. The student's program must include a physical education component and a statement of needed related services.

This chapter examines the variables that determine and enhance the least restrictive educational environment for physically handicapped students. Discussed here are techniques for identifying physically handicapped students in need of special educational help, the continuum of special education services available to physically handicapped students, considerations in matching the individual learner's needs to the appropriate placement, and, finally, methods for facilitating placement in the least restrictive environment.

REACHING THE UNSERVED OR UNDERSERVED

Before an educational program for the physically handicapped can be effective, the needy children must first be found. In school systems with long-established programs, public and professional awareness generally channels most children with special needs to the appropriate program; but in those school districts where special education programs for the physically handicapped are new and unfamiliar, the lines of communication must be opened. The incidence of physically handicapped school-age children is small — the U.S. Office of Education estimates 0.5 of the total school-age population (1971) — but only a very unusual school district would have no children in need of this special help. Thus, in all likelihood, school districts without programs for the physically handicapped have children who are unserved or underserved.

Unserved children and young people include those who were turned away from school in the past because no programs were available, and parents may not be aware of doors that are now open. The unserved also include those children whose parents have never tried to enroll them in school for a variety of reasons — family shame, neglect, overprotection, and the feeling that the schools probably would not do anything anyway.

Underserved children are those who, although enrolled in some sort of school program, are not developing to their fullest potential because they are not in the *right* program. Included here are those children who are on homebound instruction because of the lack of in-school programs for the physically handicapped, as well as those children in regular classrooms who are falling behind because of a lack of understanding of their special learning needs.

School districts initiating programs have an obligation to spread the word so that unserved and underserved physically handicapped children can receive the best possible education. The following are some "child find" ideas that some districts have found helpful (Clark, 1976; Zehrback, 1975):

1. One district appointed a full-time "child-find specialist" whose job was to locate unserved handicapped children. She began the job by spending 8 hours a day calling every agency and institution that might be able to put her on the trail of a handicapped child.
2. Information packets can be sent to agencies, physicians, clinics, and public health nurses. Each should contain a short explanatory letter, a brief set of criteria, and a request that the letter be posted in a prominent spot. Area clergy should be sent similar packets.
3. The media can be used in a variety of ways, including: public-service announcements on radio and TV, stories in newspapers, and posted notices in public places (e.g., supermarkets, laundromats, and libraries).
4. The school system itself can assist in locating children with special needs. The director of special services or the teacher of physically handicapped children should present inservice programs to all schools in the district, requesting assistance in identifying physically handicapped children who need special help. School officials should be questioned concerning any handicapped children whom they may have had to turn away in the past. Talks can be given to Parent-Teacher Associations. Notices can be sent home with children already attending the schools.

Child-find programs depend heavily on public awareness — on letting people know that programs do exist for handicapped children no matter how difficult their situation may seem.

A CONTINUUM OF SPECIAL EDUCATION SERVICES

Because physical disabilities may interfere with learning to any degree from mild to severe, the available educational alternatives must provide a continuum of services that also range in degree, from mild intervention to a total support system. Deno (1970) describes a cascade of special education services to meet these diverse needs: Most handicapped children can be served in regular classrooms; a smaller number will need the special help of supplementary instructional services, such as part-time (or resource) special classes, full-time special classes, and homebound instruction. A still smaller number will need instruction in hospital or residential settings.

This continuum is called a cascade because of the considerable difference in the number of children involved at the different levels of intervention. The cascade system is designed to make available whatever different-from-the-mainstream setting is required to control the learning variables deemed critical for the individual student (Deno, 1970). This arrangement of services facilitates the tailoring of treatment to individual needs, rather than sorting out children to fit rigid categories and conditions.

Alternatives within this continuum of services are discussed below, with attention directed to student eligibility for inclusion, teacher-pupil ratio, and teaching practices. The responsibilities of parents, teachers, and school officials (especially principals and directors of special education) are also discussed. Because the goal of the programs is to provide learning situations that are as much like regular education settings as possible, the alternatives are presented in order from least to most restrictive.

Regular Classroom

For many physically handicapped children, the regular schoolroom provides the best educational situation. These children demonstrate a reasonable acceptance of their handicapping conditions, and are able to function academically in the regular classroom setting, and can compensate adequately for the limitations imposed by their disability.

The teacher-pupil ratio is stipulated by the guidelines for class enrollment issued by each state's department of education according to the grade level of the student. In most states, this means that the elementary student will attend classes with 18-25 peers, while the secondary youth may have as many as 22-50 classmates.

Students who require supportive therapy (for example, speech or physical therapy) may be absent from the classroom for short periods of time. Some students will also require medical treatments that may have to be scheduled during school hours.

Although the student is carried on the teacher's roll rather than on a special education roll, the teacher must be able to demonstrate that the instruction is geared to the educational goals as delineated by the student's placement committee. There will be an annual evaluation of the student's progress toward these stated goals; if, at any time, the student does not appear to be maintaining steady growth in the desired areas, the placement committee will be charged with the responsibility of discussing the situation with the teacher(s) and re-evaluating the placement decision.

School administrators are responsible for providing for the needs of the physically handicapped students within their school building. Medical considerations and architectural alterations are discussed later in this chapter.

Careful selection of the regular teachers of disabled students is considered of paramount importance. Battaglia (1977) states that dumping or forced mainstreaming causes difficulties for both the teacher and the child in a regular class. The school administrators should seek and identify those teachers with positive attitudes toward working with handicapped children.

The teacher must have an understanding of what is "normal" for the classroom, and she should have adequate information about the handicapping conditions (an understanding of the causes, the limits of ability, and the prognosis). The teacher should know the individual child as a person: his interests, academic aspirations, and previous academic achievement. In addition, the teacher should be aware of available resources — persons in the building or district who can provide suggestions for materials and techniques —, understand his own feelings about the handicapped, and recognize and acknowledge any personal fears and doubts he may have about teaching a handicapped student (Klein, 1977). (See Table 5-1 for further details about the responsibilities of the special education personnel.)

Teaching Practices in the Regular Classroom   The majority of the physically handicapped pupils enrolled in regular programs will have motor disabilities. Their lack of manual dexterity and/or ambulation will require the teacher to make alterations in some of the regularly assigned learning experiences of these children. Taking notes may be impossible for a mildly involved cerebral palsied student; however, tape recorders make it possible for students to record those portions of the teacher's comments that they will need to review later. In some cases, the manner of testing the handicapped student's learning will have to differ from the method used with the other class members. Interview, discussion, or multiple examinations by stylus may be necessary for those children with limited manual dexterity.

Students who are non-ambulatory or who have limited use of their legs may require no educational alterations other than those necessary to accommodate this particular disability. Classrooms in which this student will be taught must be easily accessible to ramps or elevators, and classroom furniture and equipment must be located conveniently.

Table 5-1. Physically handicapped students in a regular classroom

Classroom Teacher	Responsibilities of the... School Official	Parent
1. Meet with parents to discuss instructional goals for each child.	1. Plan (with teachers) instructional strategies and curriculum modifications as needed.	1. Tour the school building with your child and point out to school officials any needed changes in the facilities.
2. Discuss the amount of homework to be assigned; suggest how much time should be allotted for these assignments at home.	2. Periodically evaluate each student's progress.	2. Notify the school personnel of any medication, medical treatment, or allergies that might affect your child's school work.
3. Adjust and adapt the curriculum when necessary.	3. Adapt the scholastic environment — both physical and personnel components — to facilitate the mainstreaming of students.	3. Give permission to the school personnel to contact your child's physician in case of treatment-related educational questions.
4. Formulate an IEP for each handicapped child.	4. Select the handicapped child's teacher carefully to guarantee a responsive and accepting classroom situation.	4. Have the child ready for school transportation at the appropriate time.
5. Be informed concerning each child's disability and its prognosis. Know each child as a person; know his personal aspirations.	5. Conduct inservice faculty workshops on the needs of the physically handicapped.	5. Share with your child's teachers any information that will help them to understand him as a special person.
6. Maintain accurate records indicating progress made toward educational goals.		6. Notify school personnel when your child will be unable to attend classes or when there is a change in his condition.
7. Be alert for changes in a student's health that might point to the need for consultation with a physician, school special-service personnel, or other professionals.		7. Attend meetings of school and parental organizations and action groups.

The toileting needs of some physically handicapped children may be of special concern to classroom teachers. Easy access to barrier-free bathrooms is essential for the physically handicapped child in a regular setting. Parents should be consulted concerning the need for scheduling or special equipment.

Special consideration should be given to the physical education programs of handicapped students. A medical excuse may placate a parent and be the most expeditious course for an administrator, but by no stretch of the imagination is it in the best interest of the student (Vodola, 1973). A high-quality, regular physical education program uses the adaptive approach, offering individualized instruction and opportunities to develop physical fitness, skill in sports activities, good body mechanics and rhythms, and relaxation techniques for all the students in the program (Arnheim, Auxter, and Crowe, 1973).

Resource Room Programs

Students participating in the resource program are enrolled in the general educational curriculum and go to the resource room on a regularly scheduled basis for special support, most often of an academic nature. The student, having been referred for special services, is thoroughly evaluated on an educational basis, after which a school committee determines whether resource room intervention on a part-time basis will be beneficial for this student (Hawisher and Calhoun, 1978). The resource room may be categorical, serving children with one particular kind of disability (such as physical handicaps), or may be non-categorical, serving children with a variety of special learning needs. The resource teacher is a certified special education teacher.

The teaching caseload for a resource room is 20-33 students, who are scheduled into this classroom for one or two periods each school day. The students are seen individually or in small groups of no more than four. Physically handicapped students enrolled in the resource program are those who meet the eligibility requirements for regular class placement but have accompanying mild learning problems that need attention. In addition to academic work, the resource teacher may help the physically handicapped student with communication and independent living-skill development, self-esteem issues, and in adapting materials for use in the regular classroom.

The resource teacher works directly with the students and also serves as a curriculum and materials consultant to their regular classroom teachers. It is her responsibility to coordinate the instruction in the resource room to support and facilitate the student's regular classroom education. (See Table 5-2 for an example of a resource room schedule.)

Table 5-2.   Resource room schedule

8:00- 9:00	Planning/Conferences
9:05- 9:50	Group A
10:00-10:45	Group B
10:55-11:40	Group C
11:45-12:15	Lunch
12:15- 1:00	Group D (or Conferences)
1:00- 1:55	Group E
2:00- 2:45	Group F
2:45- 3:30	Planning/Conferences

Groups A, B, and C are comprised of students requiring a heavy concentration of remedial assistance. The groups are small, having no more than four students in each. Groups D, E, and F lend themselves to alternate scheduling: Group D, for example, could be split into D^1 and D^2. The students in D^1 would attend resource room class on Monday, Tuesday, and Wednesday; D^2 students would attend the class on Thursday and Friday. The D^2 time period could also be reserved for observations and conferences. Group F also meets at a time of day that is suitable for rewarding students who had controlled specific target behaviors as delineated in their planned behavior management programs (Hawisher and Calhoun, 1978).

Teaching Practices in the Resource Room   Tutorial services (in the tool subject areas for elementary students, and study skills and content areas for middle and secondary students) are of major emphasis in the resource room. The instructional program, determined by educational assessment procedures, is matched to the student's educational goals as established by the placement committee. For physically handicapped students, non-academic areas, such as communication, mobility, independent living, and self-concept may constitute some of these goals.

Typical teaching materials and equipment used in the resource room include magnetic card readers, listening stations and earphones, overhead projectors, tape recorders, and tape players. The techniques of teaching employed include learning centers, one-to-one instruction, and small-group work. Table 5-3 gives further details of the specific responsibilities of special education personnel.

Itinerant Teacher Program

The term "itinerant class" is a misnomer in that it seems to imply that the class members or even the classroom itself is mobile and moves about the school district. There are instances in which an equipped van serves as a mobile schoolroom; however, usually the term "itinerant class" refers to a situation in which the teacher moves from one school building to another, providing specialized instructional services to the students enrolled in her class. The itinerant program is helpful in school districts that are sparsely populated, predominantly rural, have transportation problems, and/or have only small numbers of physically handicapped children.

The itinerant teacher shares the responsibility for the student's educational planning with the general education teacher because the student will be attending classes in both sectors of the school's program. The students served by this teacher generally exhibit mild or moderate physical involvement and are able to function in the regular classroom with the aid of supportive services as provided by the itinerant teacher and district special-service personnel. Approximately 22-30 pupils will be served by the itinerant teacher, meeting with her individually or in small groups.

The nature of this model means that the itinerant teacher is not a "full-fledged" faculty member of any particular school building; therefore, since this teacher is not in one particular school during the entire week, the ability to communicate and maintain precise records (as well as proficient teaching ability) are necessary skills for the itinerant teacher. Working effectively with others is another essential skill.

On her visits to the schools the itinerant teacher provides instruction either directly (as a tutor) or indirectly (as a teacher consultant) for those students on her rolls. She confers with each student's regular teachers concerning classroom progress and suggests materials or adaptations as appropriate. Good communication among teachers is necessary to ensure that the instructional programs of the regular classrooms and the special support instruction provided by the itinerant teacher are closely correlated and/or complementary. This special support may be in the form of remedial or supplementary teaching, or adapting curricular materials to facilitate the handicapped's school experiences.

Teaching Practices in the Itinerant Program   The academic program in the itinerant model is either skill oriented in the tool subjects, study-skill oriented in the content areas, or of a teacher consultant nature. When direct student service is provided by the itinerant teacher, the students are assigned to this teacher for a specified number of class periods each week. Each student should reasonably be seen for approximately 120 minutes a week.

In programs providing indirect student services the itinerant teacher team-teaches with the regular class teacher, offering support through material selection or construction, or assisting the student in completing his assignments.

The distance between schools and the number of students in each building are factors that influence the establishment of a schedule. Samples of working schedules are found in Table 5-4.

The responsibilities of the parents, the school officials, the classroom teachers, and the itinerant teacher are the same as those already discussed under the topic of resource room programs.

The Self-Contained Classroom (and the Special School)

There are those physically handicapped students whose conditions preclude mainstreamed education. Along with a physical disability, these children have learning problems that are severe enough to preclude regular/

Table 5-3. Physically handicapped students in a resource room

| | Responsibilities of the… | | |
Resource Room Teacher	Classroom Teacher	School Official	Parent
1. Schedule each child's resource room sessions to permit maximum successful participation in the regular classroom.	1. Meet with parents to discuss instructional goals for their child.	1. Plan (with the regular and resource teachers) the necessary instructional strategies and curriculum modifications for each student.	1. Visit the school and tour the building. Point out any necessary changes in the school facilities that you feel would permit your child to be more independent.
2. Coordinate the instructional program with the regular classroom program.	2. Discuss the amount of homework to be assigned with parents; suggest how much time should be regularly allotted for after-school assignments.	2. Periodically evaluate each student's educational progress to ascertain the degree of program success.	2. Notify school personnel of any medications or medical treatments necessary for your child.
3. Formulate an IEP for each student.	3. Adjust and adapt curriculum when necessary; request the assistance of the resource teacher in planning.	3. Adapt the scholastic environment — both the physical and personnel components — to facilitate the mainstreaming of handicapped students.	3. Give permission to the school personnel to contact your child's physician in case of treatment-related educational questions.
4. Meet with students individually or in small groups of no more than 4 children per group.	4. Be informed concerning the child's disability and its prognosis. Know the child as a person; know his personal aspirations.	4. Select the handicapped students' regular classroom teachers carefully.	4. Talk to the regular and resource teachers; understand the contributions of each to your child's educational program. Determine which teacher you should contact if particular questions arise.

5. Communicate frequently with each child's other teachers to share successes, solve problems, and make decisions.
6. Observe the child in his regular classes.
7. Confer with parents to share information.
8. Be alert to any changes in a child's condition that may warrant the attention of a physician.
9. Maintain accurate records of placement, instructional time, conferences, lesson plans, and student progress.

5. Maintain accurate records indicating progress made toward educational goals and adjustments to the educational placement.
6. Be alert to any changes in health, learning, or behavior that might necessitate consultation with the child's physician, school special-service personnel, or other professionals.

5. Conduct inservice training for building personnel on the needs of physically handicapped students.
6. Include the handicapped students with regular school students on the daily attendance rolls.

5. Have your child ready for school transportation at the appropriate time.
6. Notify school personnel when your child is unable to attend school and when there is a change in his condition.
7. Attend meetings of school and parental organizations and/or parent action groups.

Table 5-4.   Itinerant teacher's schedules

Example 1
The two schools visited by this teacher are within a short driving distance. Twenty minutes are allotted for travel.

8:00- 9:00	Planning/Conference
9:05- 9:50	Group A
10:00-10:45	Group B
10:55-11:40	Group C
11:45-12:00	Conference/Planning
12:00-12:30	Lunch
12:30- 1:00	Travel/Planning
1:00- 1:30	Planning/Conference
1:30- 2:15	Group A
2:20- 3:00	Group B
3:00- 3:30	Conferences/Planning

Example 2
The schools visited by this teacher are far enough apart to warrant full-day attendance at each school. The itinerant teacher will then follow the schedule as established for a resource room teacher, but switch schools during the week.

School A	Monday, Tuesday, Wednesday
School B	Thursday, Friday

resource classroom programming. They may have hearing or visual problems, or be mentally retarded, or severely learning disabled. Their physical disabilities may so restrict mobility and speech, or their stamina could be so limited, that appropriate adaptations in a regular classroom are not possible. Because of these difficulties, a committee of educators and parents may determine that the best placement is within the school district, but apart from academically related interactions with their peer group.

There is some similarity in the instructional programming of a self-contained or special class and the special school placement; the primary and notable difference between these two settings, however, is in the availability of social interaction with non-handicapped learners.

The special school houses the more severely handicapped pupils from within a given school district. The available peer group is composed of handicapped students; thus, the student is deprived of associations with the normal school-age population. Special schools are advantageous from an administrative standpoint because specialized equipment and personnel can be housed in a central location.

To minimize the expense of special education for physically handicapped students with concomitant learning problems, several school districts may form a consortium. The consortium arrangement gathers together enough pupils to meet the state guidelines for the employment of a specially certified teacher. The combined school districts locate a centralized classroom to which students are transported from their home school areas.

Another method of serving the student with very special needs involves a contractual agreement between two school districts or the school district and a special service agency. Dade County, Florida, for example, uses contractual agreements when a student exhibits characteristics of an exceptionality that is so profound or complex that no special education available in the district can appropriately meet the educational plan (Dade County Board of Education, 1976).

The self-contained classroom is the site of all academic instruction for those handicapped students who would find few successful experiences in a regular classroom situation. It is possible for these students to be integrated with the non-handicapped in those school activities that are non-academic in nature: lunch, recess, and music and art classes.

In either setting the teacher is a certified special educator, trained to teach physically handicapped students. The caseload should be approximately 8–15 students, and in many states an aide is also assigned to this classroom.

Teaching Practices in the Self-Contained Class Self-contained class members present a variety of learning problems and needs. The teacher must be prepared to provide instruction in daily living skills, tool subjects, and content areas. In the case of accompanying visual, hearing, or severe learning problems, the teacher may work cooperatively with itinerant teachers who are specialized in these areas.

Teaching in these settings is highly individualized, with an emphasis on behaviorally stated instructional objectives. Learning centers, one-to-one instruction, peer tutoring, and small-group work are frequently incorporated techniques. (See Table 5-5 for further details.)

Home-Based Educational Programs

A child may be eligible for enrollment in a home instruction program if his parents have a signed statement from a licensed physician, psychiatrist, or public health officer to the effect that the child has a handicapping condition that prevents his attendance at school. Certain diseases, such as hemophilia, sickle cell anemia, and rheumatic fever, may prevent a child's participation in a regular classroom for extended periods. Children enrolled in home instruction programs will return to their regular classroom setting when sufficient improvement is made in the condition to warrant this change.

Some limitations are placed on program enrollment: Children with communicable illnesses are usually not accepted, because they may reasonably be expected to return to a less restrictive school environment within 20 days. Home instruction, while beneficial, is not a suitable substitute for a more conventional educational placement and is not undertaken without careful consideration and planning by the student's placement committee.

Table 5-5.   Physically handicapped students in a self-contained classroom

Responsibilities of the. . .	
Teacher	School Official
1. Carefully delineate the teaching methods and instructional goals for each student.	1. Maintain attendance dates on enrolled students.
2. Assign non-teaching responsibilities to the classroom aide.	2. Evaluate program effectiveness and student achievement.
3. Coordinate classroom instruction with the stated objectives of the itinerant teacher(s) serving students.	3. Assist with the scheduling of ancillary support services to be available to enrolled students.
4. Formulate an IEP for each student.	
5. Maintain precise records of instructional time, lesson plans, and student achievement.	
6. Confer with parents and other concerned persons when planning for the students.	

The greatest misuse of home instruction occurs in situations in which a child is denied school placement because of problems with the school (architectural barriers, for example) rather than because of his own health problems.

The pupil-teacher ratio is approximately 6-10 students per teacher. Although it is recommended that the teacher possess certification in special education, this is not necessarily a requirement. The teacher must hold a state teaching certificate and should be certified to teach the majority of the enrolled students. When the home instruction is conducted by a teacher certified in regular education and the student has learning limitations, the placement committee should suggest team teaching collaboration with a special education teacher. This collaboration may be in the form of suggestions of materials and teaching techniques or it may include a visit by the specialist prior to the initiation of the actual instruction.

After a caseload has been established for the teacher of home-based instruction, she will formulate a schedule for visits. When preparing this schedule, the teacher should allow time for conferences with the regular teachers of her students and with any coordinating agencies that are also providing services to the child or his family. The schedule assists the teacher in preparation and planning, helps the student and his family approach home learning seriously, and serves as a means of communication with others who are concerned with the child's progress.

Teaching Practices in Homebound Instruction   If the teacher selected to provide homebound instruction is not acquainted with the student, it will be necessary to precede the home visit with teacher conferences and a review of all records of academic achievement.

The first visit with the student should be directed toward establishing rapport and informal assessment of the student's skills, either in the tool subjects for the elementary school pupil, or in the content areas for the secondary student. During this visit the teacher will determine what formalized assessment is necessary prior to the initiation of instruction. Useful instruments for this procedure include diagnostic reading and arithmetic tests, criterion-referenced scales, end-of-chapter discussion questions, multiple-choice questions provided by the publisher of a given text, and teacher-made tests on specific assignments.

The subject areas to be taught are determined according to the individual student's current course of study. Assignments for homebound instruction should closely approximate the work being done by the student's peer group. The texts used should be the same as those that will be in use when the student returns to school. It is often possible to use the handouts and assignments that are prepared by the student's regular teacher.

For secondary students who anticipate a long-term home instruction program, correspondence courses may be considered. Credit for units or subjects completed would be the same as if the student were attending school on a regular basis. Attendance in a home instruction program is usually based on 3–5 teacher visits a week. The number of visits per week and the length of each visit are recommended by the student's placement committee in accordance with state guidelines for home-based instruction.

Adaptation of methods, techniques, and materials is usually necessary to meet individual needs. Recorders, records, cassettes, home-to-school telephones, and educational television are useful aids in home education. (See Table 5-6 for further details.)

Hospital Educational Programs

In many instances, learning is therapeutic as well as educational. For the hospitalized student (who is first a hospital patient and secondly a student) education can surely be considered part of the therapeutic process. The educational program within the hospital represents "normalcy" in an abnormal setting (Fryburg, 1975). This program permits the continuation of education for children whose conditions necessitate lengthy hospital stays. Hospital education is less responsive to the needs of children with acute illness problems because severe illness and rapid recovery preclude intensive and sustained instruction (McKnight-Taylor, 1975).

Hospital instruction may be conducted in either a classroom setting or at the bedside. If the students are ambulatory, it is preferable to simulate a normal learning environment, encouraging students to dress for classes, and meeting on a regular school basis. The students should meet with the

Table 5-6. Physically handicapped students in a homebound program

	Responsibilities of the...		
Teacher of Homebound Students	Classroom Teacher	School Official	Parent
1. Introduce yourself to each child's parents and inform them that you have been assigned to teach their child. Give them your telephone number.	1. Cooperate with the home teacher in planning the instructional program for each student.	1. Provide the proper certification forms to parents.	1. Visit the school your child attends or would attend and ask the principal to send a teacher to your home.
2. Confer with the classroom teachers concerning each student's assignment.	2. When necessary, provide or assist in processing instructional materials (such as texts, keys, and worksheets) for the home teacher.	2. Select a certified home teacher.	2. Obtain the required forms for your physician's signature and comments.
3. Obtain instructional materials necessary for teaching each student. Adjust and adapt the curriculum as necessary.	3. Request progress reports and grade recommendations from the home teacher.	3. Plan (with the teacher and the parents) the initiation of the home instruction program.	3. Establish a time and work area for home instruction. Gather the necessary supplies.

4. Formulate an IEP for each student.

5. Arrange for communication between the students at school and the home-bound student.

6. Be available for conferences with classroom teachers, parents, medical personnel, and school officials.

7. Report progress in writing, recommend grades, and maintain up-to-date lesson plans and records.

4. Provide the home teacher with useful observations concerning each student's previous behavior.

4. Correlate the individual education program of each student with that of the class he would ordinarily attend.

5. Periodically evaluate each student's progress to determine when transfer back to the classroom is feasible.

6. Account for the attendance of each student.

4. Notify the teacher when your child is unable to have his lessons on any given day.

5. Be available when the teacher arrives.

6. Inform the school principal when the physician says your child is ready to return to school.

Adapted from *Education of Homebound and Hospitalized Students.*

teacher either individually for bedside instruction, or in a group of no more than 8-10. The length of the instructional periods is determined by the student's stamina and therapy and treatment schedules.

The hospital teacher should be a well-educated, inquisitive person who is willing to meet the demands of a variety of students who are at different grade levels and who have a wide range of concomitant problems. The Division on Physically Handicapped, Homebound, and Hospitalized Children of The Council for Exceptional Children suggests that the teacher of hospitalized students meet the following criteria:

be flexible
adjust quickly to situational changes
have a broad general education
be willing to continue acquiring knowledge
have some special education background
be especially knowledgeable concerning physically handicapped and other-
     wise health-impaired students
be able to organize schedules, work, and timing
be realistic and child-oriented
be inclined to accentuate the positive.

Teaching Practices in a Hospital Setting   Hospital teaching is very challenging. Not only are the student's disabilities varied, but their ages, abilities, and educational needs are also diverse. The hospital classroom is not an educational setting that promotes group instruction. Individual instruction is generally necessary and planning requires the same assessment procedures as those used by the teacher of the homebound student (see Table 5-7).

Because the hospital student is primarily a hospital *patient,* the teacher's program is often at the mercy of the staff doctors, therapists, and laboratory schedules and personnel. Although it is considered good educational practice to teach in the morning hours when students are rested and fresh, the hospital routine may interfere. It is not uncommon for laboratory work, therapy programs, and doctors' rounds to be scheduled during the morning — these procedures naturally take precedence over the classroom program. Moreover, a trip to the therapist, a visit from the doctor, or laboratory experiences may exhaust the student, making an afternoon class little more than a visit from a concerned adult friend. It is not unusual for a hospital teacher to revise bedside planning on the spur of the moment when she discovers a very weakened, unhappy, or anxious student with so many fears and curiosities that the sound of a short "a" or the concerns of America's founding fathers temporarily seem tremendously irrelevant.

Hospital teaching materials include the student's regular class textbooks, and the curriculum should be augmented with audio-visual mate-

Table 5-7. Physically handicapped students in a hospital

Hospital Teacher	Responsibilities of the... Classroom Teacher	School Official
1. Cooperate with each child's school and parents in planning the program.	1. Help each student maintain communication with his classmates.	1. Include the hospital teacher as an itinerant staff member.
2. Formulate an IEP for each child.	2. Cooperate with the hospital teacher by sharing information about assignments, appropriate materials, tests, and teacher's manuals.	2. Make provisions for the hospital teacher to confer with each child's classroom teachers for mutual planning and continuing evaluation.
3. Adapt a schedule to the needs of the child and his family.	3. Remain flexible in assigning grades for work accomplished.	3. Commit yourself to the idea that each child is a member of the student body despite the fact that he is a hospitalized student.
4. Aim teaching at each child's needs; bolster his strengths; be supportive.	4. Assist the hospital teacher, if necessary, in areas of specialized instruction.	
5. Remain aware of each student as an individual; help enrich his environment.		
6. Establish communication with school officials to make re-entry as smooth as possible.		
7. Observe and record student behaviors and the situations in which they occur.		
8. Evaluate each student's educational status, progress, and achievements.		

From *Division of Physically Handicapped, Hospitalized and Homebound Journal* (1973) p. 13.

rials and a great deal of student involvement. The creative teacher searches for activities that are of interest to the student and that can be used as a nucleus for an original "learning by doing" experience. The combination of arts and crafts, hobbies, and skills and talents with academics fosters motivation — a most important ingredient in teaching a hospitalized student.

Residential School Placement

For a small minority of physically handicapped students, the goal of mainstreaming is unrealistic. These few exceptional children may have severe mental or emotional problems compounded by a very limiting physical handicap. In some cases, the physical disability is multiple or so severe that the child's presence in the home for any period of time is a tremendous hardship on the other family members because of the requisite nursing care. There are also some children who do not have parents or guardians to provide for them so that their only option is residential placement.

The residential educational program is not unlike the program for hospitalized children (see Table 5-8). The residential school is similar in function to a hospital, except that the residential school's focus is usually on handicapped persons of all ages; the clinical support services of a hospital are available to residential clients, either on an in-building or a contractual basis. Therapy programs, psychological and social services, the services of paraprofessionals (such as nursing aides and caregivers), and special education programs are carefully coordinated to provide the most stimulating and appropriate environment for the client.

Because there are seldom shared responsibilities between several agencies in a residential placement, the responsibility of providing an enriching, beneficial experience for the client clearly rests with the institution itself. The full commitment of all personnel is essential for program integrity.

The teacher of the residential student holds a state certificate in the education of physically handicapped students and is prepared to teach basic daily living activities as well as academics. She must demonstrate creative problem-solving and teaching abilities because many of her students will exhibit unique conditions that are nonconducive to learning. She must be able to communicate effectively with others because she will be one of an interdisciplinary team planning for this child.

Teaching Practices in a Residential Setting   The special educator synchronizes the educational program with the on-going activities of one or more therapists. The student may be spending time with the occupational therapist for small muscle development or for instruction with adaptive appliances, with the physical therapist for movement and large muscle activities to enhance postural control, and with a speech and language therapist to improve communication skills. As in all programs in which the child is served by many professionals, the need for coordination of activities and communication of progress is extremely important.

Table 5-8. Physically handicapped students in a residential school

Parent/Guardian	Responsibilities of the... Teacher	School Official
1. Investigate your school district's capabilities and determine whether residential placement offers the best possible educational program for the child.	1. Formulate an IEP for each child.	1. Facilitate admission procedures for each student.
2. Complete all requirements for your child's admittance to the residential treatment center.	2. Plan instructional activities so as to meet the goals stated in the IEP.	2. Plan (with teachers, therapists, and each child's parents) all treatments, therapy routines, and learning activities.
3. Confer regularly with school personnel concerning your child's activities and progress. Request a written summary of these meetings.	3. Coordinate classroom activities with other treatment programs provided for each child.	3. Conduct staff training sessions to familiarize all ancillary personnel with the needs of each child.
4. Attend meetings of parent action groups regularly.	4. Suggest after-school activities that will benefit each child during his leisure time.	4. Maintain accurate records that document the activities of each child during residential placement.
	5. Maintain accurate records of instructional time, lesson plans, and students progress.	5. Schedule regular staff meetings so that the persons working with each child can share information and discuss the progress being made.
	6. Meet regularly with other persons working with each child to share information, solve problems, and make decisions.	6. Report at regular intervals to each child's home school district so that, if the child's progress warrants it, the school district may resume responsibility.

The teacher not only is concerned with the education of the student in the classroom, but also demonstrates concern for, and contributes to, the leisure activities of her pupils. The teacher, the occupational therapist, and the music and art therapists often work together in suggesting games, projects, and musical and audio-visual productions to be carried out by nursing and caregiving personnel in the late afternoons or the early evenings.

Assessment procedures that precede educational instruction are behaviorally stated and criterion-referenced. Reinforcement and operant techniques are the preferred educational approaches for severely multiply handicapped students.

THE MATCH: STUDENT AND SERVICE

A continuum of services is necessary to properly meet the needs of all the handicapped children in a given school district. The delivery system is, of course, necessary, but in and of itself, not sufficient to ensure learning (Gickling and Dickinson, 1977). The careful matching in educational programming of the child's learning needs to the focus and capabilities of a particular program or classroom within the delivery system is crucial. This matching decision determines the least restrictive setting in which the child can receive an appropriate education.

As has been noted, the least restrictive environment is not automatically (or necessarily) a regular classroom or even a regular classroom with ancillary supportive services. Cruickshank (1977) warns that:

> the child placed in a so-called least restrictive situation who is unable to achieve, who lacks an understanding teacher, who does not have appropriate learning materials, who is faced with tasks he cannot manage, whose failure results in negative comments by his classmates and whose parents reflect frustration to him when he is at home, is indeed being restricted on all sides.

The concern of the educator in determining the least restrictive setting is what classroom or learning situation is best designed to help the student meet his educational goals. What teacher-pupil ratio, instructional time frame, and environment will foster achievement at the least distance from the regular education program?

Residential settings and hospital and home-based programs permit the non-ambulatory, dependent, and/or semi-dependent student to receive instruction with a minimum of exertion and inconvenience. These settings also lend themselves to the necessary therapists' visits, medical treatments, and various other health care requirements of the severely handicapped population.

Special schools, including itinerant and resource room models, emphasize the "look of school." These classrooms are located in the school building; this fact alone can boost a student's motivation and enthusiasm.

For the physically handicapped student whose needs are predictable and/or manageable, these placements are preferred.

Delivery selection is carefully made by a committee comprised of educators, the student's parents or guardians, and, in some cases, the student himself. Placement errors do happen, however, in spite of the best efforts of these concerned persons. Problem factors not recognized or anticipated, such as sudden changes in the student's condition, inconveniences erroneously thought manageable, or the student's negative reaction to the classroom, may necessitate a revision of the placement decision. If an error in placement is suspected, the committee will reconvene and recommend an alternative strategy for the student's education.

Described below are several systems designed to minimize the likelihood of placement errors and the accompanying feelings of insecurity, distress, and "differentness" to which the incorrectly placed student is often subject.

Placement Systems

Adamson and Van Etten (1972) suggest a system called the "fail-save" model. The authors interpret the model name as "the 'fail' represents the system's failure to meet all children's needs, not the child's (failure). The 'save' represents the adaptation of the system to the child's individual need and 'saves' him."

This model is an outgrowth of Adamson's (1972) data collected over a 3-year period on 308 learning disabled and educable mentally retarded children at the Olathe, Kansas, Educational Modulation Center. The data indicate that there were significant changes in the achievement rate in reading for 70% of the enrolled students, while 80% showed improvement in their self-concept, and 90% exhibited improved classroom behavior.

The fail-save model utilizes the services of an itinerant special education teacher (itinerant methodological and materials specialist) who, upon referral of a child by his regular education teacher, conducts a basic skills evaluation and shares the results with the regular teacher. The specialist visits and observes the child in the regular classroom, after which the two teachers pinpoint one task or behavior to be remediated. The child's parents are included in this educational decision and are encouraged to assist at home in a prescribed fashion. Throughout the 10-week period of the fail-save intervention, the specialist does not act as a tutor or remedial teacher — her services are provided to the regular teacher.

At the end of the intervention period, the teachers and parents confer to decide what future action is necessary. The decision may be one of three alternatives:

1. continued services, as described, for an additional 10-week period, with an accompanying revision of goals and objectives

2. student referral to a resource room/regular classroom program for 90 days
3. the return of the student to the regular classroom without the continuation of services provided by the specialist

If the child is enrolled in the resource/regular classroom plan for a 90-day period, the specialist will then provide the appropriate supportive services to both teachers and assist in the careful coordination of their activities. At the end of 90 days, a conference is again scheduled with educators and parents to select one of the following alternatives:

1. a return to the 10-week itinerant services cycle in the regular classroom
2. a continuation of resource/regular classroom programming for an additional 90 days
3. a special class/resource room arrangement for not more than 9 months (Adamson and Van Etten, 1972)

The contract system recommended by Gallagher (1972) outlines a contract system designed to place mildly handicapped children back in regular education situations and to provide a method for combating the overassignment of minority group children to special education. The special education contract proposal is based on the following assumptions:

1. Exiling children to special education is too easy an escape for general education and must be made more difficult if it is going to be stopped as a general practice.
2. Bureaucracies (such as educational systems) move institutionally only under threat or duress; otherwise, they take the path of administrative ease.
3. Special education assistance is necessary for many children who have mild handicaps — a way should be found to apply it.
4. A special education program should continue to operate separately from general education for severely handicapped children and those children in need of a more intensive remedial program than is possible through the aid of a resource person to the regular teacher or a resource room.

The placement of a mildly handicapped primary student in a special education unit requires a signed agreement or contract between parents and educators stating the educational goals. The term contracted for cannot exceed 2 years and the only way to renew the contract is through a formal hearing process. The termination of the contract means the transfer of the major teaching responsibility for the student to regular education; services from special education are available as needed.

A third method of placement is suggested by Christie and McKenzie (1975). This process is based on the behavior of the student as matched by the entry/exit behavior requirements for various programs within the district (e.g., resource rooms and self-contained classes). Minimum objective systems appear to offer solutions to at least three of the problems associated with mainstreaming handicapped learners: namely, how to determine a child's entry into, or eligibility for, special education services; how to evaluate the effectiveness of those services; and, finally, how to determine when the child is ready to leave this special situation and can be successfully maintained by the regular classroom teacher (Christie and McKenzie, 1975).

A behavioral approach eliminates comparison with peers and estimation of potential. If the child's performance does not meet the minimal expected objectives for all children at his same level in schooling, the educator then knows that added special services may be warranted (Christie and McKenzie, 1975). Alterations and rearrangement of the child's learning environment are initiated until the child exhibits an accelerated rate of acquisition of those behaviors that comprise the minimal instructional objectives.

The establishment of minimal objectives for the student and the delineation of classroom services along a continuum of programs throughout a given district's special education system greatly enhance the likelihood of making good decisions in the placement of handicapped learners.

These placement systems all emphasize the need for periodic re-evaluation and appropriate goal setting to ensure that progress is made. While a physically handicapping condition may be lifelong in nature, the need for special education intervention may be short-term. Whenever possible, then, regular class settings, at least for part of the day, are preferred.

A California survey of directors of special education and principals responsibile for programs for physically handicapped students revealed that the following criteria were most often considered important in the decision of whether a child could best be served in a regular class:

academic achievement (79%)
speech (68%)
psychological adjustment (61%)
mobility (48%)

When the same persons were asked who, in their school or district, generally initiated the mainstreaming of orthopaedically handicapped students, it was reported that the special education teacher plays the most important role (Best, 1977).

Variables to Consider in Student Placement

To make the right placement decision, the placement committee must examine a number of important variables. By closely examining the needs of the student and what various teachers and classrooms in the continuum have to offer, the most appropriate match of service to student can be made. It must be noted once again that the school district has an obligation to provide the most appropriate placement, even if such a placement does not currently exist within that district.

Student variables to be considered in the placement decision are as follows:

1. What physical needs exist?
2. How are those physical needs to be met?
3. What is the pupil's level of stamina?
4. What should be the length of instructional periods?
5. What are the educational goals to be met?
6. What ancillary/support services are recommended?
7. How will support services be scheduled in coordination with classroom activities?
8. What are the student's chronological age and physical size?
9. What is the pupil's attitude toward placement alternatives?
10. What is the anticipated learning rate?
11. What special learning problems exist?
12. What degree of openness in a classroom can be tolerated?
13. What communication problems exist?
14. What is the student's level of psychosocial adjustment?
15. To what degree is the student mobile?
16. What special health problems exist?

Teacher variables to be considered are these:

1. What are the teacher's areas of expertise?
2. What is the teacher's area of certification?
3. What is the teacher's attitude toward this student and his physical needs?
4. Is teaching structured, open, small-group, lecture, tutorial, developmental, or eclectic?
5. Is the teacher a creative problem solver?
6. Is the program rigid or flexible? Can adjustments be easily accomplished?
7. What is the teacher's caseload or class size?
8. Can the teacher gear instruction to meet the educational goals for this student?
9. If necessary, is the teacher receptive to assisting in exercise therapy and self-care skill development? Can this be done without disrupting other students?

Important classroom variables include:

1. Where is the classroom located?
2. Do instructional time periods fit the students stamina level? If not, what adjustments can be made?

3. How many students will share the teacher's time?
4. Do the scheduling mechanics of the setting lend themselves to the student's educational goals?
5. What degrees of interaction between student and teacher and among students are possible?
6. Will there be a problem with crowding, privacy, or territoriality?
7. To what extent will learning be influenced by lighting, noise levels, color, and temperature?
8. What architectural barriers must be eliminated?

FACILITATING MAINSTREAMING

For many physically handicapped children, moving about in the mainstream of education can be as difficult as a salmon's up-river swim. Contemporary educational practices are not always carried out in modern school structures that feature carpeting, adjustable tables, ramped walkways, and widened doorways. Many schools will require varying degrees of renovation before the physically handicapped student is able to participate in the educational programs.

The physically handicapped student often encounters another major difficulty in mainstreaming: a lack of acceptance by peers and teachers stemming from feelings of prejudice, fear of the unusual, and the accompanying concerns about how to be "helpful." Withdrawal and/or avoidance of physically handicapped students by their non-handicapped peers, although perhaps not unexpected, is a most undesirable way of handling these feelings.

This section describes some methods of eliminating obstacles — people-related as well as physical — for the mainstreamed physically handicapped student. Faculty inservice programs, techniques that enhance peer acceptance, and renovations of school buildings are discussed.

Teacher Acceptance

Attitudes are learned behaviors. They are not innate, nor are they a result of constitutional development and maturation (McGrath, 1964). An attitude is not vague, but *specific:* a specific response to a specific social referent (Sherif and Sherif, 1956). Thus, an attitude toward the physically handicapped, because it is a learned behavior, can be altered. Changing a negative attitude has been found to be most effective when the persuasive attempts are modest (Kiesler, Collins, and Miller, 1969). In other words, an attempt to change attitudes toward the physically handicapped should proceed with small steps, first providing new information about the handicapped population, and then offering opportunities for the audience to practice new behaviors or ways of reacting toward the persons.

The attitudes of teachers toward handicapped children influence the intellectual, social, and emotional adjustment of these students (Haring, 1957). Faculty inservice programs are often recommended and used as a viable technique for creating a positive effective environment for children with handicapping conditions. (The rationale to support inservice training is based on theory related to the development and subsequent change of attitudes.)

Harasymiw and Horne (1975) recommend that efforts to educate classroom teachers in working with handicapped students be based on the attitudes already held by those teachers, and developed through workshops and inservice experiences. Mathey (1975) investigated the way in which two-day inservice workshops for regular classroom teachers (K-6) affected their attitudes toward the integration of handicapped children into the regular classroom; the workshop's focus on feelings about self and the various disabilities resulted in a positive change in teacher attitudes.

Singleton (1977) compared two methods of inservice training to determine the respective successes of each in creating positive attitudes toward the acceptance of mainstreamed educationally handicapped children in the elementary school. Recommendations based on her findings indicate that direct assistance in the regular classroom by a specialist more successfully resulted in a positive attitude change than did a workshop or inservice program that provided instruction-related information.

Klein (1977) states that teachers should have information concerning the handicapping condition, knowledge of available resources, and must recognize and admit their own feelings toward the handicapped in order to teach effectively.

Thus, the components of faculty inservice programs for the effective facilitation of mainstreaming based on the stated research include:

1. the provision of information regarding handicapped conditions
2. the opportunity for teachers to examine their feelings about the handicapped
3. assisted interaction in the regular classrooms with a physically handicapped student

The inservice program can be conducted by qualified district personnel (Lavin and Sanders, 1976), or by nearby college or university faculty, where the program can be accompanied by graduate course credit (Prehm, 1977). Regardless of the choice of presenter, the inservice training is made relevant by a preliminary needs assessment to pin point problem areas and establish priorities for training. It is essential that the information-providing and practical, instruction-related components of the training workshop correspond. These instructive aspects of training are continued through ongoing, direct teacher assistance in the classroom.

Clark (1976) investigated teacher attitudes toward the integration of handicapped children into the classroom. In a follow-up study conducted four years after a staff development program was initiated, it was concluded that:

1. A handicapped child has more in common with the total population of children than s(he) has in common with others who share the same handicap.
2. There was a desire among the teachers studied to make the child well and move him/her toward normalcy.
3. The nature of the handicap is not as important to class functioning as is the degree of severity of the handicapping condition.

Acceptance of the physically handicapped into mainstreamed education can be anticipated, providing the student is placed in a realistic educational setting (and therefore is capable of achieving at a rate commensurate with the other class members) and the teacher has accumulated the knowledge necessary to be comfortable with her ability to teach according to the student's special needs.

Pell's (1973) study revealed that teachers who had recommended the removal of a physically handicapped student from the regular classroom and the return of that student to a special class had a significantly lower degree of acceptance in attitude than did those teachers who felt the student could remain in the regular class. This study supports Battaglia's (1977) statement that dumping, or forced mainstreaming, creates difficulties for both teacher and student in regular programs.

Peer Acceptance

Learning achievement is closely related to self-concept. Major factors that contribute to feelings of self-esteem are the reactions or perceived reactions and responses of "significant others" (Gordon, 1972). In the school environment significant others are the teacher and classmates of the handicapped student. Marsh and Friedman (1972) state that the attitudes of children and their teachers influence the handicapped child's standard of conduct as well as his selection of friends in the classroom.

Sociometric investigation by Force (1956) incorporated three criteria: friends, playmates, and workmates. Although the conclusions of this twenty-year-old study may not be valid today, they do point to some serious obstacles to effective mainstreaming:

1. The physically handicapped student is not well accepted in the elementary class.
2. The psychological integration of the handicapped student is not achieved by his physical presence.

3. The child's physical handicap magnifies his difficulties in gaining the social acceptance of his normal peers.
4. The student with cerebral palsy is the lowest on a social value scale of the physically handicapped.
5. Few physically handicapped children have enough positive assets to off-set the negative effect of being handicapped.
6. Children as young as six have negative feelings toward the physically handicapped.

Klein (1977) cautions that no child profits from being the object of ex-cessive attention or constantly being singled out in the classroom. Too much teacher attention can be as harmful for the handicapped child as neglecting his special needs.

Classroom teachers should use subtle and persuasive techniques in an attempt to foster peer acceptance of physically handicapped students. Hawisher (1977) studied the use of curriculum intervention to create an ac-cepting scholastic environment for the physically handicapped. Among other conclusions, this study mentions a stated change in the attitudes and perceptions of classroom teachers toward physically handicapped students as a result of teaching a curriculum unit on the feelings of such handi-capped youngsters to first grade students. In addition, there was a notice-able positive change in the students' behavior toward handicapped young-sters.

Cerreto's (1977) study of the effects of empathy training on children demonstrates that role-playing techniques are generally more effective methods of facilitating positive change in attitudes and behaviors toward the handicapped. Likewise, emphasizing the similarities between handi-capped and physically normal individuals is recommended. Cerreto's work supports the earlier work of Clore and Jeffery (1972) and Wilson and Alcorn (1969), who had college students assume handicapping conditions while en-gaged in campus activities. This technique is also effective for high school students, according to Jones and Gottfried (1965), who found that the atti-tudes held by these younger pupils were similar to those held by college stu-dents.

School districts or individual teachers interested in developing peer ac-ceptance are well advised to plan curriculum interventions to include the following techniques:

1. film (or filmstrip) introductions to the physically handicapped popula-tion (including the needs of the elderly)
2. role-playing or simulation exercises to allow students to experience the inconveniences of a physical handicap
3. interaction with a physically handicapped student

4. guidance about the best way to approach a handicapped person when offering assistance

(Appendix C offers some suggested material for this training.)

Because physical presence in the classroom alone does not guarantee peer acceptance, the handicapped student requires assistance to learn his social interaction skills. It is unrealistic to expect that the physically normal student will do all the learning and giving in a friendship relationship with the physically handicapped student. The handicapped student will need skills in:

1. accepting and directing well-intentioned assistance
2. developing fine interpersonal skills
3. recognizing non-verbal communication signals that suggest a need for altered behavior

The necessary guidance can effectively be given by resource or itinerant teachers, school counselors, or a district psychologist. Once again, the understanding of personal feelings and attitudes must precede this training, which incorporates role playing, simulations, and discussions.

Acceptance: The Physical Environment

Access to the classroom is a common-sense prerequisite to the procurement of an education. As physically handicapped students enter the mainstreamed educational program, it becomes necessary to examine the environment closely for actual or potential obstacles to the student's use of the facilities.

Architectural barriers are segregating instruments; they remind the handicapped individual of his inferiority and prevent his participation in activities, employment, and opportunities that are available to others (Harris and Harris, 1977). A flight of stairs seen from a wheelchair or while supported by Candian crutches, or a slippery floor negotiated with braces and canes, can arouse feelings of frustration, anger, helplessness, loneliness, sadness, self-depreciation, isolation, segregation, and failure.

The Rehabilitation Act of 1973 prohibits the exclusion of handicapped persons from any program receiving federal funds. The Education for All Handicapped Children Act of 1975 ensures the availability of a free and appropriate public education to all handicapped children. Monies for the renovation of existing structures into barrier-free environments are available from appropriated funds from the Education for All Handicapped Children Act of 1975 (P. L. 94-142).

Before school districts mainstream physically handicapped students, it is necessary to prepare the school building to allow the student maximum independent activity and equal participation in the educational program — extracurricular as well as academic.

At least seven general areas must be considered to make schools barrier-free and accessible to handicapped students:[1]

I. Access to the Classroom
    A. Parking lots
    B. Walk and curbs
    C. Ramps
    D. Stairs and rails
    E. Entrances and doors
    F. Elevators
    G. Corridors and floors
II. Classroom Facilities and Materials (These are discussed in Chapter 7.)
III. Play Spaces
IV. Sanitary Facilities
V. Other Facilities
    A. Auditorium
    B. Dining hall
    C. Laboratory
    D. Library
    E. Water fountains
VI. Controls and Warning Signals
VII. Telephones

A representative group of therapists, teachers, students, parents, school board members, and architectural designers should be assigned the task of examining the school buildings and facilities for needed renovations, which might include the carpeting of floors to prevent slipping, and the installation of signs with raised lettering, hand rails, and ramps. There may be a need for the cutting of curbs and widening of doorways. (A form to facilitate the appraisal of physical plants is found in Appendix B.)

Districts considering the construction of new school buildings and special education facilities will find assistance in planning and designing from a checklist developed by Birch and Johnstone (1975). This list includes questions such as:[2]

Does the location facilitate scheduled participation in regular classes and transfer to and from regular classes when the educational needs of the exceptional child can best be met by such arrangements?

---

[1]From: *Barrier-free School Facilities for Handicapped Students.* Educational Research Service, Inc. (1977).

[2]From Birch and Johnstone (1975) pp. 103-105.

Does the location provide maximum opportunities for exceptional children to test reality, to have lifelike problems to meet and to overcome?
Is participation with normal children in the following school activities facilitated by the location of:
sports and physical education?
music, orchestra, band?
newspaper and yearbook?
social events?
auditorium programs?
business education programs?
Is maximum use made of:
school library?
school cafeteria?
shops?
gymnasium?
outdoor recreation area?
Does the location facilitate transportation?
Does the location increase the likelihood that children from the same neighborhoods will attend school together?

Construction of new, barrier-free buildings and the elimination of existing barriers from the environment ensure the safe and extensive use of public buildings by all members of our society (Aino, 1977). Environmental barriers present obstacles to many persons other than the physically handicapped. Harris and Harris (1977) describe the results of a survey at the University of Kansas following the installation of curb cuts in sidewalks and parking lots:

> Nearly 90 percent of the students thought the curb cuts were installed to aid bicycle riders on campus. The service and delivery personnel thought the curb cuts were there to help them move their paper towels and soft drink bottles in and out of buildings. The buildings and grounds people thought that the curb cuts would help them move their gardening and snow removal equipment up and down the sidewalks. Each group polled interpreted changes in the environment differently and according to their specific needs. They all were impeded by architectural barriers.

SUMMARY

There are numerous elements to consider when seeking the least restrictive environment for a physically handicapped student, including the continuum of services provided by the school district. A wide variety of options are available through the utilization of programs offered in the regular classroom, the resource and itinerant teacher's classrooms, the self-contained special class, and the special school. For those students unable to attend the public schools in their home districts, home instruction and hospital-based programs are available. Similarly, for handicapped persons with severe complications that prevent attendance in a regular school, educational opportunities are available in residential settings. Placement models exist that guarantee a careful match of the student with the educational setting that is most appropriate and least restrictive according to individual needs. By eliminating barriers — people-made and architectural barriers — each placement is made more effective. The "least restrictive environment," then, means the environment that is as close to regular education as possible, provides the most appropriate learning experiences possible, and through attitudes of teachers and peers and architectural access, permits and encourages the growth of the handicapped child as a person.

LITERATURE CITED

Adamson, G. 1972. Final report of the educational modulation center, Olathe, KA: Olathe Public School, 1970. In: Adams, G., and Van Etten, G. Zero Reject Model Revisited: A Workable Alternative. Except. Child. 38:735-738.

Adamson, G., and Van Etten, G. 1972. Zero Reject Model Revisited: A Workable Alternative. Except. Child. 38:735-738.

Aino, B. A. 1977. Access For All. The Ohio Governor's Committee on Employment of the Handicapped and Schooley Cornelius Associates, Columbus, Ohio.

Arnheim, D. D., Auxter, D., and Crowe, W. C. 1973. Principles and Methods for Adapted Physical Education. C. V. Mosby Company, St. Louis, Mo.

Battaglia, M. 1977. Mainstreaming from plan to program: from the perspective of the regular classroom teacher. Paper presented at the 55th annual convention of the Council for Exceptional Children, March. Atlanta. (ERIC Reproduction Service No. ED 139 230).

Best, G. A. 1977. Mainstreaming characteristics of orthopedically handicapped students in California. Rehabil. Lit. 38:205-209.

Birch, J. W., and Johnstone, B. R. 1975. Designing Schools and Schooling for the Handicapped. Charles C Thomas Publisher, Springfield, Ill.

Cerreto, M. C. 1977. The effects of empathy training on children's attitudes and behaviors toward handicapped peers. Dissert. Abstr. Int. 38, 1394.

Christie, L. S., and McKenzie, H. S. 1975. Minimum objectives: a measurement system to provide evaluation of special education in the regular class. Except. Child. Abstr. (ERIC Reproduction service No. ED 102 786).

Clark, E. A. 1976. Teachers' attitudes toward integration of children with handicaps. Educ. Training Ment. Retard. 11:33-35.

Clore, G. L., and Jeffrey, K. M. 1972. Emotional role playing, attitude change and attraction toward a disabled person. J. Personal. Soc. Psychol. 23:105-111.

Council for Exceptional Children, Division on Physically Handicapped, Homebound, and Hospitalized. 1972-73. Tips for the Development of Programs for the Homebound and Hospitalized. Reston, Va.

Cruickshank, W. 1977. The least restrictive placement: administrative wishful thinking. J. Learn. Disabil. 10:5-6.

Dade County Procedures for Providing Special Education for Exceptional Students. 1976. Dade County Division of Elementary and Secondary Education, Miami. (ERIC Reproduction Service No. ED 136-497).

Deno, E. 1970. Special education as developed capital. Except. Child. 37:229-237.

Education for All Handicapped Children Act of 1975. (Public Law 94-142).

Educational Research Service. 1977. Barrier-Free School Facilities. Arlington, Va.

Force, D. G. 1956. Social status of physically handicapped children. Except. Child. 23:104-107.

Fryburg, E. L. 1975. Individualizing Instruction for Physically Handicapped and Mentally Retarded Children in Special Schools. New York City Board of Education, New York. (ERIC Reproduction Service No. ED 136 462).

Gallagher, J. J. 1972. The special education contract for mildly handicapped children. Except. Child. 38:527-535.

Gickling, E. E., and Dickinson, D. J. 1977. Delivery systems and instructional delivery: necessary distinction when providing services for mainstreamed children. Paper presented at the 55th annual convention of the Council for Exceptional Children, March, Atlanta. (ERIC Reproduction Service No. ED 139 166).

Gordon, I. J. 1972. Children's View of Themselves. Association for Childhood Education International, Washington, D.C.

Harasymiw, S. J., and Horne, M. C. 1975. Integration of handicapped children: its effect on teacher attitudes. Education 96:153-158.

Haring, N. G. 1957. A study of classroom teachers' attitudes toward exceptional children. Dissert. Abstr. 17:103-104.

Harris, R. M., and Harris, A. C. 1977. A new perspective on the psychological effects of environmental barriers. Rehabil. Lit. 38:75-78.

Hawisher, M. F. 1977. An evaluation of an experimental early childhood curriculum designed to create an accepting scholastic environment for the mildly physically handicapped youngster. Unpublished doctoral dissertation, University of South Carolina.

Hawisher, M. F., and Calhoun, M. L. 1978. The Resource Room: An Educational Asset for Children with Special Needs. Charles E. Merrill Publishing Company, Columbus, Ohio.

Johnson, R. A. 1975. Models for alternative programming: perspective. In: Meyen, E. L., Vergason, G. A., and Whelan, R. J. (comp.), Alternatives for Teaching Exceptional Children. Denver: Love Publishing Company, Denver.

Jones, R. L., and Gottfried, N. W. 1965. The social distance of the exceptional. Paper presented at the annual meeting of the American Psychological Association, Chicago.

Kiesler, C. A., Collins, B. C., and Miller, N. 1969. Attitude Change: A Critical Analysis of Theoretical Approaches. John Wiley & Sons, Inc., New York.

Klein, J. 1977. Teaching the special child in regular classrooms. ERIC clearinghouse on early childhood education, Urbana, Ill. Office of child development, Washington, D. C. (ERIC Document Reproduction Service No. ED 136 902).

Lavin, R. J., and Sanders, J. E. 1976. Inservice Training for Professional Educators: Case Study of a Program Implemented in the Region Served by the Merrimack Education Center. Chelmsford, Mass. (ERIC Document Reproduction Service No. ED 135 189).

McGrath, J. E. 1964. Social Psychology: A Brief Introduction. Holt, Rinehart & Winston, Inc., New York.

McKnight-Taylor, M. 1975. Summer Program for Hospitalized Handicapped Children. New York City Board of Education, Brooklyn, New York. (ERIC Document Reproduction Service No. ED 136 460).

Marsh, J., and Friedman, R. 1972. Changing public attitudes toward blindness. Except. Child. 38:426-428.

Mathey, J. P. 1975. The effects of an inservice teacher training workshop for regular classroom teachers on their attitudes toward handicapped children. Dissert. Abstr. Int. 35:6659A.

Oregon Board of Education and Oregon College of Education. 1970-71. Handbook on Home and Hospital Instructional Programs for the Physically Handicapped. Portland, OR.

Pell, D. M. 1973. Teacher acceptance and perception of behavior of physically handicapped pupils transferred from special to regular classes. Dissert. Abstr. Int. 33:4209A.
Prehm, H. J. 1977. Personnel training to facilitate mainstreaming. Paper presented at the 55th Annual International Convention of The Council for Exceptional Children, March, Atlanta.
Rehabilitation Act of 1973. (Public Law 93-112).
Sherif, M., and Sherif, C. W. 1956. An Outline of Social Psychology. Harper & Row, New York.
Singleton, K. W. 1977. Creating positive attitudes and expectancies of regular classroom teachers toward mainstreaming educationally handicapped children: A comparison of two inservice methods Dissert. Abstr. Int. 38:186A-187A.
Slack, G. 1976. Child find. Am. Educ. 12:29-33.
Smith, R. M., Neisworth, J. T., and Greer, J. G. 1978. Evaluating Educational Environments. Charles E. Merrill Publishing Company, Columbus, Ohio.
U. S. Office of Education. 1971. Estimated Number of Handicapped Children in United States, 1971-72. U. S. Office of Education, Washington, D.C.
Vodola, T. M. 1973. Individualized Physical Education Program for the Handicapped Child. Prentice Hall, Inc., Englewood Cliffs, N.J.
Wilson, E. E., and Alcorn, D. 1969. Disability simulation and development of attitudes toward the exceptional. J. Spec. Educ. 3:303-307.
Zehrbach, R. R. 1975. Determining a preschool handicapped population. Except. Child. 42:76-83.

6

PSYCHOLOGICAL
AND EDUCATIONAL
ASSESSMENT

Figure 6-1. Psychological assessment of physically handicapped student requires a careful selection of test items.

Consider the following challenge for the psychological or educational evaluator in a professional situation involving three children, each of whom has very special individual needs: One child is experiencing a progressive degeneration of his muscles and has recently been confined to a wheelchair. The other two children are so limited by cerebral palsy that they cannot speak or move independently. The task for the evaluator is to identify the childrens' learning strengths and weaknesses so that the best possible educational program can be planned. The traditional tools of the evaluator are not appropriate and there also exists the danger of underestimating the children's intellectual capacities because of the enormity of their physical problems. This chapter explores these and similar issues in the evaluation of persons with physical handicaps and offers guidelines to facilitate the successful completion of the evaluator's task as well.

Psychological and educational evaluations have long been part of the special education services available to handicapped children. Some sort of evaluation has generally been required to determine a child's eligibility for special class placement. Although a traditional evaluation does attempt to establish educational goals for a child, its major purpose is often to confer a diagnostic label: "Yes, he is mentally retarded and belongs in a special class," or "Yes, she is emotionally disturbed; special help is needed." To obtain this special help the label had to be conferred by a diagnostic expert. For children with physical handicaps, this expert often was not a psychologist but a physician: "She has a congenital heart condition," or "He is orthopaedically handicapped."

Labeling, as part of a psychological or medical evaluation, often leads to special services for handicapped children. However, although these special services can be quite helpful, the labeling and categorization of children has had negative effects in terms of personal adaptive behavior and social relationships within the community. The diagnostic evaluation of a child with special needs, then, could lead to special services, but it could also lead to the identification of the child as someone with problems, someone who is different or set apart. The possibility of these negative effects of assessment produces many serious questions about the value of psychological testing for special educational concerns.

Apart from these broad concerns about psychological and educational evaluations, specific issues have been raised about the testing of children with physical handicaps. Traditional psychological testing has not been geared toward the special difficulties of persons with limited mobility and limited means of receiving and expressing ideas. Some examiners' lack of experience with physically handicapped people, as well as the scarcity of suitable assessment instruments, has greatly limited the effectiveness of evaluations. Teachers and parents have often heard children they care about discouragingly diagnosed as "not testable." Assessment has closed doors for persons with physical handicaps by presenting a hopeless picture. It is possible to underestimate a child in a superficial evaluation because she is unable to talk or move adequately. Other observers might make the mistake of overestimating the abilities of that same child by assuming undisclosed, unprovable, and possibly nonexistent potential (Byers, 1971). In neither case does the assessment serve the best interests of the child.

Psychological and educational assessment has great potential to benefit the physically handicapped child. It can open the doors to good school placement, effective teaching, meaningful personal and vocational guidance, and realistic planning for the future. This potential can be realized only by skilled examiners who approach assessment with a flexibile, creative, and resourceful attitude. These examiners must look not only for a diagnostic label, but for levels of accomplishment, learning rate and style, and areas of interest as well. Fortunately, Public Law 94–142 supports this kind of positive evaluation.

This chapter discusses the requirements of the law with regard to evaluation and special concerns in testing persons with physical handicaps. A review of currently available assessment tools that have been proven to be beneficial for use with physically handicapped clients and guidelines for interpreting test results are also provided. Throughout the chapter case studies of psychological and educational evaluations are presented. These reports include the instruments used and the resulting recommendations. An annotated bibliography of assessment instruments can be found in Appendix D.

EVALUATION CONCERNS RELATED TO PUBLIC LAW 94–142

The Education for All Handicapped Children Act requires that an individual be comprehensively evaluated to pinpoint his current level of educational achievement and to facilitate recommendations for the development of instructional objectives. The law requires that valid assessment instruments be administered by trained personnel according to the publisher's directions.

Other requirements of the law are as follows:

1. The manner in which the assessment is conducted should not bias the results obtained (i.e., a deaf child should not be given a verbal intelligence test).
2. No single procedure or test should be used in establishing an educational program.
3. The assessment should be conducted by a team that is multidisciplinary in nature, and the teacher is to be a part of that team.
4. A comprehensive evaluation should include all areas related to the suspected disability (i.e., a visually handicapped child would need, in addition to psychological and educational testing, an ophthalmalogic evaluation to assess functional vision) (Turner and Somerton-Fair, 1978).

These requirements for the evaluation of handicapped children have beneficial implications for persons with physical handicaps. A multidisciplinary team is better able to adequately assess a child's learning needs than is a single examiner. The teacher's inclusion on the team ensures that the child will be able to deal, at least in part, with someone he knows well. Similarly, the teacher is able to provide feedback to the other examiners regarding the degree to which the child's performance at any given time is typical.

Another strong aspect of these guidelines is the requirement that "all areas related to the suspected disability" be examined. For the physically handicapped child, this requirement generally leads to medical evaluations and assessment by a motor specialist (such as a physical or occupational therapist). This assessment provides teachers with important information concerning the child's posture, degree of mobility and physical limitations, and future possibilities. Speech, hearing, and vision evaluations are also sometimes needed for accurate planning. Chapter 9 describes the professional persons who might be included as part of a multidisciplinary evaluation and service team and details the special contributions of each.

Requiring the standardized use of valid instruments is certainly a reasonable and necessary mandate for most evaluations of handicapped persons: however, considering the nonstandardized problems faced by some physically handicapped persons in giving and receiving information, this requirement could be interpreted as counterproductive or even punitive. The *Wechsler Intelligence Scale for Children — Revised* (Wechsler, 1976), for example, yields a verbal IQ, a performance IQ, and a full-scale IQ (the combination of the other two scales). The performance IQ is determined based on the child's ability to perform such tasks as assembling puzzles, making block designs, and arranging pictures in a sequence. A child with a severe motor disability might not be able to do any of these things, not because he is unable to understand the task, but because his hands will not do the necessary work for him. If the test is administered to this child in the standardized manner, his performance IQ will be significantly depressed. It is unlikely, however, that an accurate estimate of the child's intelligence will be obtained even if a *valid* test is administered in a standardized manner. The child is done a grave disservice, utterly contrary to the spirit of P.L. 94-142, when tests and test results are used in this fashion. Creativity in choice of assessment instruments and parts of instruments is necessary to obtain the most valid possible picture of a child's academic aptitude. Creative choice is supported by the provision of the law that states "the manner in which the assessment is conducted should not bias the results obtained." The real value of a psychological and educational evaluation lies not in identifying the things a child cannot do, but in determining what things he can do and uncovering clues to lead to good teaching and learning.

JAMIE: A CASE STUDY

Jamie, a six-year-old first grader, was referred by his teacher for a psychological evaluation because "he takes an extra long time to eat his lunch at school and because he refuses to tell the teacher when he has to use the bathroom." Jamie was reported as having to be carried in the classroom because he "has a disease which affects his legs."

The referral concerns necessitated a social and medical history, which was taken by a school social worker in an interview with Jamie's father. This interview revealed that Jamie has Werdnig-Hoffman's Disease, a progressive, degenerative type of muscular dystrophy. The family medical history indicated that three maternal uncles also had had the disease and died before reaching adulthood. Neither Jamie's teacher nor his divorced father (with whom he lives) understand much about this condition. Jamie's language development has been in the average range; his motor development has been significantly delayed and he has never walked.

Tests Administered

> McCarthy Scales of Children's Abilities (MSCA)
> Wide Range Achievement Test (WRAT)
> Primary Self-Concept Scale

Test Adaptations

Because of Jamie's physical disability, he was unable to take the motor subtest of the MSCA, which is an individual intelligence test for young children. The activities on this subtest, including running, hopping, and walking a straight line, were impossible for Jamie; therefore, this segment of the test was omitted. However, the MSCA yields a general cognitive index score, which is an indication of academic aptitude. Because this score is a composite of the scores gained on the verbal, perceptual, and quantitative subtests and does not include the motor score, a valid measure of academic aptitude could be obtained.

Test Results

On the MCSA, Jamie's overall functioning was in the slow learner range. His academic achievement (WRAT) was at grade level in reading and spelling, but mildly delayed in math. A self-concept measure indicated that Jamie feels sad and lonely, both at home and at school.

Recommendations

1. Jamie's family was referred to a field representative for the state Muscular Dystrophy Association. This representative can help obtain for Jamie appropriate orthopaedic devices (such as a wheelchair for school), a complete medical evaluation by a specialist in neuromuscular disease, and many other supportive services. The field representative also met with Jamie's teacher and principal to explain Werdnig-Hoffman's Disease.

2. Jamie was placed in a resource class for children with orthopaedic handicaps that is newly available in his school. He will spend one period each day in that class for help with his toileting and feeding skills and mobility in school and for additional assistance to facilitate his progress in math. The toileting program will involve scheduled trips to the bathroom, a system of cueing to help Jamie be aware of when he needs to go to the bathroom, and a positive reinforcement approach to reward Jamie both for asking to go to the bathroom and for staying dry. Additionally, peer tutoring and a "buddy system" (bring-

ing a friend to the resource room each Friday) will be implemented to help Jamie develop friendships in school.

Comments

This evaluation did not demand any particularly dramatic adaptations. The creativity of this relatively standard psychological assessment lies in the gathering together of Jamie, his family, and his teacher with helpful, knowledgeable persons who can make school a much better place for this little boy.

CAUTIONS IN TESTING CHILDREN WITH PHYSICAL HANDICAPS

Different Experiences

Academic aptitude and intelligence tests are designed to determine how much a person has learned from previous experience. These tests also measure how quickly this person can learn new things, and how effectively he can use that information in his dealings with the environment. There is some degree of risk involved in comparing the academic aptitude of physically handicapped persons to that of the population as a whole because it may not be valid to assume that the physically handicapped person has the same basic underlying experiences as non-handicapped children. The early learning experiences of creeping, crawling, and physically exploring the environment may have been denied the handicapped child. Later experiences of independent play and interaction with other children may have been severely limited. Thus, a child with a physical handicap may be in a real sense "environmentally disadvantaged," and this disadvantage may depress his test scores. Although it may be of some use to determine the student's relative standing on an aptitude or achievement test in comparison to the "normal world," extreme caution should be exercised in accepting this score as a valid indication of intellectual potential.

Effects of Medication

A second caution in interpreting test scores for persons with physical handicaps, according to Schlenoff (1974), is the possible effect of any medication these persons may be taking. The physically handicapped are frequently placed on antispasmodic, anxiety-inhibiting, or anticonvulsant medications. Many of these drugs directly affect the central nervous system, and may have effects that can easily interfere with the testing procedure, as well as the results obtained. Therefore, the examiner should determine whether this possibility exists before testing begins. If the child is regularly taking medication, the physician should be contacted concerning possible side effects that could interfere with learning and behavior. Someone who knows the child well should also be contacted regarding medication-related changes in behavior.

Appropriate Instruments

It is of the utmost importance that the tests administered to physically handicapped persons suit each individual's physical condition. Although this guideline hardly seems revolutionary, it must be stated, because rigid, inappropriate test selection in the past has penalized many children. It should be remembered that in the fairly recent past non-English-speaking children were sometimes diagnosed as mentally retarded because they so poorly handled intelligence tests administered in English (*Diana* v *California State Board of Education,* 1970). Thus, just as it makes sense that a Spanish-speaking child should have the opportunity to tell what he knows in Spanish, so it is only right that a child who cannot speak be given the opportunity to respond on a performance test. Similarly, a child who is immobile or incoordinated should not be tested solely on instruments that demand fine motor precision. Before testing, the examiner should find out how the physically handicapped person receives information — can she see and hear? — and how she expresses ideas. Does she have understandable speech and/or gestures? Are her fine and gross motor skills age-appropriate? This information can then be used in the thoughtful selection of a test battery. Guidelines for this selection follow.

CHOOSING A TEST BATTERY

The psychological and educational evaluation of a physically handicapped person should yield the following information to assist in the establishment of educational goals: current levels of social maturity and educational achievement, aptitude for future learning, relative strengths and weaknesses in achievement and learning style, and the existence or possibility of barriers to the fulfillment of the person's academic potential.

To collect this information, it is essential to obtain an adequate and representative sample of the person's behavior. Much of this behavior sample will be obtained through the administration of standardized psychological and educational tests. Observation, interviews with persons who know the client well, and the child's medical and social history aid in the selection of an appropriate test battery, as well as providing important information for educational planning.

A client's medical records should be reviewed by the examiner before she sees the client. Written permission for the release of information must be obtained from the client (if he is of legal age), or his parent or guardian. Reports of previous hospitalizations and psychological evaluations should also be reviewed. The specific diagnostic category of the physical handicap, and related disorders, and the prognosis are all of help in educational planning.

The medical records should indicate if the client sees and hears adequately. If this information is not available, the *Psychoeducational Evaluation of the Preschool Child* (Jedrysek et al., 1972) provides some sensory status screening items that are appropriate for use beyond the preschool years. This evaluation explores visual acuity and pursuit, depth perception, auditory acuity, and the ability to use touch and vision together. Some examiners are trained to use the *Keystone Telebinocular* as a screening tool for vision. The speech pathologist can conduct a hearing screening using a *pure-tone audiometer*.

Before scheduling testing sessions with a physically handicapped client, it is of great value to observe that client in an everyday setting (such as home or school) and to interview someone who knows him well. The client's parents or teacher will have important observations to share and concerns to express. The ideal interview would be conducted with the parent or teacher while observing the child unobtrusively (as through an observation mirror) in the classroom.

Observation combined with the informed help of the parent or teacher assists the examiner in understanding how the client gives and receives information, as well as what physical tasks the client may be capable of performing. Through observation the examiner can determine whether the client uses speech and, if so, whether that speech can be understood by persons who do not know the client well. If his speech is not functional, the client may use gestures or some other communication system. Observation will provide the examiner with an opportunity to learn the communication system and to make a judgment about its reliability. Optimal seating arrangements for comfort and head control, and the positions in which the client can best use his eyes and hands should also be noted in observation.

It is best to conduct the interview with a knowledgeable informant in such a way that the examiner is able to make some judgments about the client's social maturity and general level of functioning. Scales like the *Balthazar Scale* (1971), the *AAMD Adaptive Behavior Scale* (Nihira et al., 1974), and the *Vineland Social Maturity Scale* (Doll, 1953) provide the examiner with questions designed to assess the client's ability to care for himself, to interact with others, and to perform age-appropriate activities (such as crossing a street or counting change) independently. Although physical disabilities may limit a client's potential to perform many of these tasks, the examiner can focus on those items for which physical limitations would not be a barrier. The information yielded by a social maturity scale is a beginning in establishing educational goals. The determination that a mildly handicapped child is severely delayed in independent activities and self-care may point to the possibilities of overprotection and lack of opportunity. The finding that a severely physically handicapped but mentally alert child has no independent leisure activities could lead to the adaptation of games and crafts and the opportunity to use them.

For some adolescent and adult clients, it is best to dispense with the knowledgeable informant interview and conduct a personal session with the client in his home or school. Questions from the adaptive behavior scales can be used to explore the ways in which the client spends his time, manages transportation, self-care, and homemaking, what his future plans are, and what barriers he sees to the fulfillment of his dreams. Some special problems of adults with physical disabilities are explored in the *Purdue Handicap Problems Inventory* (Wright and Remmers, 1960); this self-administered scale may be of help in determining those areas that should be explored in the evaluation.

In summary, the interview and observation, and a review of the client's records will aid the examiner in choosing a battery of more formal tests by providing:

1. the nature of the physical disability and its related disorders, and the prognosis (medical records)
2. the sensory status — how well the client receives information from the environment (medical records and screening)
3. preliminary knowledge of the client's physical capabilities, and which positions are most comfortable and facilitate performance (observation)
4. the effectiveness of the client's communication abilities (observation and adaptive behavior interview)
5. a general sense of the client's level of social maturity and functioning (observation and adaptive behavior interview)
6. any special needs or problem areas (observation and adaptive behavior interview)

The test battery selected for the more formal part of the evaluation should reflect the insights gained through the preliminary work. The tests chosen must match the physical and sensory status of the client, even if this necessitates some adaptations. Whether the educational evaluation is focused on academic achievement, preacademic work, or nonacademic areas will depend on what information is gained in the preliminary work concerning the client's current levels of functioning. Special problems (such as inappropriate behavior or the lack of an effective means of communication) should be explored through trial teaching.

After gathering information through record review, observation, and interview, the examiner may conclude that a standard test battery using an appropriate, individual test of intelligence and academic achievement will fit the client's specific needs perfectly. On the other hand, the conclusion may be that only limited standardized items can be used, and informal trial teaching will be the most valuable source of information. In either case, the preliminary knowledge prepares the way for a valuable testing session.

Table 6-1. Handicap problems inventory

INSTRUCTIONS: With a soft pencil, blacken the space between the vertical lines in back of all problems caused by or added to by your disability. Skip over, do not mark, those problems which you do not have or which you feel have nothing to do with being handicapped. The way you truly feel is the "right" or best answer.

As you read through the Handicap Problems Inventory mark between the two lines (||) after the items which have something to do with your handicap.

#	Item		#	Item
1.	Feel discouraged more easily		26.	Cannot make friends easily
2.	Feel left out with own family		27.	Feel unsure about earning a good income
3.	Do not get out with people enough		28.	Feel embarrassed by experiences caused by the handicap
4.	Lose confidence in work ability		29.	Do not have good relations with opposite sex
5.	Do not like being around other handicapped people		30.	Feel unsure about future home life
6.	Feel more need for religion because of handicap		31.	Think others dislike working with a handicapped person
7.	Love someone without being loved		32.	Think about not being equal to normals
8.	Feel embarrassed by others		33.	Feel bitter toward the world
9.	Do not apply self at work		34.	Feel despair when not treated as normal by others
10.	Feel bothered because people do needless things to help		35.	Fear losing job to one who isn't handicapped
11.	Do not get along with family members		36.	Fear having more handicap later
12.	Do not like entering into social gatherings and parties		37.	Cannot have sex relations
13.	Find two strikes against a handicapped person job hunting		38.	Want to be more popular
14.	Find trouble in accepting handicap			
			50.	Hold a grudge against those who feel superior
			51.	Wonder if family did enough to prevent handicap
			52.	Seem not liked because of handicap
			53.	Work harder to succeed than if not handicapped
			54.	Become less careful about own well being
			55.	Do not take part in all the family does
			56.	Do not feel free to enter into social events
			57.	Get discouraged because not fit for all work
			58.	Envy people who aren't handicapped
			59.	Get too little chance for hobbies and pastimes
			60.	Feel bothered that no one else in family is handicapped

15. Want to be normal ==
16. Have less chance for a normal family life ==
17. Do not like pity shown by other people ==
18. Need to get extra education for suitable job ==
19. Have trouble in finding happiness ==
20. Think family doesn't show enough respect ==
21. Lack a well-rounded social life ==
22. Require special privileges on the job ==
23. Feel inferior ==
24. Feel unhappy ==
25. Wonder what family thinks about handicap ==

39. Fear loss of ability to work ==
40. Find it is harder to face life ==
41. Feel it better to suffer in silence ==
42. Cannot financially support family ==
43. Feel unsure what others think about the handicap ==
44. Find fellow workers take advantage of handicapped people ==
45. Worry about overcoming handicap ==
46. Feel not treated as normal by some in family ==
47. Get angry when not treated by others as normal ==
48. Hold no chance of making good in life's work ==
49. Blame handicap upon someone else ==

61. Feel pushed aside as being in the way ==
62. Fear having to take up "pan-handling" (begging) ==
63. Want to talk about the handicap ==
64. Seem to be treated as an inferior person by family ==
65. Feel dissatisfied with treatment from sweetheart or mate ==
66. Prefer work with other handicapped people ==
67. Need to find substitute joys and pleasures ==
68. Feel comforted by fact that some handicaps are worse ==
69. Fear losing loved one ==
70. Require change of job plans ==

By George N. Wright and H. H. Remmers. Reprinted with permission of Purdue Research Foundation.

ADAPTATIONS OF TESTS AND TEST ITEMS

Many individual tests of academic aptitude explore a number of different kinds of abilities, all of which fall under the general heading of intelligence. The more complex general intelligence tests, such as the *Stanford-Binet* (Terman and Merrill, 1973) and the *Wechsler Intelligence Scales* (Wechsler, 1974), frequently require that the child answer test questions verbally or make quick, complex, fine motor responses, gaining points for speed. Obviously, this kind of testing situation is inappropriate for many persons with physical handicaps, and the adaptations that must be made often result in a less comprehensive evaluation.

For the child with poor speech but good use of her hands, performance tests could be appropriate. Cruickshank, Hallahan, and Bice (1976) suggest the following tools: the *Ravens Progressive Matrices* (1965), a nonverbal analogy test in which the client selects the proper element for completion of an abstract design; the *Columbia Test of Mental Maturity* (Burgemeister, Hollander, and Lorge, 1959), which requires no verbal response and only a minimal motor response to select the right multiple choice answer to 100 questions; or the *Peabody Picture Vocabulary Test* (Dunn, 1965), which yields a receptive language score and requires that the child indicate the picture named from a selection of four choices.

Dunn and Harley (1959) studied the comparability of these three tests with 20 cerebral palsied children, ages 7-16. They also studied the correlation of these test measures with reading and arithmetic achievement scores. They concluded that each of the above-named performance scales was effective in predicting school success for children with cerebral palsy. In two other studies, Ando (1968) and Nicholson (1970) found independently that the IQ score yielded on the *Peabody Picture Vocabulary Test* (*PPVT*) (Dunn, 1965) was substantially higher than those yielded on other tests. While the correlations are high, there is apparent evidence that cerebral palsied children score higher on the *PPVT* than they do on other measures.

For children with functional speech but poor motor control, verbal tests may take priority. The verbal scale of the *Wechsler* tests may be used, for example, as might certain portions of the *Illinois Test of Psycholinguistic Abilities* (Kirk, McCarthy, and Kirk, 1968).

These assessment alternatives, although having the distinct advantage of being within the range of physical capabilities for handicapped children, have been criticized because they do not assess a full range of cognitive abilities. Nicholson (1970), for example, suggests that the *PPVT* evaluates only concrete mental skills through assessment of vocabulary, while the *Columbia Test of Mental Maturity* evaluates concrete as well as some abstract concepts through a single task, and that the *Ravens Progressive Matrices Test* evaluates abstract concepts. To obtain a more comprehensive evaluation,

Nicholson (1970) has suggested the possibility of combining certain portions of these tests. Other researchers have suggested adapting selected items from an even broader range of assessment tools. Cruickshank, Hallahan, and Bice (1976) suggest that occasionally a child can tell the examiner how to perform a specific task although he cannot do it himself, and the results can be scored on that basis. Test materials can be modified to suit the child's physical needs; for example, a child who cannot pick up small blocks may be able to handle larger ones. These researchers caution the examiner against making the mistake of thinking that the modified test is the same as the test administered in the standard fashion.

A comprehensive guide to test adaptation for persons with physical handicaps can be found in Taylor's (1971) description of psychological evaluations of children with cerebral deficits. Taylor (1971) describes the types of tasks that are found in comprehensive evaluations of cognitive abilities and suggests possible modifications of each. The result is not a standardized test battery, but a physically possible sampling of a number of cognitive skills. Because these items are adapted from standardized tests, such as the *Stanford-Binet,* age norms are often available to provide a rough sense of the child's developmental level in handling the task. The following are the types of tasks described by Taylor (1971):

1. blocks
2. pictures
3. paper and pencil
4. fitting and assembling
5. following, finding, retrieving, noticing, and reaching out
6. matching, sorting, and grouping
7. designs
8. learning and memory
9. judgment and reasoning
10. common knowledge and comprehension
11. factual information
12. vocabulary

Another promising approach to the comprehensive assessment of the intellectual capabilities of physically handicapped persons is the development of standardized instruments that require minimal responses from the subjects to assess a variety of cognitive skills. One such test is a modified version of the *Stanford-Binet* (Sattler and Anderson, 1973). In this modification, all tests are nonverbal and require the minimal response of a "point" or yes-no indication. This modified version was administered to 100 preschool children, 80 of whom were normal, and 20 of whom were cerebral palsied. High correlations between *Stanford-Binet* and modified *Stanford-Binet* IQs (rs = .83, .91) and mental ages (rs = .92, .95) in normal and handicapped groups support the use of modified forms of the test for persons with physical handicaps.

The *Pictorial Test of Intelligence* (French, 1974) has all the functional advantages of other pictorial tests and can also be used to assess a broad range of mental abilities. Designed to assess the intelligence of normal and handicapped children between the ages of 3 and 8, the test is a revision of the *North Central Individual Test of Mental Abilities,* and consists of six subtests: 1) picture vocabulary, 2) form discrimination, 3) information and comprehension, 4) similarities, 5) size and numbers, and 6) immediate recall.

The accuracy of the *Pictorial Test of Intelligence* (PTI) as used with physically handicapped children, has recently been the subject of two investigative studies. Harper and Tanner (1974) administered the test to 40 inpatients in a children's rehabilitation hospital and compared the results with *Stanford-Binet* scores. Of the 40 children tested, 25 were cerebral palsied; 8 had myelomeningoceles; 4 had encephalopathy; 2 had congenital anomalies; and 1 had Riley Day Syndrome. Twenty-three were quadriplegic; 13 were paraplegic; and 1 was hemiplegic. A correlation of .79 was demonstrated in the comparison of the *PTI* and *Stanford-Binet L-M.*

Coop, Eckel, and Stuck (1975) compared the results of the *PTI* to those of the *Peabody Picture Vocabulary Test* and the *Columbia Test of Mental Maturity.* The scores of 46 cerebral palsied children between the ages of 4 and 7 were studied. The children's performance on the *PTI* was also compared with their school or preschool achievement. It was found that the *PTI* has a high concurrent validity with the *Columbia* (r = .88) and the *PPVT* (r = .83), and the *PTI* is a better predictor of academic achievement than the other two tests. These two studies would appear to indicate that the *PTI* is a valid instrument for the assessment of the intellectual capabilities of young physically handicapped children: it samples a broader range of mental abilities than do other performance tests and has the additional advantages of broad standardization, objective scoring, ease of administration, and moderate testing time.

In addition to estimating a child's overall intellectual potential, the evaluation should also assess the child's present level of educational achievement. The widely used *Peabody Individual Achievement Test* can be administered to many persons with physical disabilities (Dunn and Markwardt, 1970). This widely standardized test, normed for kindergarten through 12th grade, measures achievement in mathematics, reading recognition and comprehension, spelling, and general information. The arithmetic, reading comprehension, and spelling subtests are presented in a multiple choice format in which four choices are presented and a pointing response is required. For the handicapped person who has difficulty in speaking or writing, this test can yield an effective sampling of academic achievement.

For preschool children (or others functioning in the preacademic range of achievement), the *Psychoeducational Evaluation of the Preschool Child* (Jedrysek et al., 1972) is an important educational tool. This manual is based on the work of Else Haeussermann, a pioneering teacher of young children with cerebral palsy. The assessment approach is designed to permit the examiner to observe the handicapped child learning under standardized conditions and to explore his capacity to master new learning in a variety of ways. In addition to physical functioning and sensory status, perceptual functioning, competence in short-term retention, language competence, and cognitive functioning are also studied. The main testing procedures are followed by a graded series of teaching probes to facilitate the precise identification of the child's level of achievement and learning style. No age norms are presented. This evaluation does not allow the examiner to compare the child to any group; rather it provides a detailed description of an *individual's* educational needs. Because the materials involved were initially developed for young children with cerebral palsy, required motor responses are minimal.

One important aspect of the issue of educational testing of physically handicapped persons is the need to explore the possibility of specific learning disabilities. Because many physically handicapped persons are brain-injured, uneven growth patterns, maturational lags, and discrepancies between potential and achievement can result in a confusing pattern of learning strengths and weaknesses. Taylor (1971) noted some of these patterns in her clinical practice. Children with spastic hemiplegia, she has noted, are often slow in language development and encounter difficulty in form discrimination and orientation. A child with hydrocephalus and spastic paraplegia may have advanced speech and social skills and still be motor-handicapped and generally mentally retarded. Uneven patterns of strengths and weaknesses may have an even more complex origin than the physical limitations alone. Neurological dysfunction can interfere with learning in subtle and uneven ways.

In addition to measuring academic aptitude and achievement, the evaluation should also initiate exploration into methods of making learning more comfortable and exciting for the child. Giving a reinforcement inventory to determine a child's favorite foods, television shows, games, and free time activities can provide very valuable information to a teacher who is developing learning materials or a reward system (Hawisher and Calhoun, 1978). A child who is unable to respond to a reinforcement inventory can be given a variety of toys and learning materials, and favorable responses can then be noted.

The evaluation, then, should provide the examiner with a sample of a child's behavior in a variety of learning situations that is sufficient to permit tentative conclusions concerning intellectual potential and current levels of educational achievement to be made. The sample should also suggest to the educator ways to make learning a positive, exciting experience.

DEREK: A CASE STUDY

Derek, a five-year-old boy in need of help in educational planning, was referred for evaluation at a federally funded developmental disabilities clinic. He is a severely involved, athetoid cerebral palsied child, currently enrolled in a United Cerebral Palsy preschool program. Derek is confined to a wheelchair, with little voluntary control over his upper extremities. His expressive language is limited to a few vowel sounds and the consonant sounds /k/, /b/, and /n/.

In spite of his severe physical handicaps, Derek gives every indication of being mentally alert. He indicates his awareness and interest in the environment by smiling and using his eyes. He indicates a "yes" response by raising, and a "no" response by lowering, his head and eyes. Derek's whole body is involved in giving these answers; this form of responding is quite fatiguing.

Tests Administered

Pictorial Test of Intelligence
Peabody Picture Vocabulary Test
Illinois Test of Psycholinguistic Abilities — auditory reception subtest

Test Adaptations

All tests were adapted to use the "yes-no" response. On the PPVT, for example, because Derek was unable to point to the picture named, the examiner pointed to each one in turn, asking "Is it this one?" Because this was a laborious and quite tiring process for Derek, the testing was conducted in three one-hour sessions, and Derek was allowed to rest every 20 minutes.

Test Results

Derek consistently scored in the superior range on all the abilities measured.

Recommendations

1. Derek should enter the first grade next year in a self-contained class for children with orthopaedic handicaps. His program should include occupational, physical, and speech therapy. Part of his school day should be spent in a regular first grade classroom; opportunities for rest should be provided.
2. Derek's school program should focus on developing a more effective communication system, possibilities for which include a communication board with stylus, eye-blink responses — perhaps in Morse code, and an electric typewriter with stylus.
3. Beginning academic work in reading and math should be initiated with the help of technological teaching aids, such as *Talking Books.*

Comment

Derek's severe physical disabilities do not mask his alert cognitive abilities. Nonverbal tests requiring minimal motor responses confirmed his parents' and teachers' impressions of above-average intelligence. While it is unlikely that Derek will ever be able to function as a totally independent adult, his good mind and pleasant disposition make meaningful work and personal relationships a good possibility.

SPECIAL CONSIDERATIONS IN THE EVALUATION OF SEVERELY/PROFOUNDLY HANDICAPPED PERSONS

For clients who have significant mental retardation as well as physical handicaps the use of standardized assessment procedures is even more severely limited. Turner and Somerton-Fair (1978) suggest that a transdisciplinary approach over an extended period of time may best comply with the intent of P.L. 94-142.

Transdisciplinary Approach

The transdisciplinary approach employs those team members with whom the child is most familiar to perform most of the direct assessment. It is quite difficult to elicit responses from many severely/multiply handicapped persons. The best responses are generally obtained by examiners with whom the client is most comfortable, probably his parents or teachers. Because it is unlikely that parents and teachers will be trained to administer the tests required, however, specialists (such as psychologists or speech pathologists) can feed information to the examiners, who will then try different things in the diagnostic observation period.

This approach is called transdisciplinary rather than multidisciplinary. In a multidisciplinary approach, each specialist works with the client in his own particular area of expertise. In the transdisciplinary approach, the persons in direct contact with the client are not necessarily those with discipline-specific skills; they are the people who know the client best. Specialists cut across disciplinary boundaries by suggesting test items and procedures to the primary evaluation team, as well as by sharing in observation and interpretation of results.

Extended Testing Period

The challenge in testing severely/multiply handicapped persons is to determine specifically what they *can* do, for it is all too obvious what they *cannot* do. It is unlikely that the best estimate of a severely handicapped person's abilities can be made in a quick testing session. Because responses may be minimal and may occur infrequently, testing is best conducted over a period of days (perhaps as many as thirty) to obtain a comprehensive picture of the client's abilities. This on-going evaluation process makes good use of the selected criterion-referenced tests that have recently been developed for use with the severely handicapped.

Assessment Instruments

For severely/multiply handicapped persons, the best assessment tools are those that lead directly to a careful teaching plan. These tests are criterion-referenced; they do not compare the client to any group. Rather, these tests determine what things the client is presently able to master and what things he cannot currently do. In addition, they provide a criterion (stated level of achievement) to alert the examiner when a specific task is mastered.

The *Pennsylvania Training Model Educational Planning System* (Somerton and Turner, 1975) is an example of this kind of assessment device. This procedure uses test results, checklists, and naturalistic observations to develop a specific educational plan. First, a broad assessment is conducted in the areas of sensory, motor, language, cognitive, and social skills. A screening in these areas, which can be performed in 20 minutes, indicates areas of greatest concern. A more specific evaluation is then conducted to explore 1) cues — how the examiner can communicate with the pupil, 2) responses — how the pupil tells the examiner that he understands, and 3) motivation — those circumstances required by the pupil for the performance of an activity.

Other criterion-referenced assessment and teaching methods for the severely handicapped include the *Behavioral Characteristics Progression* (Vort Corporation, 1973), the *Learning Accomplishment Profile* (Sanford, 1974), the *Portage Project* (Shearer et al., 1972), and the *Radea* (1977).

Assessing the Cognitive Development of Deaf-Blind Persons

While all physically handicapped persons present certain challenges to the psychological examiner, perhaps no one group has been more consistently labeled difficult-to-test than those children termed "deaf-blind." Most deaf-blind children have some functional vision and hearing but are significantly impaired in both of these sensory areas (Tweedie, 1975). These children are significantly limited in what information they can receive from their environment. Most tests are therefore inappropriate, and most test results are suspect.

For those deaf-blind children who have been termed "untestable" by means of sophisticated psychological, audiological, and educational instruments, an alternative method for gathering behavioral data is proposed by Curtis and Donlon (1972). These researchers suggest the use of videotape to permanently record behavior, to provide a basis for group discussion regarding the child's current level of functioning, and to give future evidence of accomplished growth. Standardized items from the criterion-referenced

Table 6-2.   Behavioral Characteristics Progression (BCP): Wheelchair Use

Behavioral Characteristics Progression (BCP)

NAME _____

TEACHER _____

SCHOOL _____

53	WHEEL CHAIR USE

1.0	2.0	3.0	4.0	5.0	6.0	7.0	8.0
Lifts head while lying on stomach.	Reaches for, grasps and releases objects while lying on stomach.	Sits with maximum support (e.g., prone sitters, car seats).	Sits with minimum support (e.g., one body strap).	Holds head up when sitting with support.	Maintains sitting position when placed using hands to support self.	Touches feet to floor in saddle or sling walker.	Moves walker in any manner.

9.0	10.0	11.0	12.0	13.0	14.0	15.0	16.0
Moves walker in any manner to designated location.	Stands in maximum supportive standing table.	Sits in wheelchair when supported by two straps (e.g., chest strap and seat belt).	Sits in wheelchair when supported by one strap (e.g., seat belt).	Grips rim of wheel on wheelchair.	Releases grip on rim of wheel.	Moves wheelchair in any manner.	Stops wheelchair in any manner.

continued

Table 6-2. (continued)

17.0 Moves wheelchair forward using one push forward and release movement.	**18.0** Moves wheelchair backward using one pull back and release movement.	**19.0** Turns wheelchair in a circle to the right.
20.0 Turns wheelchair in a circle to the left.	**21.0** Sets brake on wheelchair to stop or remain stationary.	**22.0** Releases brake on wheelchair to resume movement.
23.0 Travels forward ten feet in wheelchair.	**24.0** Travels backward ten feet in wheelchair.	

25.0 Travels length of classroom (e.g., 30 feet) in wheelchair.	**26.0** Travels length of classroom in wheelchair in one minute.	**27.0** Travels using wheelchair in roomy areas to go forward, backward, and to turn at will.
28.0 Travels using wheelchair in compact areas to go forward, backward, and to turn at will.	**29.0** Travels forward through doorway.	**30.0** Travels backward through doorway.
31.0 Opens door, travels through doorway and closes door.	**32.0** Places foot rests in down position.	

33.0 Places foot on rest.	**34.0** Takes foot off rest and places foot rests in up position.	**35.0** Transfers from floor to wheelchair.
36.0 Transfers from wheelchair to floor.	**37.0** Transfers from bed to wheelchair.	**38.0** Transfers from wheelchair to bed.
39.0 Transfers from chair to wheelchair.	**40.0** Transfers from wheelchair to chair.	

41.0	42.0	43.0	44.0	45.0	46.0	47.0	48.0
Transfers from toilet to wheelchair.	Transfers from wheelchair to toilet.	Transfers from bathtub to wheelchair.	Transfers from wheelchair to bathtub.	Transfers from car seat to wheelchair.	Transfers from wheelchair to car seat.	Travels up and down incline using wheelchair.	Travels up and down curbs using wheelchair.

49.0

Follows safety rules using wheelchair (e.g., sets brake at desk).

Identifying Behaviors

O Sits only with support O Displays poor equilibrium in sitting position O Requires more than one support strap to remain in wheelchair O Drops head when sitting O Lacks strength to grip wheel O Lacks strength to move wheels of wheelchair O Moves wheelchair with feet rather than with wheel O Moves wheelchair forward or backward only a short distance O Stops wheelchair with feet rather than with brake O Turns left when wants to turn right and vice versa O Makes only wide turns in wheelchair   (see Booklet)

Santa Cruz County Office of Education © 1973

Published by: VORT Corporation P. O. Box 11132, Palo Alto, CA 94306 instruments cited above can be presented to the child; the videotape record will then facilitate the interpretation of the child's responses.

Tests designed to elicit the highest level of attainable response have been developed for use with young children. The *Peabody Intellectual Performance Scale* (Kiernan and Dubose, 1974) is an experimental test based largely on a review and adaptation of items from published scales. The test items were adapted for a high stimulus value for the sensory impaired child. No hearing is necessary to complete the test, although some usable vision is needed. An experiment with preschool deaf-blind children revealed a high correlation with traditional intelligence measures. However, the scores on the *Peabody Intellectual Performance Scale* were significantly higher, indicating that this adaptation does indeed elicit the highest level of attainable response. A similar published test is the *Developmental Activities Screening Inventory* (Dubose and Langley, 1977). The test is designed not to penalize sensorily handicapped children. It measures fine motor manipulation, cause-effect, means-end relationships, associations, number concepts, size discrimination, and seriation.

LORI: A CASE STUDY

Lori is a thirteen-year-old girl with severe quadriplegic cerebral palsy. She has mixed spasticity and athetosis. Lori has not been in school or any other program until this year, when her rural school system began a developmental day care center for the severely handicapped in compliance with P.L. 94-142.

Lori lives at home with her parents and two older sisters. The family members, all of whom express much love and concern for Lori, have had little help with her management and care over the years. In addition to being denied school placement, Lori has received only minimal services from state agencies dealing with physically handicapped persons because of her "poor prognosis." Although all the family members include her in their activities, Lori's mother has assumed almost total responsibility for her care. Lori is completely dependent for her feeding, dressing, and toileting, and her mother indicates that she currently has to rock Lori to sleep at night, only to have her awaken several times before morning.

The evaluation, including physical and speech therapy, was conducted at a regional resource center funded by the state department of education. The psychologist and special educator worked together in conducting the psychological and educational evaluations.

Tests Administered

AAMD Adaptive Behavior Scale
Peabody Picture Vocabulary Test (attempted)
Items from Taylor (1971) Psychological Appraisal of Children with
Cerebral Deficits

Test Adaptations

Because the AAMD Scale indicated that Lori has a rather consistent yes-no response using facial expressions, and that she can also point with her fist in a limited range, the *PPVT* was attempted, using first the point and then the yes-no response. The responses seemed random and inconsistent, however, and this test was therefore discontinued. The evaluation consisted largely of informal items from Taylor (1971): picture discrimination, grasp and release, visual tracking, and scribbling. Lori's mother was asked to attempt several items with her.

Test Results

Lori was not able to sit independently, and her overall muscular control was poor. Lori's head control was also poor in both the prone and sitting positions. Her spasticity increased as she rolled from her back to her stomach, a task she was unable to complete by herself.

Lori was able to visually track a moving object, hit a nerf ball with her fist (after repeated demonstration), move chalk across a chalkboard, grasp and release a rattle, and discriminate between two simple pictures by pointing with her fist. She smiled frequently, indicating possible understanding of simple conversation. She could also follow simple one-step commands for hand movement.

Recommendations

1. It was recommended that Lori's placement in the developmental day care center continue, with ongoing assessment using the *Radea Program* developmental test and curriculum guide. She should also receive speech and physical therapy at her school.
2. Short-term respite care placement in a facility capable of intensive physical therapy to facilitate head control, posture, and mobility development, should also be explored.
3. Teaching emphasis should be on activities that will increase the number of purposeful things Lori can do with her hands, improve her understanding of words, and enable her to communicate her basic needs to others.
4. Suggestions were also made to help Lori (and her family) get a good night's sleep, including: increased daily exercise, a warm bath and massage before bed, soft music, and a metronome to induce sleep.

Comment

Because of the severity of Lori's disability, a formal evaluation was not possible. The *AAMD Adaptive Behavior Scale* proved the most useful in identifying special areas of need from the family's point of view, as well as in quickly identifying the severe nature of Lori's handicaps. The evaluation itself was essentially a trial-teaching situation, seeking learning experiences of which Lori was capable, and identifying the kinds of tasks with which she should be presented in her school setting.

INTERPRETING TEST RESULTS

Predictability

After the examiner has carefully chosen, administered, and scored psychological and educational tests, there is definitely more collected information available about the child, but cautions about final conclusions must still be stated. Studies indicate that, even more than with the population as a whole, the IQ scores of a physically handicapped child should never be assumed to be the absolute, final indication of the child's potential (Cruickshank, Hallahan, and Bice, 1976). In a follow-up study conducted after an interval of four years from testing, Nielsen (1971) found that 20% of the IQ scores of children with cerebral palsy had changed more than 15 points. Klapper and Birch (1967) found even less stability in their follow-up study. After an interval of 14 years, IQ scores were stable only for the most severely retarded and intellectually normal of their physically handicapped subjects. The mildly retarded and slow-learner groups had quite variable IQs.

This same variability is especially apparent in the assessment of cognitive functioning in infants. Bayley (1970) and Goffoney, Henderson, and Butler (1971) found that tests of infant development are notoriously poor predictors of later intellectual functioning in non-retarded populations, although infant intelligence tests are highly reliable predictors of later intellectual development of multiply handicapped children. Through the administration of mental tests on two occasions to 28 multiply handicapped children, Dubose (1976) investigated the predictive value of infant intelligence scales and found a high correlation ($r = .83$) of scores for severely handicapped children.

It would seem, then, that test results for persons with physical handicaps are not as reliable in predicting future intellectual functioning as they are for the population as a whole. The exception is the severely/multiply handicapped group, for whom intelligence tests have a high predictive value.

Interpreting Results to Parents

A number of studies indicate that parental judgments about a child's physical and mental abilities often differ considerably from the evaluation results. Differences between parental and professional points of view are greater in cases of younger, more severely physically handicapped, and lower-IQ children (Keith and Markie, 1969). In almost all cases, the parental estimation of a child's potential is higher than that of the evaluators. Ozer (1977) points out that this difference is a potential source of friction that can interfere with a child's progress. Thus, an on-going collaboration among parents, teachers, and evaluators is required to serve the child well. If the parents are involved in the evaluation process, contribute to adaptive behavior ratings, and observe the same behavioral responses the evaluator observes, the chances for common goals and expectations would logically seem to be greater.

SUMMARY

The Education for All Handicapped Children Act requires a comprehensive evaluation to establish an educational plan. Evaluating persons with physical handicaps poses special challenges for the examiner: the client's different experiences, the effects of medication, and the lack of available appropriate testing instruments all impede the determination of valid estimates of ability. Tests and test items must be selected to yield the least equivocal results. This selection necessitates an initial understanding of the client's physical status, communication system, and adaptive behavior. No matter how careful the test selection and administration, caution and restraint are necessary in statements of prognosis, because testing scores for physically handicapped persons are even more variable than for the population as a whole. Psychological and educational testing must have as its ultimate goal not a final diagnostic and prognostic statement, but, rather, the best possible teaching plan based on the available evidence. Assessment is one of the many areas in which professionals who work with the physically handicapped must be creative and flexible.

LITERATURE CITED

Ando, K. 1968. A comparative study of the Peabody Picture Vocabulary Test and Intelligence Scale for Children with a group of cerebral palsied children. Cerebr. Pal. J. 29:7-9.

Balthazar, E. E. 1971. Balthazar Scales of Adaptive Behavior, Part Three: The Scales of Functional Independence. Research Press Company, Champaign, Ill.

Bayley, N. 1970. Development of mental abilities. In: P. Mussen (ed.), Carmichael's Manual of Child Psychology, Vol. 1. John Wiley and Sons, Inc., New York.

Boothroyd, A. 1971. Auditory Training Handbook. Clarke School for the Deaf, Northhampton, Mass.

Burgemeister, B., Hollander, L., and Lorge, I. 1959. Columbia Mental Maturity Scale. Harcourt Brace, Jovanovich, Inc., New York.

Byers, R. K. 1971. Introduction. In: E. M. Taylor, Psychological Appraisal of Children with Cerebral Defects. Harvard University Press, Cambridge, Mass.

Coop, R. H., Eckel, E., and Stuck, G. B. 1975. An assessment of the Pictorial Test of Intelligence for use with young children with cerebral palsy. Dev. Med. Child Neurol. 17:287-292.

Cruickshank, W. M., Hallahan, D. P., and Bice, H. V. 1976. The evaluation of intelligence. In: W. M. Cruickshank (ed.), Cerebral Palsy. Syracuse University Press, Syracuse.

Diana v California State Board of Education. Civil # 0-70-37 RFP (ND Cal, Feb. 5, 1970).

Doll, E. A. 1953. Vineland Social Maturity Scale. American Guidance Service, Circle Pines, Minn.

Dubose, R. F. 1976. Predictive value of infant intelligence scales with multiply handicapped children. Am. J. Men. Defic. 81:388-390.

Dubose, R. F., and Langley, M. B. 1977. Developmental Activities Screening Inventory. Teaching Resources, Boston.

Dunn, L. M. 1965. Peabody Picture Vocabulary Test. American Guidance Service, Circle Pines, Minn.

Dunn, L. M., and Harley, R. K., 1959. Comparability of Peabody, Ammons, Van Alstyne and Columbia test scores with cerebral palsied children. Except. Child. 16:70-74.

Dunn, L. M., and Markwardt, F. C. 1970. *Peabody Individual Achievement Test.* American Guidance Service, Circle Pines, Minn.

French, J. L. 1974. Pictorial Test of Intelligence. Houghton Mifflin Company, Boston.

Goffeney, B., Henderson, N. B., and Butler, B. V. 1971. Negro-white, male-female: eight month developmental scores compared with 7 year WISC and Bender test scores. Child Dev. 42:594–604.

Harper, D. C., and Tanner, H. 1974. The French Pictorial Test of Intelligence and the Stanford Binet, L-M: a concurrent validity study with physically impaired children. J. Clin. Psychol. 30:178–180.

Hawisher, M. F., and Calhoun, M. L. 1978. The Resource Room. Charles E. Merrill Publishing Company, Columbus, Ohio.

Jastek, J. F., and Bijou, S. 1946. Wide Range Achievement Test. Psychological Corporation, New York.

Jedrysek, E., Klapper, Z., Pope, L. and Wortis, J. 1972. Psychoeducational Evaluation of the Preschool Child. Grune and Stratton, New York.

Keith, R. A., and Markie, G. S. 1969. Parental and professional assessment of functioning in CP. Dev. Med. Child Neurol. 11:735–742.

Keystone Telebinocular. Keystone View Company, Davenport, Iowa.

Kiernan, D. W., and Dubose, R. F. 1974. Assessing the cognitive development of preschool deaf-blind children. Educ. Visu. Handic. 103–105.

Kirk, S. A., McCarthy, J. J., and Kirk, W. D. 1968. The Illinois Test of Psycholinguistic Abilities, Revised Edition. University of Illinois Press, Urbana.

Klapper, Z. A., and Birch, H. G. 1967. A fourteen-year follow-up study of cerebral palsy: Intellectual change and stability. Am. J. Orthopsychiatry. 37:540–547.

Lambert, N., Windmiller, M., Cole, L., and Figuerosa, R. 1975. AAMD Adaptive Behavior Scale — Public School Version. American Association on Mental Deficiency, Washington, D.C.

McCarthy, D. 1972. McCarthy Scales of Children's Abilities. The Psychological Corporation, New York.

Muller, D. G., and Leonetti, R. 1974. Primary Self-Concept Inventory. Learning Concepts, Austin, Texas.

Nicholson, C. L. 1970. Correlations among CMMS, PPVT, & RCPM for cerebral palsy children. Percept. Mot. Skills 30:715–718.

Nielsen, H. H. 1971. Psychological appraisal of children with cerebral palsy: a survey of 128 reassessed cases. Dev. Med. Child Neurol. 13:707–720.

Nihira, K., Foster, R., Shellhass, M., and Leland, H. 1974. AAMD Adaptive Behavior Scale Manual. American Association on Mental Deficiency, Washington, D.C.

Ozer, M. N. 1977. The assessment of children with developmental problems. Except. Child. 44:37–38.

The Radea Program. 1977. Melton Book Company, Dallas, Texas.

Raven, J. C. 1965. Progressive Matrices. Grieve, Great Britain.

Sanford, A. R. (ed.). 1974. Learning Accomplishments Profile. Chapel Hill Training-Outreach Project, Chapel Hill, N.C.

Sattler, J. M. 1970. Intelligence Test Modifications on Handicapped and Nonhandicapped Children. Progress Report of September 30, by the San Diego State College (Grant No. 15-P-5527719-02), for the Department of Health, Education, and Welfare, Social and Rehabilitation Service.

Sattler, J. M., and Anderson, N. E. 1973. The Peabody Picture Vocabulary Test, Stanford-Binet and the modified Stanford-Binet with normal and cerebral palsied preschool children. J. Spec. Educ. 7:119–123.

Schlenoff, D. 1974. Considerations in administering intelligence tests to the physically disabled. Rehabil. Lit. 35:362-363.

Shearer, D., Billingsley, J., Frohman, A., Hilliard, J., Johnson, F., and Shearer, M. 1972. The *Portage Guide to Early Education*. Cooperative Educational Service Agency 12, Portage, Wisc.

Somerton, M., and Turner, K. 1975. Pennsylvania Training Model: Individual Assessment Guide. Pennsylvania Department of Education, Harrisburg.

Taylor, E. M. 1971. Psychological Appraisal of Children with Cerebral Defects. Harvard University Press, Cambridge, Mass.

Terman, L., and Merrill, M. 1973. Stanford-Binet Intelligence Scale. Houghton Mifflin Company, Boston.

Turner, K. D., and Somerton-Fair, E. 1978. Special considerations in evaluating the severely/profoundly handicapped. Paper presented at the Annual Convention of the Council for Exceptional Children, May, Kansas City.

Vort Corporation. 1973. Behavioral Characteristics Progression. Palo Alto, Calif.

Wechsler, D. 1974. Wechsler Intelligence Scale for Children — Revised. Psychological Corporation, New York.

Wright, G. N., and Remmers, H. H. 1960. Purdue Handicap Problems Inventory. Purdue Research Foundation, Lafayette, Ind.

Wright, L. S. 1976. Chronic grief: The anguish of being an exceptional parent. Except. Child 23:3, 160-169.

7

APPROPRIATE
EDUCATION

Figure 7-1. Appropriate education requires a competent teacher, the right equipment, and an adaptive approach to the special needs of the physically handicapped child.

The appropriate education of physically handicapped students requires careful consideration of several key factors. Implementation of the mandate of Public Law 94–142, the Education for All Handicapped Children Act of 1975, can be achieved only through the careful analysis of each student's skills, abilities, and aptitudes, coupled with the careful preparation of the scholastic environment. Neither the analysis of student skills nor the preparation of the scholastic environment is a static procedure; conscientious and continual regulation, observation, and evaluation are essential.

This chapter deals with those elements of the teaching/learning environment that contribute to the appropriate education of physically handicapped students. Some of these elements are relatively stable, such as: a well-designed, safe classroom, adequate equipment, and a competent teacher. Other elements are more fluid, for example: adaptive teaching to match programs and techniques to the needs of the child, and program evaluation, or a monitoring process that provides to both the teacher and her pupils the feedback necessary to ensure continuous progress.

TEACHER COMPETENCIES

A competent teacher is the vital central component in an effective educational program. Physical settings are not without influence, of course, but the atmosphere depends on the teacher. In fact, of all the elements that contribute to the social environment in which children are educated, the competency of the teacher is by far the most decisive (Smith, Neisworth, and Greer, 1978).

Teacher responsibilities in working with physically handicapped students include: 1) to provide appropriate and relevant education, 2) to offer friendly, helpful, and encouraging support to her students and their families, and 3) to share significant information with other professionals and paraprofessionals interacting with her students and their families.

These three responsibilities are equally important to the total educational program of the handicapped. To be able to fulfill these responsibilities, the teacher must have a core of basic skills. The "basics" for competent teaching, according to the U.S. Office of Education's Institute on Professional Preparation for Educators of Crippled Children, are these:[1]

Basic Areas of Knowledge:

understanding the dynamics of child development
understanding the nature of various disabilities and how they may interfere
    with learning
awareness of the neurophysiological correlates of physical disability
knowledge of the psychological implications of handicapping conditions
ability to adapt both the physical environment and equipment for use by
    handicapped persons

Assessment and Programming:

ability to develop and to modify tools for the assessment of the child's learn-
    ing style and level of achievement
ability to plan and to modify the curriculum according to individual differ-
    ences
knowledge of and ability to use specialized equipment and media
ability to teach the subject matter

Coordination of Resources:

awareness of special resources that exist in the community
ability to serve as an effective team member
ability to integrate ancillary services and to promote interagency coopera-
    tion
knowledge of work-study programs

---

[1](Connor, Wald, and Cohen, 1970)

Teacher Preparation

Effective teaching, as specified above, requires both cognitive and affective skills. Some of these are necessary for all teachers; others are specialized requirements for teachers of physically handicapped students. Teacher education programs should reflect this need for both general and special knowledge.

Horner (1977) suggests that the basic requirements of competence be organized into clusters to form the basis of a teacher education program. It is imperative that classroom instruction be coordinated with direct experience in dealing with physically handicapped students. Supervised "hands-on" learning experiences give the student teacher an opportunity to apply textbook information to student populations with a variety of learning needs. There is no substitute for direct teacher-student interaction in the preparation of teachers to work in the field of special education. The essential function of teacher education programs is to prepare teachers to change pupil behaviors (Wilcox, 1977). The special education teacher should be prepared to help a child move from being a nonreader to being a reader, from being a person with few self-care and social skills to being a person with many such skills, from feeling overwhelmed by a physical disability to being competent and able to cope.

The Effective Teacher

The final product of teacher training, the end result of years spent in the acquisition of skills and knowledge and the development of various abilities, is a professional person. The demonstration of these professional talents in practical settings, a realistic understanding of each student and his/her own particular world, a total commitment to instilling in each student the desire to fulfill his or her ultimate potential, and the skillful blending of guidance, discipline, humor, firm resolve, and love are the essential attributes of an effective teacher. Love is not enough. The desire to help is not enough, nor is the accumulation of textbook information. All of these characteristics are necessary, but the basic teaching skills must be combined with the ability to relate to the student in an honest, open manner, both verbally and through non-verbal signs. The teacher must also accept responsibility for pupil progress. When standard measures do not work, the effective teacher seeks out new methods that will help every student to be the best person he or she can be.

THE CLASSROOM

The preparation and arrangement of the physical environment is a key factor in creating an atmosphere that is conducive to learning. The classroom should reflect the teacher's attitude of concern and understanding as well as the determination to create an environment that stimulates and promotes learning.

Classrooms typically mirror the curricular content to be studied within them: homemaking rooms are equipped with furniture and home equipment, science rooms with laboratory facilities, social studies rooms with globes, maps, and an atlas, and so on. Classrooms intended to house physically disabled students require variations on these traditional themes to meet the physical needs of students.

Physically handicapped students arrive at school with the usual student possessions (coats, books, and sack lunches) along with more unusual belongings, such as wheelchairs, braces, crutches, and canes. Therefore, the classroom housing handicapped students who use these appliances must be arranged so that the student is able to perform class-related activities with as little confusion and discomfort as possible.

Bednar (1970) suggests that teachers of the physically handicapped usually regard the classroom in one of two ways: 1) the environment should compensate completely for the student's disability, so that, after the environment has been altered to offset all of the student's needs, the classroom then represents what is a "normal" environment for the handicapped; or 2) the classroom should remain as it exists for the majority of the students, and effective means should be devised to aid the disabled student in coping with the environment.

Bednar (1970) urges teachers instead to view the classroom as an element in the total educational ecology that can be effectively manipulated and utilized as an educational aid. If the teacher views the classroom itself as one more piece of educational material, it is then possible to alter this environment to promote the acquisition of student skills and encourage pupils to reach higher levels of self-sufficiency. In other words, in September the student might enter a compensatory classroom equipped to cater to his disability; by May, he may be functioning adequately in this same classroom, which has now been revised to more nearly approximate a normal environment. Through alterations of this nature, the student grows in independence and becomes better prepared to cope with the less protected world he will encounter as an adult.

The degree of alteration required to prepare a classroom for handicapped students depends on the primary use of the classroom and the severity of the handicapping conditions involved. The self-contained classroom used specifically by physically handicapped students should be equipped to care for the special needs of all of the individual class members, as well as to provide a total instructional program. The classrooms that house mainstreamed students serve a majority of non-handicapped pupils and therefore require alteration only as necessary for those few physically handicapped students who use them for portions of the day.

Classroom Furniture

Rows of desks are usually an inconvenience in the classroom for physically handicapped students. Far more suitable are adjustable tables designed to be raised or lowered to different heights. For example, an adjustable table can be lowered for use by small children and then raised to accommodate a demonstration or display. The use of adjustable tables permits flexibility in room arrangements as well. Torrey (1960, as cited in Yuker, Young, and Feldman, 1967) suggests a pedestal-based table as a practical surface for the student in a wheelchair.

If it is necessary to use standard desks, some should be removed from the room to provide greater maneuverability. Portable lap boards (Rusalem, 1962) can serve as writing surfaces, as can specially-designed cut-out desk tops attached to the existing surface (Schoenbohm, 1962). (See Figure 7-2.)

Classroom Equipment and Design

A careful examination of existing equipment in the classroom from the perspective of a person sitting in a wheelchair can be of help in determining

Figure 7-2. Options for flexible seating in the classroom for students in wheelchairs: a) lap board; b) cut-out table; c) multiplace cut-out table. Photos courtesy of the Prentke-Romich Company

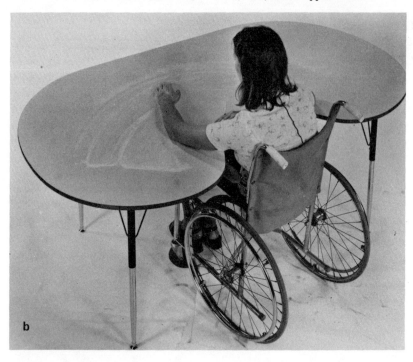

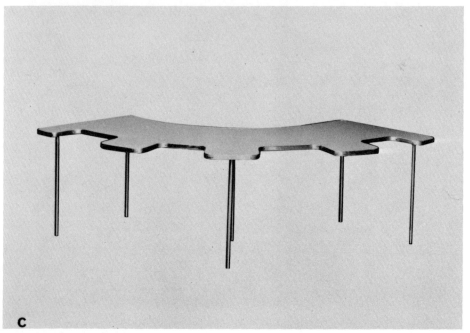

Figure 7.2. *continued*

what equipment should be relocated. Yuker et al. (1967) suggest that chalk-boards and corkboards be lowered to be accessible to the wheelchair student (see Figure 7-3). It is recommended that these boards be installed 3″–6″ from the wall.

It is usually necessary to relocate pencil sharpeners, some doorknobs, light switches, alarms, plumbing fixtures, coat hooks or racks, and lockers.

The installation of pivoting mirrors above laboratory tables enables students to comfortably watch science and home economics demonstrations. Library references — books, atlases, and card catalogues — should be on low, accessible shelves.

The following classroom design suggestions from Barrier-Free School Facilities for Handicapped Students (1977) are helpful:

1. Classrooms should have two doors, one near the front and one near the back.
2. The chalkboard should be low (24″ from the floor).
3. Doors should have automatic door checks that keep the door open for wheelchairs and crutch walkers.
4. Long grasping bars, rather than doorknobs, are recommended.
5. Classroom sinks should be accessible from three sides.
6. Faucets should be of the delayed, self-closing type.
7. Toilet facilities should be adjacent to the classroom.
8. Facilities for rest should be provided.
9. Floors should have nonskid surfaces.
10. Warm floors are essential.
11. Storage and cupboard space should have sliding doors.
12. Equipment should include easels, portable reading racks, a standing table, adjustable seats, and desks.

Classroom Safety

Student safety is a concern in any classroom; special thought must be given to the safety of physically handicapped students. First aid provisions for

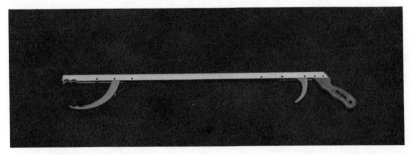

Figure 7-3. An extension arm aid to reach objects on high shelves for those with limited mobility. Photo courtesy of Maddak Inc., Pequannock, N.J.

medical emergencies and facilities for resting, changing clothes, and bathing may be required, along with the usual provisions for fire drills and/or tornado plans, with the necessary variations for the evacuation of the handicapped (see Figure 7-4).

Safety routines must be planned so that a student is not left unattended or behind during fire and tornado drills. Exit plans should be established and, if wheelchair obstacles are unavoidable, someone must be available to transport students. Edgington (1976) suggests the use of an ordinary chair as a stretcher in such a situation.

Crutches can pose a safety hazard for other class members if the students are careless about putting them down. It is usually best to place crutches on the floor next to other furniture within easy reach of the student. Placing them on the floor deliberately prevents them from falling to the floor disruptfully (Edgington, 1976).

Students using leg or body braces do not have the degree of mobility and flexibility of movement enjoyed by other children. It may be difficult for these students to examine the path underfoot and to quickly regain their balance after bumping into something unexpected. The classroom floor must therefore be kept uncluttered and litter-free to avoid unpleasant and painful falls and crashes.

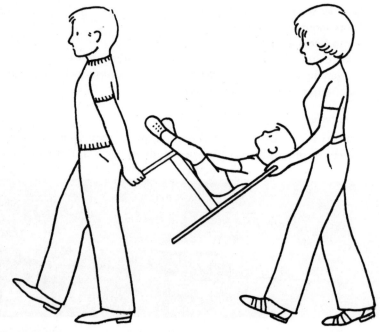

Figure 7-4. A standard chair can be used as a stretcher to transport students.

In order to prevent slips and slides, a carpeted floor, free of ridges, and an uncluttered furniture arrangement with adequate cruising space in and about the room are high priority considerations in planning the classroom for special students.

Wheelchairs, because they have small front wheels for easy steering, are stopped by even very small obstacles. Therefore, to avoid tipping and pitching accidents resulting from sudden stops, the floors in the classroom must be smooth and free of bumps.

One of the very first habits a teacher of physically handicapped students should acquire is that of automatically locking wheelchairs when they are in place. This habit should be communicated to all students and everyone else in the classroom. Other rules for wheelchair safety include:

1. Students in wheelchairs should put on brakes when transferring from the chair to the desk or other location.
2. Students should take turns leaving and entering a room.
3. Students should stay close to the wall when moving down the hall.
4. Students should look in all directions before turning or going backwards.
5. Students should push themselves whenever possible.

School personnel should be prepared for, and informed about, the expected medical emergencies and first aid requirements that might be associated with a disease or disability of the physically handicapped students. It would be wise for schools to have a nearby physician on call in case of emergency. Parents and school personnel should discuss, and decide upon, a plan or procedure should such a situation arise in order to avoid needless delay in providing medical care and treatment.

TECHNOLOGICAL AIDS

The classroom housing students with physical disabilities will be set apart from other classrooms by a number of teaching aids not typically found in schools. Teaching aids can compensate for incoordination, limited hand use, and restricted mobility; they can facilitate the understanding and expression of ideas and make the activities of daily living much easier.

The applied technology that aids teaching/learning for physically handicapped students includes such simple devices as Velcro strips, elastic tape, clipboards, four-fingered scissors, and clay-wrapped pencils. This same technology has also produced complex machines designed by skilled engineers, such as typewriters controlled by mouth pressure, electrically operated communication boards, and environmental control devices that enable even the most severely handicapped person to select radio stations and TV channels and to use a telephone.

According to Jefcoate (1977), the technology that enabled men to live and work in the moon's alien environment has benefitted mankind in many different ways. Space technology is often used to aid handicapped people — particularly in the field of communication. The use of electronic technology in the rehabilitation of the physically handicapped toward increased independence is in the very early stages of development. Jefcoate (1977) tells the story of a courageous, determined woman who, paralyzed by myasthenia gravis, was unable to move her hands, speak, or swallow. Through the use of electronic technology and the residual movement of 1/16 inch in each of her big toes, she was able to edit a magazine and raise thousands of dollars for other handicapped people. Her remarkable accomplishments encouraged others who also faced apparently insurmountable challenges.

The development of sophisticated and less complex devices stems from the need of an individual and the determination of a teacher to help his or her student overcome the obstacle of a disability that interferes with communication, learning, or independence. The creation of amazing electronic aids is the result of teaching determination plus the specialized assistance of those interested electronic experts who respond to the challenge. Such ingenuity can be found in rehabilitation centers and university electronic engineering classes, as well as in electronic engineering firms. Examples of technological aids to the development of self-help and learning skills and recreation are described below.

Teaching Machines

Teaching machines are used by many different learning populations. It is a rare elementary school classroom that does not have a magnetic card machine, a tape player, or an electronically programmed learning system. These common teaching devices can be used effectively with many physically handicapped students, if complex motor movements are not required for their operation. In addition to equipment in general use, some machines have been specifically designed for this special handicapped population. This equipment facilitates the learning situation by providing an effective means of independence in learning that would otherwise be denied to people who have trouble speaking or using a pencil.

When choosing teaching machines for persons with physical handicaps, Haskell (1973) recommends the following guidelines:

1. The machine should be able to withstand uncontrollable shaking by the handler.
2. The student should be securely positioned so that he does not slump onto the machine.
3. The machine should be able to withstand excessive or prolonged pressure on its various parts.
4. The machine must be easy to operate and repair.

Some examples of teaching machines that have been used effectively with physically handicapped learners are described below:

1. Magnetic card machines (Figure 7-5) are versatile classroom aids. A message recorded on tape is heard while the card runs through the machine, thus presenting auditory and visual information simultaneously. Programmed cards are available to teach specific predetermined skills, as are blank cards on which the teacher can create an individualized program. The magnetic card machine can be used to teach reading, spelling, and arithmetic skills, and to aid the handicapped student in communication with other students, as well as to teach Blissymbols or other communication techniques.

2. Typewriters enable students to write down their thoughts, not only by the conventional method of finger pressure, but also through the use of head wands and light-operated techniques (see Figure 7-6). Stoede et al. (1973) describe the typewriter system operated by fixing a light source to the student's hand so that a lightspot can be projected on the control panel. This system enables the quadriplegic student to use the typewriter, thereby increasing the scope of his activities. Special grids can be fixed to the typewriter keyboard to reduce the likelihood of the student's pushing a key other than the one intended. The electric typewriter, which requires only a light touch, can be used by the student with weak muscles.

3. Tape recorders are used to aid in the development of skills in language,

Figure 7-5. A magnetic card machine is used to teach beginning reading skills.

Figure 7-6. Typewriter adaptations: a) a special grid reduces the likelihood that extra keys will be punched; b) a headstick makes typing possible when hand function is inadequate.

speech, auditory discrimination, and phonics, and to direct students in individualized activities of all kinds. Earphones allow the student to use the machine without disturbing others.

4. *System80* (Figure 7-7) by Borg-Warner has gained wide acceptance as a diagnostic and prescriptive audio-visual learning system. This machine, adapted for use by severely handicapped persons by Dr. Eugene McDonald of the Pennsylvania State University, incorporates both scanning and direct selection techniques as well as a call signal. A wide selection of programmed learning materials is available for use with this machine.

5. Telephones can also be used in the teaching of physically handicapped students. Using the local telephone network, a teacher can conduct a class of up to twenty students. The homebound or hospitalized student can participate in class work via a telephone equipped with a headset. The class then operates in much the same way as a conference call; each student can hear his classmates and the teacher. The teacher's console is arranged so that she can speak with each student privately, divide the class into smaller groups, connect a tape recording to present prepared

information to the class, or transfer part of the class to another teacher in a different location for specialized instruction.

Telephone companies have many options available to facilitate telephone use by motor handicapped students. Card dialers — prepunched cards — can be inserted into the phone to automatically dial a specified number. Automatic dialers can store hundreds of frequently called numbers on magnetic tape. To dial a desired number, the caller simply presses one button; the phone does the rest. The teacher can promote independence by educating students and their families about the availability and proper usage of these and other options.

A variety of telephone holders are available to facilitate use by motor handicapped persons. An example is the flexible telephone holder (Figure 7-8).

6. Talking Books are available not only to the blind, but also to those children and adults with disabilities that prevent them from handling books comfortably. Talking Books and talking book machines are distributed by the Library of Congress at no cost to the user. Books for children and adults, with a wide range of topics, as well as current magazines, are available on loan. Teachers generally find Talking Books to be helpful additions to the classroom and home experiences of the handicapped student.

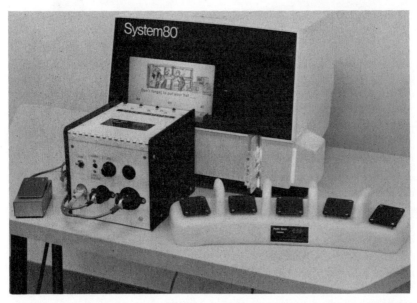

Figure 7-7. System80 Interface, a teaching machine shown here with arm slot control. Photo courtesy of Prentke-Romich Company.

Figure 7-8. Flexible telephone holder: the phone may be used with free hands. The headset may remain attached to the extension arm at all times. A bar is pressed to make and break contact. Photo courtesy of Maddak Inc., Pequannock, N.J.

Aids to Mobility and Independence

A physically handicapped student may have to be wheeled about, fed, clothed, toileted, and bathed by others. This extreme dependence discourages any feelings of control, power, or success. Special equipment or technological devices can often encourage increased independence and learning by compensating for a lack of power or control. The right kind of seating, for example, can promote better eye-hand coordination and facilitate movement from place to place.

Several aids to mobility and independence are illustrated below. The use of this kind of equipment should be guided by physical and occupational therapists, who can recommend the most helpful posture, balance, and mobility aids for each student. (Complete coverage of aids to independence can be found in Robinault's [1973] *Functional Aids for the Multiply Handicapped:* the items described include aids to travel, transfer, mobility, feeding and eating, dressing, and personal hygiene.) Chapter 8 provides teaching suggestions for facilitating independence in the activities of daily living.

Some of the aids just discussed are illustrated in Figures 7-9 to 7-14.

Recreation Equipment

In addition to equipment designed to facilitate academic and daily living activities, programs for physically handicapped students require equipment for play. Toys, whether adapted standard versions or special designs,

Figure 7-9. Travel chairs have adjustable legs for changing seating positions and feature well-balanced handling. Photos courtesy of Orthokinetics, Inc.

Figure 7.9. *continued*

can give physically handicapped children the stimulation necessary to encourage learning, to improve physical and perceptual control, and to reduce the handicap itself (Jefcoate, 1977) (Figure 7-15).

The match of a specific toy to the needs of a particular child should not be based solely on the child's physical ability to manage the object: the toy should also be matched to the child's intellectual abilities and interests. Objects selected should present progressive challenges to the students. It is important first that the child enjoy the activity. Second, the child should be given toys that encourage strategy and improve performance. A good resource for adaptive toys is the Alpha Chi Omega *Toy Book*.

Monster Dash (Figure 7-16) is a simple game that can be played by severely handicapped children. The teacher can create new games by using blank overlays. The game is effective as a reward in classroom management

Figure 7-10. The relaxation chair promotes good sitting posture. The footrest is adjustable to accommodate growth. Photo courtesy of Hausmann Industries.

Figure 7-11. The UNIVERSAL desk is a sophisticated solution to postural and other problems that handicapped students face in work and study situations. The adjustments can be made in many cases by the handicapped person himself. Photo courtesy of Maddak Inc., Pequannock, N.J.

systems as well as a valuable source of informal diagnosis of the student's basic number skills.

Playground equipment can be designed to encourage therapeutic play. Tunnels and obstacle courses, things to crawl over, under, through, around, across, and between, all promote goal-directed play. Basketball nets at a lower-than-regulation height tempt wheelchairbound students to shoot a basket. A permanently installed batting tee enables one person to "play ball." Sand and water entice children to participate in many activities — even some that are a bit messy!

Games for the physically handicapped should not be confined to those of a sedentary nature. Games that require exertion, from mild to vigorous,

Figure 7-12. The automatic page turner is an example of highly skilled technology applied to educational needs. Various types of control systems are available (push button, hand or chin switches, and finger control). The puff and breath switch is shown. Photo courtesy of Maddak Inc., Pequannock, N.J.

should be encouraged. Parachutes, relays, shuffleboard, and adapted volleyball and basketball provide avenues for activities that are therapeutic, recreational, and educational. Chapter 8 offers some ideas for recreation and leisure activities.

ADAPTIVE TEACHING

Adaptive teaching means applying existing knowledge about curriculum and learning goals, sometimes in unique and creative ways, to the special needs of a particular child. Adaptive teaching requires that the teacher possess, or at least be open to, skills held by other members of an interdisci-

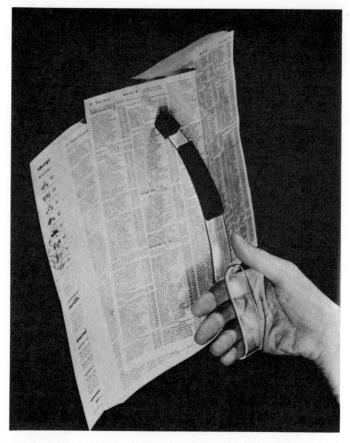

Figure 7-13. Page turners may also be of this type, with a spring action clip to fit the hand. Photo courtesy of Maddak Inc., Pequannock, N.J.

plinary team. According to the nature of a particular student's disability, a variety of trained personnel (including physical, occupational, and speech and language therapists, specialists in vision and hearing) may be part of that team (Scheuerman, 1976). Scheuerman points out that the teacher's role is not to replace these important people, but to extend their services because time and financial constraints do not permit these specialists to devote their undivided attention to any one particular student. The teacher is better able to incorporate therapeutic techniques into her daily teaching routine if she has a basic understanding of the development, function, and rationale of a recommended therapy.

In addition to understanding therapeutic techniques, the teacher must also understand the nature of the task presented to the child — what demands the task makes on the child, and what skills are required of the

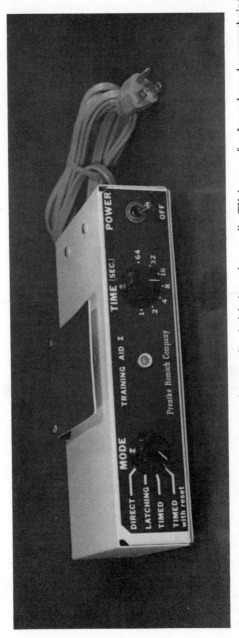

Figure 7-14. The Training Aid I was designed to give control over an electrical device such as a radio, TV, lamp, or fan. It may be used to assess the individual's ability to comprehend the concept of control. Ideally, this could lead to the prescription and use of one of the more sophisticated communication aids, such as an environmental control system. Photo courtesy of Prentke-Romich Company.

Figure 7-15. Toys can encourage learning and personal growth.

teacher to help the child master this task. The teacher must find an effective means of communication so that instruction can be given and progress can be monitored.

Adaptive teaching, then, requires that the teacher possess skills in the interdisciplinary process, communication skill development, and task analysis. Chapter 9 discusses the interdisciplinary process; communication methods and task analysis are discussed below.

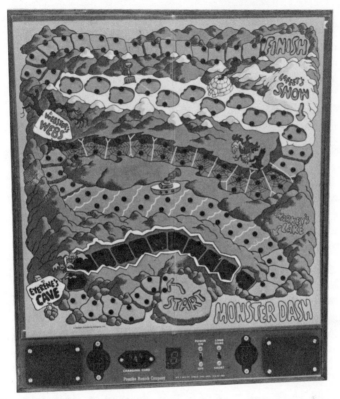

Figure 7-16. Monster Dash game. Photo courtesy of Prentke-Romich Company.

Communication

Communication Aids   The interaction between teacher and student that is typical of teaching in the usual sense is often stifled when the student is physically handicapped. The physically handicapped student with intact cognitive abilities and upper extremity motor control may not require communication procedures that are any different from those used with non-handicapped learners. However, for those children with neurological involvement, the traditional teaching methods must be evaluated, and perhaps altered or even discarded.

A normal child develops language as a result of interaction with his environment. In order for this phenomenon to happen, the child must first have a sensorium that receives and interprets information concerning the events that take place around him. This does not mean, however, that he must have an intact motor system. Many children with severe motor handicaps demonstrate well developed receptive language, as well as good manipulation of language in another modality (McDonald, 1976).

Speech is the usual evidence of language aptitude. For the child with a speech impairment severe enough to render him incapable of functional oral language, alternative methods of expressive communication must be developed.

Vanderheiden (1976) identifies these steps in the development of a communication system for the non-vocal, severely handicapped student:

1. selecting/developing a technique or aid to provide the child with an effective means of indicating the elements of his message
2. selecting/developing a symbol set and vocabulary system that are compatible with the child's current abilities
3. developing in the child the necessary communication skills to enable him to use his symbol set in a manner that is clearly understood by the message receiver

Facilitating expressive language for the non-vocal, physically handicapped learner generally requires some sort of modification of the three basic approaches of scanning, encoding, and direct selection (Vanderheiden, 1976).

The scanning technique (Figure 7-17), used with persons who have very limited control, is a slow method of communication, presenting numerous unwanted choices in the search for the correct response (Vanderheiden, 1976).

Encoding (Figure 7-18) is a faster method of communication than scanning, provided that the individual has good cognitive skills and some form of quick movement. Many encoding procedures can be automated for adaptation to suit individual needs in both operation and the display of print-outs (Vanderheiden, 1976).

The direct selection approach (Figure 7-19), most frequently demonstrated by a communication or letter board, is useful for students with limited intellectual abilities as well as for severely involved persons who have fine cognitive skills trapped inside an extremely disabled body.

Fingerspelling can be taught to students who have control of their finger muscles. The disadvantage of this method, however, is that the "listener" or receiver must also be skilled in fingerspelling to interpret the communication. This obviously limits the social interaction possibilities of the "speaker."

Blissymbols, a system of pictographs related to meaning, are more frequently used as an alternate means of communication.

A cerebral palsied child may be too involved motorically to engage in fingerspelling and signing. Manual picture and communication boards may frustrate the child with their associated slowness. Harris-Vanderheiden

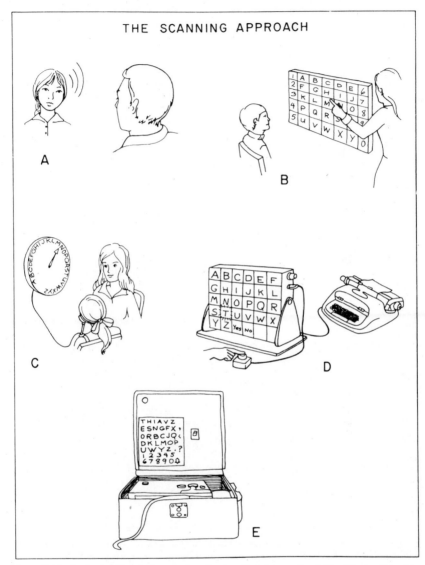

THE SCANNING APPROACH

Figure 7-17. Examples of techniques using the scanning approach: a) Yes/No guessing; b) manual scanning of communication board; c) rotating pointer communication; and d) printing communication board using row column scanning; e) portable printing communication aid. From Vanderheiden (1976). Reprinted with permission.

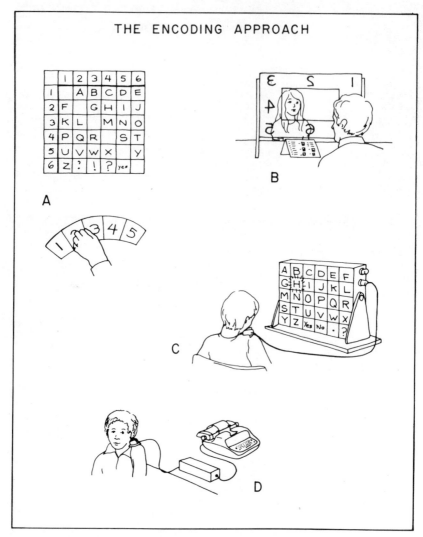

Figure 7-18. Examples of techniques using the encoding approach: a) two-movement encoding with number line, b) two-movement encoding using eye gaze; c) Morse code decoder/display being controlled with shoulder (shrug); d) Morse code decoder controlling typewriter. From Vanderheiden (1976). Reprinted with permission.

(1976) suggests the following criteria for consideration when deciding whether Blissymbols (Figures 7-20, 7-21) are an appropriate communication device for mentally retarded, and/or physically handicapped students:

1. the student can establish eye contact
2. the student demonstrates object permanence

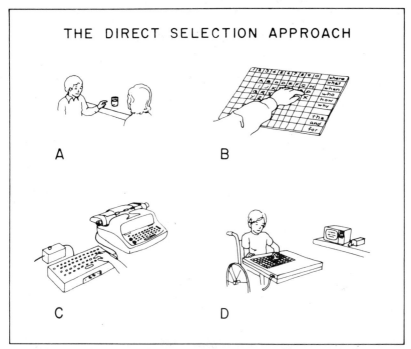

THE DIRECT SELECTION APPROACH

A   B

C   D

Figure 7-19. Examples of techniques using the direct selection approach: a) direct indication; b) pointing communication board; c) expanded, recessed keyboard; d) portable printing communication board. From Vanderheiden (1976). Reprinted with permission.

3. the student can attend to a task for at least 5 minutes
4. the student is able to follow oral directions
5. the student demonstrates a desire to communicate
6. the student does not possess functional language skills

The selection of Blissymbols, in the experience reported by Harris-Vanderheiden (1976), was based on the realization that the children were non-vocal and needed a functional communication system that would not cause frustration.

McNaughton (1976) supports the use of the Blissymbolic system. A young student must retain a visual sequence or configuration to learn words; Blissymbols are pictorial representations whose configurations indicate the objects or ideas they portray. Blissymbols are composed of visual elements that are related to meaning; written words are composed of visual elements that are related to sound. Both the word and the Blissymbol equip the child for communication. Words are used in typing and reading. Blissymbols can facilitate learning to read. When the printed word is presented

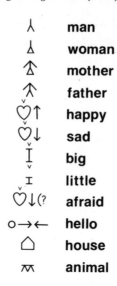

λ	man
λ	woman
$\hat{\Uparrow}$	mother
$\hat{\wedge}$	father
$\overset{\vee}{\heartsuit}\uparrow$	happy
$\overset{\vee}{\heartsuit}\downarrow$	sad
$\overset{\vee}{\text{I}}$	big
I	little
$\overset{\vee}{\heartsuit}\downarrow(?$	afraid
$\circ\rightarrow\leftarrow$	hello
$\triangle$	house
$\overline{\wedge\wedge}$	animal

Figure 7-20. Examples of Blissymbols. Reprinted with permission of Blissymbolics Communication Institute, Toronto, Canada.

Figure 7-21. Blissymbol scanner. Photo courtesy of Prentke-Romich Company.

with the Blissymbol, the student is given the opportunity to learn the printed word through incidental experience (McNaughton, 1976).

Communication boards are frequently used to enable the non-verbal student to express ideas and wants, as well as to answer questions. Language boards provide the child with a means of two-way communication and facilitate language development (McDonald and Schultz, 1976). Too often, the effort required to attempt to talk to others and the associated tension and anxiety prevent the cerebral palsied student from entering into and initiating conversations. The early use of communication boards may minimize these problems (McDonald and Schultz, 1976).

The child should be positioned so that he can indicate his choice of pictures or symbols on the board with a minimum of effort. The teacher may wish to consult the physical therapist when planning a board to ensure efficient muscle movement, thereby maximizing the speed and accuracy of pointing.

The elements of the communication board should be consistent with the student's ability. Communication boards must be dynamic; elements must be changed as the child develops. It is not possible to make a board for a young child that will meet his needs for the rest of his life. Boards may require changes and additions as often as every few days as the child adds to his vocabulary or has new experiences that he wants to discuss (McDonald, 1976). Figures 7-22 and 7-23 are examples of communication boards.

Figure 7-22. A beginning communication board for young learners.

here	I it we you my me	love can come find need	go help is look	make play run said work	drink food bathroom TV story maybe yes
where					
why					

green   red orange yellow blue purple black

| 1 | 2 | 3 | 4 | 5 | 6 |

| 7 | 8 | 9 | 0 | Thank you | please |

My name is Ginger Cook. Mother teacher
                          Daddy   friend

Figure 7-23. A word communication board.

Electronic communication boards are available from many different sources. One such machine is the *Auto-Com,* a device developed by the Cerebral Palsy Instrumentation Group at the University of Wisconsin in Madison. This machine was created to help a bright but severely handicapped young man express his thoughts and ideas. The *Auto-Com* increased the speed with which he acquired a reading and writing vocabulary by providing immediate visual feedback and an additional incentive for learning. Ultimately, it also enhanced his self-image (Wendt, Sprague, and Marquis, 1975).

Teachers involved in field testing of the *Auto-Com* reported that it greatly aided students in the acquisition of, and progress in, educational skills, especially in the areas of math, sentence structure, vocabulary, and reading (Harris-Vanderheiden, 1976). Displaying comments and responses on a TV screen (an available option) enables the teacher to include the student in classroom discussions.

Electronic communication devices that can provide voice output for severely speech handicapped individuals are also available. One example is the *Handi-Voice* (Votrax), with a pre-stored, self-contained vocabulary of over 400 words. This product makes spoken communication possible for speech handicapped individuals, who have only to select the word to be spoken.

Task Analysis

Once a communication system has been established, future goals must be set. Task analysis is a helpful approach to establishing a teaching/learning plan.

Adaptive teaching utilizes a task analysis approach. Task analysis guides decisions about 1) what to teach next, 2) where students have difficulties when attempting, but not completing, tasks, 3) what steps are probably necessary to accomplish the entire task, 4) how adaptations can aid task accomplishments, and 5) what options exist for disabled persons for whom accomplishment of a particular task is not feasible (Bigge and O'Donnell, 1976).

Task analysis is a logical process that identifies all the subskills essential to mastering a task (Frank, 1974). These subskills are then listed in a teaching sequence from the easiest to the most difficult. This sequence, or task ladder, can be used as a road map for skill development. Tables 7-1, 7-2, and 7-3 are examples of task ladders appropriate to different educational undertakings.

Table 7-1. Task ladder for motor development

Objective:
    The student will hold his head erect without support when on his stomach or held over your shoulder after attaining five consecutive position responses to a verbal command on each step of the task analysis.

Task analysis steps:

The student will:
1. let you hold his head up
2. let you hold his head up, and he will look at a dangling toy
3. let you hold his head up, and he will maintain this position for two seconds while looking at a dangling toy
4. let you hold his head up, and he will maintain the position for three seconds while looking at a dangling toy
5. let you hold his head up, and he will maintain the position for four seconds while looking at a dangling toy
6. let you hold his head up, and he will maintain the position for six seconds while looking at a dangling toy
7. let you hold his head up, and he will maintain the position for eight seconds while looking at a dangling toy
8. let you hold his head up, and he will maintain the position for ten seconds while looking at a dangling toy
9. lift his head to receive a reinforcer

From Popovich (1977). Reprinted with permission.

Table 7-2. Task ladder for self-diapering

Sit on a cot.
Put crutches on floor.
Take fresh diaper out of bag and place it on cot.
Place bag near cot on floor.
Raise legs to cot with hands.
Turn and lie down with legs extended.
Place diaper to left at level of buttocks.
Roll to left.
Pull pants with elasticized waistband down.
Roll to right.
Pull other side down.
Lie on back.
Pull pants down further.
Unsnap used diaper.
Lower front of diaper.
Reach into bag for tissue.
Wipe self.
Place tissue between legs on soiled diaper.
Roll body to the left.
Pull diaper and plastic cover away with right hand.
Place diaper and cover on floor.
Lie on back.
Roll to right.
Pull fresh diaper and cover under buttocks with left hand.
Roll to left and straighten diaper, etc.

From Bigge and O'Donnell (1976). Reprinted with permission.

PROGRAM EVALUATION

Physically handicapped students are so varied in their learning needs, their expression of learning accomplishment, and their aptitude to learn that few truisms are applicable to the total population. Effective teaching is evidenced by a desirable change in the student's behavior.

Program evaluation refers to the effect upon the learner of the curriculum, the environment, the materials, and, of course, the teacher. Evaluation of an education program is always happening in an informal manner:

"I hated school today." (student)
"What did you learn today in school?" (parent)
"I really felt on top of it today — a great day." (teacher)
"This classroom is always an active, busy place." (principal)
"What an attractive classroom!" (a school visitor)
"Are you certain this program justifies the expense?" (a school board member/taxpayer)

The following discussion of program evaluation reviews methods of compiling more formal data for reporting to concerned persons.

Table 7-3. Academic task ladders

TASK: Tell time on the hour

Recognize that the hour is indicated by the number that the short (hour) hand is pointing to when the minute hand is pointing to the top center of the clock face.

Recognize that the long hand points to the top center of the clock face when the clock reads _____ o'clock.

Recognize the function of the two hands on the clock.

Place numerals on clock face in correct order.

Say names of the numerals 1-12.

Recognize the numerals 1-12.

TASK: The word in the box is "baby." Find another word that begins with the same letter as "baby."

| baby | dog   bird   cow   run

Visually finds identical elements at the beginning of written words.

Visually discriminates letters of the alphabet.

Understands the concept "begins."

Understands the concepts "same" and "different."

From Calhoun (1976). Reprinted with permission.

Educational Achievement

The student's individualized educational plan, or IEP (see Chapter 8), lists educational goals, describes the manner of assessment of achievement of these goals, and states the criteria for successful education of a particular student.

Assessment may be as simple a procedure as pre- and posttesting with a standardized instrument. In this case, the degree of change between these two test scores indicates educational achievements. Table 7-4 shows how this comparison is accomplished using grade equivalent scores.

Table 7-4. Use of pre- and posttest scores to measure academic achievement in grade equivalents

Skill	September, 1978	May, 1979	Change
Reading	5.8	7.1	+ 1.3
Spelling	5.1	6.8	+ 1.7
Arithmetic	5.6	6.5	+ 0.9

The measurement of change can be recorded using criterion refer-
enced instruments — counting the number of accomplished skills. This
technique can be applied to academic or cognitive tasks, self-help skills, or
developmental activities. In fact, any behavior that can be subdivided into
a task ladder or sequential skill levels lends itself to a tallying approach to
assessment of acquired behaviors. However, Uzgiris and Hunt (1975) point
out that the performance of some skills is more significant than the performance of others. The performance of cognitive (reasoning) skills, for example, should have a greater merit value than the performance of skills related
to self-help. The simple tally provides a number; because of the lack of standards available, however, this number should not be used to compare one
student to another individual or group of students (Williams and Gotts,
1977). The tally is intended to serve simply as decisive evidence that the student is currently capable of more than he was a year ago.

A child's developmental age may provide still another means of assessing educational accomplishments. Awareness of these data in pre-interven-
tion assessment later enables the teacher to measure pupil progress by cal-
culating percentage changes in the rate of development. A measure of this
rate is obtained by dividing the child's developmental age in one skill area
— language, gross motor, fine motor, and so on — by his chronological age
(*Learning Accomplishment Profile Manual,* 1976). For example, an eight-
year-old child with a developmental age of four years in the area of gross
motor skills has a rate of development of 50% (of the normal developmental
rate):

12 months × 4 years (developmental age) = 48 months
12 months × 8 years (chronological age) = 96 months
developmental rate   = 48/96 = 50%

Nine months later the child is posttested and this formula is applied again:

developmental age = 58 months
chronological age = 105 months
developmental rate = 58/105 = 55%

The change in developmental rate in this case, then, is an increase from
50% to 55% of the normal growth rate, an indication of positive change.

Although this type of measurement does not attempt to explain the
cause of the increase or to predict the maintenance of the current developmental rate, it does indicate a change (where it exists) in the rate of a child's
development after participation in the intervention program (Sanford,
Learning Accomplishment Profile Manual, 1976).

Other commonly used systems assess change in terms of percentages,
the amount of time spent in an activity or completing a task, and the
number of trials required to reach a criterion (i.e., 4 out of 5, or 6 out of 8).

In any program, the method of data collection and the measurement tactic must be chosen on the basis of the individual pupil's response characteristics and the nature of each task (Haring, 1977).

Reporting Educational Progress

The teacher will be required to share collected data with the student, his parents, school district personnel, and other concerned persons. Generally, the greater the distance the report has to travel, the more formal it must be in style.

Weekly conferences with the student should be informal, providing an opportunity for the teacher to point out, reward, and encourage progress. The student must frequently be made aware that the teacher, although always demanding more, recognizes the extremely important gains he has made.

"You have been doing very well in spelling this week, much better than before. Your 82% correct on this week's work is wonderful!" This kind of positive comment focuses on specific achievements.

Hawisher and Calhoun (1978) recommend maintaining a 3×5 index card file of the skills learned by each student. Thumbing through a batch of cards that represent learning achievements can be a very rewarding experience for the student, evidence of how proud others are of his accomplishments.

Other teachers who work with this student, although perhaps not requesting a formal statement of his progress, are surely interested in the information. Because casual conversation is often forgotten or misunderstood, a written comment is preferred. A brief quickly penned statement accompanying the casual discussion has much more value than a verbal communication alone.

Parents usually receive a grade card. When the grade card is not an appropriate means of communicating progress, however, the teacher should prepare a written summary of each child's progress and present it during a teacher-parent conference. If parents have questions about its content, the teacher can answer them at that time. If parents are unable to attend a school meeting, the teacher should add a phone number and mail the report.

School districts generally have more formalized procedures for reporting student data. Information requested usually includes:

pre- and posttest data
lesson plans
anecdotal records
attendance reports

The district may also distribute questionnaires on the attitudes of others toward physically handicapped students or on the attitudes of the physically handicapped students and their families regarding the school's program.

The collection of data, regardless of their nature, is fundamental to the goal of continued appropriate education. Data collection and subsequent progress reports enable concerned persons to examine the educational program, to communicate their expectations for the students, and to reaffirm their desire to make each day learning-filled for every student.

SUMMARY

Appropriate education requires a teaching/learning environment that reflects competence, flexibility, and caring. Appropriate education also requires a creative approach to problem-solving. The solutions to those problems that impede student progress cannot always be found in texts, journals, or guides. Often the teacher must examine the impediment, locate and clearly define the point of frustration, and develop a technique, material, or approach that seems promising. Well-designed classrooms, good equipment, and effective communication skills all make a positive difference, but an effective teacher is the key. Program evaluation provides the assurance that progress is being made (or signals a warning if it is not). This information must then be shared with students, parents, teachers, and district personnel.

LITERATURE CITED

Alpha Chi Omega. Toy Book. Indianapolis, In.

Barrier-free School Facilities for Handicapped Students. 1977. Educational Research Service, Inc., Arlington, Va.

Bednar, M. J. 1970. Notes on educational environment for crippled and other health impaired children. In: F. P. Connor, J. R. Wald, and M. J. Cohen (eds.). Professional Preparation for Educators of Crippled Children. Teachers College of Columbia University, New York.

Bel-Art Products. Pequannock, N.J.

Bigge, J. L., and O'Donnell, P. A. 1976. Teaching Individuals with Physical and Multiple Disabilities. Charles E. Merrill Publishing Company, Columbus, Ohio.

Borg-Warner Educational Systems. Arlington Heights, Ill.

Calhoun, M. L. 1976. Teaching task analysis skills to teachers: A comparison of three methods. Paper presented at the 54th International Convention of the Council for Exceptional Children, April, Chicago. Cited in M. F. Hawisher & M. L. Calhoun. 1976. The Resource Room. Charles E. Merrill Publishing Company, Columbus, Ohio.

Connor, F. P., Wald, J. R., & Cohen, M. J. (eds.) 1970. Professional Preparation for Educators of Crippled Children. Report of a special study institute, funded by USOE under P.L. 85-926, as amended. (#03G-0-70-3072 [603]), December, West Point, N.Y.

Edgington, D. 1976. The Physically Handicapped Child in Your Classroom. Charles C Thomas Publisher, Springfield, Ill.

Frank, A. R. 1974. Breaking down learning tasks: A sequential approach. Teaching Except. Child. 5:16-19.

Haring, Norris G. 1977. Measurement and evaluation procedures for programming with the severely and profoundly handicapped. In: E. Sontag (ed.), Educational Programming for the Severely/Profoundly Handicapped. The Council for Exceptional Children, Mental Retardation Division. Reston, Va.

Harris-Vanderheiden, D. 1976. Field evaluation of the Auto-Com. In: Vanderheiden, G. C., and Grilley, K. (eds.), Non-vocal Communication Techniques and Aids for the Severely Physically Handicapped. University Park Press, Baltimore.

Haskell, S. H. 1973. Arithmetic Disabilities in Cerebral Palsied Children. Charles C Thomas Publisher, Springfield, Ill.

Hausmann Industries. Northvale, N.J.

Hawisher, M. F., and Calhoun, M. L. 1978. The Resource Room: An Educational Asset for Children with Special Needs. Charles E. Merrill Publishing Company, Columbus, Ohio.

Horner, R. D. 1977. A competency-based approach to preparing teachers of the severely and profoundly handicapped: Perspective II. In: E. Sontag (ed.), Educational Programming for the Severely/Profoundly Handicapped. The Council for Exceptional Children, Mental Retardation Division, Reston, Va.

Jefcoate, R. 1977. Electronic technology for disabled people. Rehabil. 38:4, 110-115.

McDonald, E. T. 1976. Design and application of communication boards. In: Vanderheiden, G. C., and Grilley, L. (eds.), Non-vocal Communication Techniques and Aids for the Severely Physically Handicapped. University Park Press, Baltimore.

McDonald, E. T., and Schultz, A. R. 1976. Communication boards for cerebral palsied children. J. Speech Hear. Disord. 38:73-88.

McNaughton, S. 1976. Blissymbols — An alternative symbol system for the non-vocal pre-reading child. In: Vanderheiden, G. C., and Grilley, K. (eds.), Non-vocal Communication Techniques and Aids for the Severely Physically Handicapped. University Park Press, Baltimore.

Popovich, D. 1977. A Prescriptive Behavioral Checklist for the Severely and Profoundly Retarded. University Park Press, Baltimore.

Prentke-Romich Company. Shreve, Ohio

Robinault, I. P. 1973. Functional Aids for the Multiply Handicapped. Harper and Row, New York.

Rusalem, H. 1962. Guiding the Physically Handicapped College Student. Teacher's College of Columbia University, Bureau of Publications, New York.

Sanford, A. R. (ed.). 1976. Learning Accomplishment Profile Manual. Kaplan Press, Salem, N.C.

Scheuerman, N. 1976. A teacher's perspective. In: M. A. Thomas (ed.), Hey, Don't Forget About Me! Council for Exceptional Children, Reston, Va.

Schoenbohm, W. B. 1962. Planning and Operating Facilities for Crippled Children. Charles C Thomas Publisher, Springfield, Ill.

Smith, R. M., Neisworth, J. T., and Greer, J. G. 1978. Evaluating Educational Environments. Charles E. Merrill Publishing Company, Columbus, Ohio.

Stoede, M., Stassen, H. G., VanLunteren, A., and Luitse, W. J. 1973. A lightspot operated typewriter for severely physically handicapped patients. Ergnomics 16:6, 829-844.

Torrey, F. Rehabilitation research furniture study. Unpublished manuscript, Cited in Yuker, H. E., Young, J. H., and Feldman, M. A. The modification of educational equipment and curriculum for maximum utilization by physically disabled persons. Albertson, N.Y.: Human Resources Center, 1967.

Uzgiris, I. C., and Hunt, J. McV. 1975. Assessment in Infancy. University of Illinois Press, Chicago.

Vanderheiden, G. C. 1976. Introduction and framework. In: G. C. Vanderheiden and K. Grilley (eds.), Non-vocal Communication Techniques and Aids for the Severely Physically Handicapped. University Park Press, Baltimore.

Vanderheiden, G. C., and Grilley, K. (eds.) 1976. Non-vocal Communication Techniques and Aids for the Severely Physically Handicapped. University Park Press, Baltimore.

Votrax. Vocal Interface. Houston, Texas.

Wendt, E., Sprague, M. J., and Marquis, J. 1975. Communication without speech. Teaching Except. Child. Fall:38–42.

Wilcox, B. 1977. A competency-based approach to preparing teachers of the severely and profoundly handicapped: Perspective I. In: E. Sontag (ed.), Educational Programming for the Severely/Profoundly Handicapped. The Council for Exceptional Children, Mental Retardation Division, Reston, Va.

Williams, W., and Gotts, E. A. 1977. Selected considerations on developing curriculum for the severely handicapped student. In: E. Sontag (ed.), Educational Programming for the Severely/Profoundly Handicapped. The Council for Exceptional Children, Mental Retardation Division, Reston, Va.

Yuker, H. E., Younng, J. H., and Feldman, M. A. 1967. The Modification of Educational Equipment and Curriculum for Maximum Utilization by Physically Disabled Persons. Human Resources Center, Albertson, N.Y.

8

INDIVIDUALIZED EDUCATION PROGRAMS AND CURRICULUM GOALS

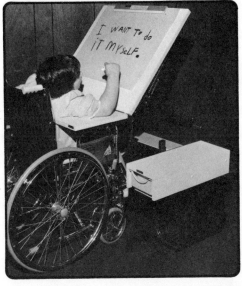

Figure 8-1. The best individualized education programs help physically handicapped students be the best they can be. Photo courtesy of Bel-Art Products.

Individualized education is essential for physically handicapped students. Although individualized education does not necessarily imply one-to-one instruction, it does mean the careful planning of goals for an *individual* student, with due consideration for his unique needs, strengths, and weaknesses. P.L. 94-142 mandates this kind of careful, creative planning through the requirement of an individualized education program for every handicapped student. This chapter explains exactly what the individualized program entails, provides an example of a completed program, and offers curriculum suggestions for students with physical handicaps.

INDIVIDUALIZED EDUCATION PROGRAM

The individualized education program (IEP) is the hallmark of P.L. 94-142. To ensure the suitability of a handicapped child's education, the law requires that a written program for each handicapped child be developed, with specific goals and measurable objectives that are subject to review. Consider Abeson and Weintraub's (1977) definition of the IEP:

Individualized means that the program must be addressed to a specific child rather than to a group of students.

Education refers specifically to the special education and related services that the child needs.

Program is a statement of what will be provided to the child as opposed to a plan that provides guidelines from which a program must be developed.

IEPs are defined in the law as: "a written statement for each handicapped child developed in any meeting of a representative of the local educational agency or an intermediate educational unit who shall be qualified to provide, or supervise the provision of specially designed instruction to meet the unique needs of handicapped children" (Section 4 [a] 19).

The law further specifies the persons who should serve on the team that writes the IEP: an administrator, a teacher, the child's parents or guardian, and, when possible, the child himself. Other district personnel may be included as needed. For physically handicapped students, "other personnel" might be a speech therapist, physical therapist, a classroom teacher, or a psychologist. It is important to note the great extent to which the teacher is involved in the development of the program. In the past, programs for handicapped students were too often developed with little input from persons who knew the child well. The inclusion of parents and teachers is an effective solution to that problem.

Because many handicapped students require unique, diverse, and extensive services in order to profit from their educational experience, P.L. 94-142 provides for the inclusion of such services in the individualized education program as needed. To enhance instruction, the following related services might be included (Sirvis, 1978): audiology and speech pathology, early identification, physical and occupational therapy, student and parent counseling and training, psychological, recreational, school health, and medical services, social work in the school, and special transportation.

The written program, designed to provide a guide for high-quality, student-specific instruction, must include at least this information (Hedbring and Holmes, 1977):

1. assessment of current level of educational performance
2. statements of both short-term and instructional objectives and expected annual achievement
3. evaluation procedures, together with objective criteria
4. schedules for determining on at least an annual basis whether specified goals have been met.

The IEP can be viewed as both a problem and a solution for special educators (Sirvis, 1978). It is a problem because the paperwork involved can seem overwhelming and there does exist the dangerous possibility of a perfunctory, going-through-the-motions approach. Reynolds (1978) expresses a realistic fear that bureaucratic machinations may overtake and mutilate the high intentions of the law.

The IEP can be a solution, however, to the problem of accountability — Is the child being served adequately and well? Is the program doing the job? These issues are addressed by the statement of appropriate goals and effective evaluation procedures. The IEP can also be a solution to the problem of decision-making about handicapped children. It should mean the development and implementation of better assessment procedures and a shift in focus from finding a good *place* for a child to finding good *instructional* techniques for a child. Finally, the IEP is a solution to the problem of developing good teaching strategies for hard-to-teach children. By requiring the statement of specific objectives and providing for at least an annual review of progress, the law supports the teacher in thinking through complicated issues and developing creative solutions.

The following pages provide a complete IEP for Lori, the severely handicapped child described in Chapter 6. The format used here is not the only one possible, but it is one example of a program that meets the requirements of the law. It was developed in two parts, based on the Idaho plan (Russell et al., 1976). The Total Service Plan lists present levels of achievement, annual goals, needed services, evaluation criteria, and review dates. This type of plan is developed by the interdisciplinary team.

The second part of the program, the Implementation Plan, is generally developed by the clinicians who will provide direct services to the child. The Implementation Plan is a breakdown of the annual goals into instructional objectives. Instructional stategies, techniques, and materials are listed, as are evaluation criteria and a time line for service.

The Individualized Education Program should reflect the good thinking of the interdisciplinary team members (see Chapter 9) and provide for a systematic review often enough to ensure effective changes in the program if progress is not being made.

Cabell County Schools Individualized Education Program

Name	Lori Moore	DOB	11-1-65
Parent(s)/Guardian	Mr. & Mrs. Braxton Moore	Age	13-5
Address	109 Truelight Road	Current placement	Cabell County Day Care Program
	Waxhaw, NC 29733		
Phone	222-1888		

IEP date   4-4-79

Review date   4-80

Program Development Participants

1. Case coordinator   M. Jarrell

2. Parent/Guardian   Mr. & Mrs. Moore

Team Members

Name	Title	Discipline/Agency
S. Clark	Certified School Psychologist, Level II	Psychology, Cabell Cty. Schools
M. Jarrell	Special Education Teacher	Special Ed., Cabell Cty. Schools
C. Sturkey	Speech Pathologist	Speech Path., Cabell Cty. Schools
E. Kleppel	M.S.W., Social Worker	Social Work, Cabell Cty. Schools
T. Carole	Physical Therapist	Physical Therapy, Crippled Children's Services
A. Bailey	Program Director	Special Education, County Day Care Program

Narrative Description

Background data: Lori is a 13-year, 5-month-old white female with severe cerebral palsy, mixed type, and seizures. She lives at home with her father, mother, two older sisters, and maternal grandmother. Prenatal history was uneventful. During delivery, the umbilical cord came first and became detached, and oxygen to Lori was cut off. Lori has been severely handicapped since birth. Mrs. Moore, who assumes almost full responsibility for caring for Lori, indicates poor sleep patterns as a major problem. Presently, Lori attends the County Day Care Center for exceptional children. Prior to her enrollment 1 year ago, Lori had received little help from the state agencies because of "poor prognosis."

Summary of test results: Psychological and educational testing found Lori to be functioning in the severely retarded range. She was socially responsive and had a rather consistent yes-no facial expression, but no meaningful sounds were noted. Lori could grasp and release an object. Physical therapy testing found Lori's overall body tone to be floppy and hypotonic. She has little head control but good range of motion in all joints of her upper extremities. She has limited hip flexion. Speech and hearing testing found that Lori is able to localize sound and frequently appears to listen to conversations at this time. Lori was able to drink from a cup in a semi-upright position. She exhibited a severe tongue thrust and had a great deal of trouble chewing and swallowing. She cannot sit independently, and her mobility is severely restricted.

Client _____ Lori Moore

Total service plan

Annual goals (in order of priority)	Services needed	Person(s) responsible	Evaluation criteria	Review date
1. Lori will remain in her current placement in the developmental day care center but will receive increased services.	environmental stimulation	A. Bailey	Is Lori receiving training in all appropriate areas?	7-1-79
	speech therapy (30 min each day, as part of mealtime program)	C. Sturkey	Is she receiving speech therapy every day?	7-1-79
	physical therapy (consultation with PT once a week) 30 min therapy daily with PT assistant	T. Carole	Is she receiving physical therapy every day?	7-1-79
2. Lori will improve her vegatative patterns (swallowing, lip closure, chewing).	speech therapy	C. Sturkey	Teacher's rating of daily performance will show significant improvement.	9-1-79
3. Lori will improve her motor skills.	Lori's physical education program should be directed by the PT	T. Carole	Lori's head control, rolling and sitting balance will be rated as improved by PT.	9-1-79
4. Lori will increase the number of purposeful things she can do with her hands.	10 minutes of directed activity each hour	M. Jarrell	Teacher will list at least 6 new purposeful activities Lori can do with her hands.	10-1-79

5. Lori will improve her understanding of words and her ability to communicate.	total program	C. Sturkey M. Jarrell	Lori will correctly identify at least 20 pictures when presented 2 at a time.	10-1-79
6. Lori will sleep for longer periods at night.		parents	Lori's parents report longer sleep periods.	10-1-79

Client ____ Lori Moore

T. Carole/Physical Therapist
Signature of implementor completing this form

Implementation plan

Goals	Objectives	Strategies/Techniques	Materials/Resources	Evaluation criteria	Date begun	Date Acc.
Lori will improve her motor skills.	1. Lori will improve head control.	Physical therapy consultation for 30 min each week.	Johnson, J. L. Programming for early motor responses within the classroom. *AAE SPH Review* 1978, 5–13.	PT assistant will record performance data on a daily basis to see if progress is being made. Among the kinds of information to be gathered are: *latency* — how long it takes Lori to assume a position;	5-1-79	
	2. Lori will improve her ability to roll over.	Physical therapy with PT assistant for 30 min each day.				

continued

Implementation plan — *continued*

Goals	Objectives	Strategies/Techniques	Materials/Resources	Evaluation criteria	Date begun	Date Acc.
	3. Lori will improve her sitting balance.	Lori will be positioned on a mat with arms extended in front. She will be encouraged to lift her head by placing toys in her field of vision, offering bites of food at high level, and stroking her spinal column. Lori will be placed on her back. PT will flex left hip and raise left buttock. Stretch Lori's right arm out and upward. PT will roll Lori toward her right side. Roll a number of times in the same direction, then reverse. Lori will be placed on mat with legs extended in front. PT will support back and hips.		*duration* — how long she is able to maintain a position; *frequency* — how often she performs a movement within a specified length of time; and the *amount and type* of assistance she needs to begin or maintain a particular behavior.		

Client _____ Lori Moore

M. Jarrell/Special educator

Signature of implementor completing this form

Implementation plan

Goals	Objectives	Strategies/Techniques	Materials/Resources	Evaluation criteria	Date begun	Date Acc.
1. Lori will increase the number of purposeful things she can do with her hands.	1.1 Lori will make random patterns in shaving cream. 1.2 She will make random patterns in finger paint. 1.3 She will grasp a rattle. 1.4 She will pick up a clutch ball. 1.5 She will punch a balloon. 1.6 She will spin the bubble on the Fisher-Price mobile.	10 minutes of directed activity each hour	Popovich, D. *A Prescriptive Behavioral Checklist for the Severely and Profoundly Retarded.* Baltimore: University Park Press, 1977. *Radea Program*	1. Lori's teachers will list at least 6 new things she can do with her hands.	5-1-79	

continued

Goals	Objectives	Strategies/Techniques	Materials/resources	Evaluation Criteria	Date begun	Date Acc.
2. Lori will improve her understanding of words and her ability to communicate her basic needs to others.	1.7 She will spin the handle on the Fisher-Price mobile.					
	2.1 When presented with 2 pictures, Lori will be able to indicate (with her right fist) the named picture for at least 20 basic pictures.	Lori's best field of vision for this type of activity seems to be to her right at about a 45° angle from her body (in a sitting position).	4" × 6" picture cards covered with clear contact paper of such concepts as: tree water boy bread girl bell airplane coat kitten horse mother hand father house car table hat duck doll chair book rabbit sun dog cake bed money flower	2.1 When presented with 2 pictures, Lori will correctly identify the named picture for 20	5-1-79	
	2.2 Lori will develop a signal for needing to go to the bathroom.	Lori's mother has indicated that Lori seems to have a certain facial expression right before she empties her	After Lori has developed some facility in pointing to pictures, a simple communi-	2.2 Does Lori have a a recognizable signal for needing to use the toilet?	5-1-79	

3. Lori will sleep for longer periods at night.	bladder. Lori's parents and teachers should be cued to this signal and should place Lori on the toilet when it occurs. Lori should be told that it is good to use the toilet and that her signal helps her parents and teachers know when to take her. She should be rewarded with a favorite snack when she uses the toilet. The following are some suggestions to facilitate Lori's getting a good night's sleep: 1. Her youth-bed sides should be padded with soft quilts. 2. She should have a warm bath and be massaged with lotion before sleeping.	cation board could be devised which could have pictures of a toilet, a cup, something to eat. Lori could be taught to point to these to indicate basic needs. The communication board should be fixed to her chair tray with clear contact paper.	3. Do Lori's parents report longer periods of uninterrupted sleep? 5-1-79

continued

Goals	Objectives	Strategies/Techniques	Materials/resources	Evaluation Criteria	Date begun	Date Acc.
		3. Soft music (FM radio) and/or metronome set at 60 beats per minute should be used to induce sleep. 4. Parents should explore with physician possible changes in medication, i.e. muscle relaxant or increased valium at night.				

Client _____ Lori Moore

C. Sturkey/Speech Pathologist

Signature of implementor completing
this form

Implementation plan

Goals	Objectives	Strategies/Techniques	Materials/ Resources	Evaluation criteria	Date begun	Date Acc.
Lori will improve vegetative patterns.	1. She will improve her swallowing pattern.	Be certain Lori is seated properly with needed support. If Lori's tongue is protruding, squirt a sweet liquid into her mouth and apply pressure under chin. Tongue will retract and you can further reward with social or tactile reinforcement. Do 3 times a day 5 times each session.	Squirt bottle	1. Lori will gain control of her tongue for purpose of swallowing with 50% accuracy.	5-1-79	
	2. She will improve lip closure.	2.1 Close lips after brushing around the mouth for 30 seconds. Do 3 times a day. 2.2 Close lips after applying ice around mouth 3 times a day.	One-inch brush	2. Lori will keep her lips closed after attaining 5 consecutive positive responses.	5-1-79	

continued

Implementation plan—*continued*

Goals	Objectives	Strategies/Techniques	Materials/Resources	Evaluation Criteria	Date begun	Date Acc.
	3. Lori will improve chewing pattern.	2.3 Pinch lips together as you pull spoon out of her mouth. 3.1 Lori will let SP manipulate her jaw in a chewing motion. (Put a piece of bubble gum in a warm glass of water to soften it. Wrap softened gum in a piece of gauze. Attach a long piece of string [tightly] to bubble gum wrapped in gauze.) 3.2 Lori will let SP manipulate her jaw to bite the bubble gum 3.3 Lori will let SP manipulate her jaw in a chewing motion while gum is in her mouth. 3.4 Lori will move her jaw in a chewing motion while gum is in her mouth.	Spoon String, gauze, bubble gum	3. Lori will approximate a chewing pattern.	5-1-79	

CURRICULUM GOALS FOR PHYSICALLY HANDICAPPED STUDENTS

The choice of appropriate annual goals for physically handicapped students is one of the most important jobs of the special education teacher. At least ten curriculum areas should be considered in developing the IEP (Sirvis, 1978):

1. gross motor skills — including mobility
2. fine motor skills — including eye-hand coordination
3. self-help skills — feeding, toileting, bathing, dressing
4. cognitive skills — preacademic and academic
5. communication skills
6. affective education
7. prevocational and vocational skills
8. physical education and recreation
9. family living
10. independent living

It will not be necessary to address all areas for all students. The selection of goals from these areas should be based on the child's age, intellectual potential, the nature and severity of the physical disability, any related disorders, and any special needs at the time of planning. Academic goals are almost always the most important for those physically handicapped students who are functioning in the average or near-average range of intellectual potential. However, a 1977 follow-up survey of cerebral palsied students who attended a special school indicates that other goals should be considered as well (Magyar, Nystrom, and Johannsen, 1977). According to this study, the areas of self-care, mobility, and leisure activities should have received more emphasis in the school program. For severely handicapped students, goals in the areas of motor development, self-help, and communication generally take priority.

The following pages present sample goals in the ten curriculum areas named above. These pages are not an attempt at an exhaustive list of goals; rather, they are suggestive of the kinds of special emphases that might be appropriate for students with physical handicaps. Communication alternatives — ways to help the student receive and express ideas so that he can attain his goals — are discussed in Chapter 7.

CURRICULUM AREA: _____ GROSS MOTOR SKILLS

Developmental Level: _____ Severely handicapped

Objectives	Activities	Facilities/Materials/ Equipment/Modifications/Adaptations	References
1. The student will improve head control in the prone and supine positions.	1.1. Position the child on his stomach with his arms extended in front. Encourage the child to lift his head by placing a toy in his field of vision.	These activities should be done under the guidance of physical and occupational therapists	Johnson (1978)
	1.2 Position the child prone on a large beach or therapy ball. Holding the child at hips or knees, slowly roll the ball forward.	Therapy ball	
	1.3 Place the child in a prone position on a scooter board and encourage him to move it.	Scooter board	
	1.4 Lay the child supine on a mat, hold his shoulders or upper arms, and slowly pull him to a sitting position.		
	1.5 Sit the child on the teacher's lap and gently bounce him until his head begins to lift upward.		
2. The student will gain improved trunk control.	2.1 Lay the child on his back. Flex his left hip and raise his left buttock. Stretch his right arm out and upward so it will not be caught under his body. Physically guide him at the hip and/or shoulder and roll the child toward		Johnson (1978)

Johnson (1978)

his right side. After a number of rolls in one direction, reverse.

2.2 Place the child on one end of a blanket with his legs together and straight. Lift up the end of the blanket until the child is forced to roll.

2.3 Place the child in a sitting position on a mat. The teacher should sit behind the child with her hands controlling the child's hips. The child should be encouraged to look at the teacher, thus turning his trunk and shoulders.

3. The student will improve sitting balance.

Corner seat

3.1 Seat the child on a flat surface with his legs extended in front of him. From a sitting position behind the child, the teacher provides support at the lower back and hips. Leg positions may be altered to provide different bases of support.

3.2 Place the child in a corner seat on the floor or a chair. Gradually increase the time the child is in the seat as his strength and tolerance allow.

3.3 Place the child on the teacher's lap facing away from the teacher. Place the child's hands on the teacher's knees and encourage him to support himself in the upright sitting position. Be sure that his head remains in midline with his body.

continued

Objectives	Activities	Facilities/Materials/ Equipment/Modifications/Adaptations	References
	3.4 Sitting with his legs in a ring or Indian position, the child can use his arms to provide support. Extend the child's arms in front of his body with his palms or fists on the mat. Applying control at the shoulders, gently and slowly lean the child forward. Return him to the upright position and repeat the exercise.		
4. The child will develop protective extension.	4.1 Place the child prone on a large beach or therapy ball. Holding him at the hips or knees, roll the ball so the child moves forward. Look for an extension of the arms as the child moves. It may be necessary to guide the movement starting at the shoulder and working out to the hand.	Protective extension with the arms is an equilibrium reaction that is automatic in normal individuals. It protects a person who is falling or losing balance. Sitting, standing, and walking are dependent on this reaction.	Johnson (1978)
	4.2 Place the child in a stable sitting position. Push him to one side by applying pressure on the opposite shoulder. Physically guide the child to catch himself by extending his arm in the direction in which he is falling.		
	4.3 Place the child in a kneeling position with his lower legs and feet under his buttocks and his trunk upright. The teacher kneels behind the child with his legs spread apart around the child. Extend the child's arms in front of his		

5. The student will develop independence in mobility to the greatest extent possible.	body parallel to the floor. The teacher's arms are around the child, with the teacher's hands over the child's hands. Smoothly bring both bodies forward and down until the child's hands are touching the floor. Raise the child to the original position and repeat.	The teacher should be in constant contact with the physical therapist regarding the most effective and appropriate way for the child to move from one place to another. The teacher should seek guidance from the therapist regarding the facilitation of: reciprocal creeping crawling pulling self to a standing position walking with a walker walking with crutches propelling a wheelchair

continued

CURRICULUM AREA: FINE MOTOR SKILLS

Developmental Level: Severely handicapped/Primary

Objectives	Activities	Facilities/Materials/ Equipment/Modifications/Adaptations	References
1. The student will squeeze an object with one hand.	1.1 Set a wastepaper basket on one side of the room. Tell the pupil to crumple a sheet of wastepaper with one hand unassisted by the other hand. Have the student try to make a basket.	*BCP Method Cards — Motor Skills.* Santa Cruz, CA: Special Education In-formation Management Systems, 1977. Wastebasket Paper	*BCP Method Cards* (1977)
2. The student will use thumb in opposition with 2 fingers to grasp.	2.1 Collect 8 1-pound coffee cans and 8 dozen spring-type clothespins. Paint the coffee cans primary colors. Paint clothespins primary colors to match cans. Instruct students in pinching clothespins onto the matching cans.	Cans Clothespins	*BCP Method Cards* (1977)
	2.2 Cut four 2″ pieces of masking tape. Put a piece of tape on the student's nose, chin, and the back of his hands. Leave at least 1″ of tape sticking up. Have him pull the tape off.	Masking tape	
3. The student will pick up small objects between the thumb and index finger.	3.1 Use a piggy bank with a large slot and easy opening bottom. Have the student pick up pennies with the thumb and forefinger of his dominant hand and drop them in the bank.	Piggy bank Pennies	*BCP Method Cards* (1977)

			Popovich (1977)

4. The student will increase eye-hand coordination skills.

3.2 Guide the student's hand in picking up small edible items with thumb and index finger.

The student will:
4. 1 make random patterns in shaving cream
4. 2 make random patterns in finger paint
4. 3 grasp a sound tube
4. 4 release a sound tube
4. 5 pick up a clutch ball
4. 6 punch a balloon
4. 7 reach for a soap bubble
4. 8 turn the knob on a busy box
4. 9 push the car on the busy box
4.10 spin the wheel on the busy box
4.11 press the button on the surprise box
4.12 flip the switch on the surprise box
4.13 place 3 pegs on a peg board
4.14 remove stacking rings
4.15 stack rings
4.16 nest nesting blocks
4.17 place a circle in a form board
4.18 place a square in a form board
4.19 place a triangle in a form board
4.20 assemble a 3-piece puzzle
4.21 trace a horizontal line with finger
4.22 trace a circle with a template

Raisins, cereal bits, goldfish crackers

Popovich, D. *A prescriptive behavioral checklist for the severely and profoundly retarded.* Baltimore: University Park Press, 1977.

Popovich provides a teaching plan for each of the activities to the left. It is important for all of these activities that the student have a work surface within easy reach — a table at the right height, or a wheelchair tray.

CURRICULUM AREA: _____ SELF-HELP

Developmental Level: _____ Severely handicapped

Objectives	Activities	Facilities/Materials/ Equipment/Modifications/Adaptations	References
1. The student will be able to: keep his tongue in his mouth; keep his lips closed; open his mouth; close his mouth; swallow; chew; and bite with strength and chew.	1.1 With a tongue depressor, apply pressure to the back of the student's tongue. The tongue will retract; reward immediately with a liquid reinforcer.	These activities should be planned and discussed with a PT, an OT, and speech pathologist.	Popovich (1977) Crickmay (1970)
	1.2 If the student's tongue is protruding, squirt a liquid into his mouth and apply pressure under the chin. The tongue will retract and the teacher can further reward the student with pudding.	Rotating brush Tongue depressor Ice 1" paint brush	
	1.3 Brush the student's hard palate with a soft 1" brush. This will tickle and cause the student to retract his tongue and touch it to his hard palate.		
	1.4 Rub the student's hard palate with a piece of ice.		
	1.5 Brush lightly around the mouth and encourage the student to close his lips.	Rotary brush Ice Spoon	

	1.6 Ice around the mouth 3 times a day, using this procedure: ice, wipe, ice, wipe, ice, wipe. While you are icing, close your lips in the same fashion you want the student to imitate.		
	1.7 Using a tongue depressor, gently apply pressure to the back of the tongue. Walk the swizzle stick down the student's tongue — from front to back. Stroke as rhythmically as possible.	Swizzle stick Tongue depressor	
	1.8 Put a piece of bubble gum in a glass of warm water to soften. Wrap the softened gum in a piece of gauze. Attach a long piece of string (tightly) to the bubble gum wrapped in gauze. The student will have to bite down on the gauze to taste the sweetness of the gum. As the teacher uses the long string to pull the bubble gum from side to side in the student's mouth, the student will be encouraged to chew in a rotary motion.	String Gauze Bubble gum	
2. The student will be able to: grasp spoon; remove food from spoon; bring spoon to mouth; scoop food.	2.1 The student should be given whatever degree of assistance is necessary (full hand prompt, wrist prompt, forearm prompt, or elbow guide) and should have whatever assistive devices will be helpful.	For the child who has difficulty getting food onto a spoon, a bowl may be more useful than a plate. (Place a non-slip mat underneath.) Spoons, forks, and knives can be fitted with plastic handles for an easier grip.	Finnie (1975)

continued

Objectives	Activities	Facilities/Materials/Equipment/Modifications/Adaptations	References
3. The student will be able to drink from a cup independently.	3.1 Start by using a plastic cup with a projecting rim. Cut out an opening on one side for the nose. Tilt the cup to the point where the liquid touches the upper lip. Let the cup rest on the lip after each swallow.	The physical or occupational therapist should suggest a good posture for eating. The atmosphere should be relaxed and cheerful, with enough time allowed for a slow eater to complete a meal. Plastic cup with projecting rim. Never use a cup with a spout, because this will encourage a more primitive sucking response.	Finnie (1975)
4. The student will use the toilet as independently as possible.	4.1 Determine whether the student's diapers stay dry for at least 2 hours at a time. Perhaps a chart to record baseline information about the time of urination and bowel movements. Familiarize the student with the terms that will be used in toilet training. 4.2 Begin placing the student on the toilet at scheduled intervals when urination or bowel movement is likely to occur. Reward liberally if the student urinates or moves bowels in the toilet.		*BCP Method Cards — Self Help* (1977) Bigge and O'Donnell (1977)

continued

pointing to a sign on a communication board, raising hand, saying "toilet, please," and so on.

4.4 Determine if student is able to sit independently on the toilet. He will not be able to sit alone until he has head and trunk balanced and can sit with his hips and knees bent apart, with his feet flat on the floor.

As the young child's balance improves, it is useful at first to place the potty in a cardboard or wooden box, and later in the corner of the room.

4.5 Some students will never have total bowel and bladder control and will need help in handling routines. Various methods for the elimination of urine are used for those who have partial or no bladder control. For males, external collection devices (such as a collection bag) are worn. Collected urine is then emptied into a toilet. Boys will need assistance in learning to change the bag.

Collection bags — available commercially.

4.6 Girls with no bladder control may have a urinary diversion operation (ostomy), or a surgical opening through the abdomen into the bowel or other hollow organ from which waste material is discharged. The material is collected into an appliance. Assistance is needed in changing the bag and cleaning the area.

Objectives	Activities	Facilities/Materials/Equipment/Modifications/Adaptations	References
	4.7 Some girls with partial urinary control use disposable diapers and plastic pants. Instruction in self-diapering will lead to independence in toileting. Some girls are taught to credé themselves. In this method, the whole hand is placed on the stomach on or above the dome of the bladder to give gentle pressure as the person sits on the toilet.	For persons without bladder control, a major source of discomfort is urine odor. Keeping the urine acidic will control odor: rinse appliances in vinegar and water or commercial cleanser deodorant, put deodorant on plastic pants, and have the child drink cranberry juice every day.	
	4.8 Bowel management should focus on regular scheduling. Suppositories and laxatives may be suggested by the physician to aid in establishing regularity.		
5. The student will demonstrate appropriate skin care techniques.	5.1 Invite the school nurse to discuss these ideas: — Why have your own towel and washcloth? — Where do oils accumulate most on the face? — What causes blemishes?	Skin care products Instruction books Towels Washcloths Mitt — made from terry toweling. May be used for washing when person has use of only one hand.	Redick (1976a)

6. The student will carry out or direct someone to shampoo, dry and style hair.	5.2 Have the students read the instructions for various popular skin care products and decide what type of skin care would be helpful for them.	
	5.3 Have students demonstrate their own skin care techniques.	
	6.1 Barber and/or cosmetology students could discuss care of the hair and demonstrate on students. Get parents' permission to have students' hair trimmed, shampooed, and set.	Present easy-to-care-for hairstyles. Styles may include those that need not be set, can be blown dry or those for which a curling iron can be used.
	6.2 Take before and after snapshots of students.	A long-handled comb is helpful for those with limited reach.
	6.3 Have students develop an individual hair care plan: a. choose a shampoo for individual hair type b. decide how often hair should be washed c. decide if cream rinse or setting lotion is needed d. decide on drying or setting procedures and necessary equipment e. estimate how often hair will need to be cut or trimmed.	Redick (1976a)

continued

Objectives	Activities	Facilities/Materials/ Equipment/Modifications/Adaptations	References
7. The student will develop a plan for taking a daily bath and using deodorant (for secondary students).	7.1 Discuss the reasons for the importance of the daily bath: health, relaxation, and social acceptability. 7.2 Discuss the use of deodorant: why (to prevent unpleasant body odor) and when (daily after bath). Have students parody current deodorant commercials and look for truth and exaggeration. 7.3 In consultation with OT, each student should develop a bath plan: — Can bath be totally independent? — Are adaptive devices needed? — Does student need limited assistance or total assistance from another person? — If the student is totally dependent, sponge or bed baths might be suggested.	Some adaptations for bathing problems are: a. bathtub seats b. security grab bars c. hand-held shower.	Redick (1976a)
8. The student will demonstrate toothbrushing skills.	8.1 Invite a dental hygienist to discuss good oral hygiene: the importance of diet, brushing after meals, and flossing. Also to be discussed: any special		Redick (1976a)

		References
	gum or teeth problems that may occur as side effects of anticonvulsant or other medication. Disclosure tablets should be introduced.	

	8.2 Student should practice and then demonstrate for the teacher (or direct someone else for parts that can't be done independently):
	  a. getting out and putting away toothbrushing equipment
	  b. taking cap off toothpaste
	  c. squeezing toothpaste on brush
	  d. brushing
	  e. rinsing
	  f. flossing
		Adaptations for toothbrushes include:
		1. Fill a bicycle grip with wet plaster of paris and insert the toothbrush handle; hold in place until plaster hardens.
		2. Push the handle of the toothbrush through the middle of soft rubber ball that has been pierced with a sharp object. This is good for persons with weak hand muscles.
		3. A 1" elastic band can be tied or taped to the toothbrush for persons who are unable to close their hands. — *BCP Method Cards — Self Help* (1977)

9. The child should attain the greatest independence possible in self-dressing: — cooperates passively — moves limbs to aid in dressing	9.1 Help the child cooperate passively while being dressed. Place the child on side, with head flexed forward toward chest, knees flexed to break up any spasticity or extensor thrust and rigidity of limbs. Relax the child's arm by tapping underside to extend arm using verbal cue "give me arm." Place sleeve on the arm that has been gently extended. Roll to opposite side and repeat. Allow the child to play with a toy while pulling on pants.	Problems that a cerebral palsied child may face in self-dressing include: difficulty in looking at what he is doing insufficient balance when using two hands trying to hold and lift his clothes while pulling them over his head without falling backward inability to grasp The following positions may help: 1. Use the corner of the wall to provide support. — Finnie (1975); Bigge and O'Donnell (1977)

continued

Objectives	Activities	Facilities/Materials/Equipment/Modifications/Adaptations	References
— pulls shirt down over chest — puts arms into shirt — closes fasteners — pulls on pants from hips to waist — puts on socks and shoes — puts on jacket	9.2 Parents and teachers should work together in analyzing the child's attempts to dress himself and offer help in figuring out the trouble spots.	2. By pressing his feet against the wall, the child may be able to lift his hips to pull on his trousers. 3. Kneeling gives some children a wider and firmer base than standing and helps them pull off a coat. 4. By turning sideways while sitting on a box or bench, a spastic child may find it easier to bend one leg without straightening the other.	
10. The student will select clothing for ease of dressing and attractiveness.	10.1 Discuss styles that would generally allow ease of dressing. Individual instruction is necessary to help students choose styles that are both appealing and applicable to them.	For a person with limited use of a hand, styles that facilitate dressing include the following features: flat opening garments, wrap garments, expandable neck openings, tabs on the inside of cuff, center front or side front closings on the side of the affected hand (so the child can reach over	Cookman and Zimmerman (1961) May (1974) McCartney (1973)

Redick (1976a)

Yep (1974)

with his capable hand to perform the task), and small numbers of closings. If necessary, use Velcro, nylon coil zippers with pull rings, large buttons with elastic threat, and magnetic fasteners.

For immobile persons, styles that facilitate dressing include these features: pants with full-length side zippers, front-opening garments, loose and comfortable clothing, and tops with shorter backs.

Knits and knit blends allow for stretchability.

CURRICULUM AREA: _____ COGNITIVE

Developmental Level: _____ Primary/Elementary

Objectives	Activities	Facilities/Materials/ Equipment/Modifications/Adaptations	References
1. The student will develop preacademic skills in areas of perceptual functioning and memory.	1.1 Randomly display 6 pairs of small squares; red, yellow, blue, green, orange, and purple. Ask the child to pick out the square that matches the one the teacher picks up. Say "Show me one that is the same color as this one."	Good sources of activities: Shearer, D., Billingsley, J., Frohman, A., Hilliard, J., Johnson, F., and Shearer, M. 1972. _The Portage Guide to Early Education._ Portage, Wis.: Cooperative Educational Service Agency 12, 1972. _Peabody Early Experiences_ kit. American Guidance Services, Circle Pines, Minn. 55014.	Jedrysek, Klapper, Pope, and Wortis (1974)
	1.2 Present a formboard with 3 forms; circle, square, and triangle. Remove the forms from their holes and place them within the child's reach, each in front of its appropriate hole. Ask the child to replace the three forms in their holes.	Colored squares 3-piece formboard	
	1.3 Provide two sets of seven cards with small black dots on them. Each set bears a configuration ranging from one to seven dots. Place one set of cards on the table in random order. Say, "I will show you one of my cards and then you look around until you find one that looks exactly the same. This is the one you need to find."	2 sets of seven cards with 1–7 dots on each	

continued

1.4 Place the pictures before the child. Say, "I want you to remember what you see: Here is the comb; here is the shoe; here is the spoon. I am going to hide one picture, and you tell me which one I took away. Close your eyes." Remove one picture, and ask the child to identify which is missing.

1.5 Say, "Listen very carefully so that you can say exactly what I said, in exactly the same way." Then give the following words, phrases, or sentences, one at a time, and ask the child to repeat:
  a. Ball. Dog. Bird.
  b. Nice boy. Little kitty.
  c. Jack has a blue ball.
      The dog has a bone.

1.6 Say, "Listen to my claps to see if you can clap the same claps."
  a. one clap
  b. two claps
  c. one clap, pause, two claps
  d. two claps, pause, two claps

3 pictures: spoon, shoe, and comb

Objectives	Activities	Facilities/Materials/ Equipment/Modifications/Adaptations	References
2. The student will develop skills in reading recognition and comprehension.	2.1 The language experience approach is an essential part of the reading program no matter what other approaches are used. Because physically handicapped students have a limited experience base, direct experiences with the environment are needed to enhance reading instruction. After an interesting experience, the child dictates a story to the teacher. The stories are written down and become part of the child's reading program. As the child develops reading skills, some of the writing can be done by the child himself. The teacher should make use of school transportation (buses with lifts and so on) to take the class places that would be difficult for families to manage— grocery stores, shopping centers, and the zoo. Within the school building itself are several "language experience" possibilities: a. Visit the school cafeteria and watch preparations for lunch.	The teacher of physically handicapped students should be familiar with many teaching approaches and have access to many different types of materials. Her repertoire should include: a decoding approach a phonics method a linguistic approach a language experience approach The appropriate approach should be selected on the basis of the child's individual pattern of strengths and weaknesses. Johnson and Myklebust (1967) and Lerner (1976) offer guidelines for making that choice. Some general guidelines for teaching reading to physically handicapped children are as follows: 1. There is no direct correlation between degree of physical handicap and the ability to learn to read. Some severely physically limited people can learn to	Lerner (1976) Johnson and Myklebust (1967) Cruickshank (1961) Strauss and Lehtinen (1948) Duffy and Sherman (1972)

b. Visit the school secretary's office and use the push-button phones.

c. Take a walk around the school building and note the shapes of windows and doors.

d. Sit quietly outside and note all the sounds that are heard.

e. Visit the art room and discuss work in progress.

f. Watch a first-grade reading group and talk about what it's like to learn to read.

read well if a good communication system is devised.

2. The teacher should carefully monitor the way in which material is presented, the rate of presentation, and the kind of response required from the child so that the child can learn comfortably and progress can be monitored.

3. The teacher should be familiar with clinical techniques developed for brain-injured children: Strauss and Lehtinen (1948); Cruickshank (1961); and Johnson and Myklebust (1967).

4. Cruickshank's (1961) principle of "increasing the stimulus value" — highlighting the important part by color or space — is a very useful tool for children with problems in attending.

5. As a supplement or substitute for reading print, Talking Books should be considered. These records, and a Talking Book machine, are available on loan at no cost from the Library of Congress for physically handicapped and blind students.

continued

CURRICULUM AREA: _____ COGNITIVE

Developmental Level: _____ Elementary

Objectives	Activities	Facilities/Materials/ Equipment/Modifications/Adaptations	References
	2.2 A useful approach to beginning reading skills can be found in Strauss and Lehtinen (1948). In this approach, phonetics instruction is oral. After the child has developed adequate auditory discrimination, the letter is presented as the visual symbol for the sound. Lehtinen assigned a color to each vowel sound and taught an association between color and sound. The child is then guided to build words letter by letter by writing or using a stamp set.	The student can borrow appropriate children's books and magazines and work on the comprehension skills of getting the main idea, following a sequence, recalling facts, and making inferences while listening to, rather than reading, books.

Some good resources for word attack skills are:

Duffy, G. G., and Sherman, G. B. 1972. *Systematic Reading Instruction.* Harper and Row, New York.

Delta Design for Word Attack Growth. National Computer Systems, 4401 West 76th Street, Minneapolis, Minn., 55435.

SRA Schoolhouse: A Word Attack Skills Kit. SRA Publishing Company, Science Research Associates, 1540 Page Mill Rd., Palo Alto, Calif., 94304. | |
| | 2.3 The pay-off for reading instruction is the ability to comprehend what is read. Here are some examples of comprehension activities:
a. Select a well-written paragraph and write each sentence on a separate piece of paper. Direct the student to arrange these sentences in the correct order.
b. Teach students to use this formula as a guide to reading: "Who? Where? When? How many? What happens?" | Some resources for reading comprehension are these:

Specific Skills Series
Burnell Loft
958 Church Street
Baldwin, N.Y., 11510. | |

	c. Ask the student to see how many things he can learn while reading and keep a tally as he learns them.	
	d. Teach the SQ 3R technique as a systematic way of studying. The 5 steps are: survey, question, read, recite, and review.	
	Provides short paragraphs at grade levels 1–8 with questions that focus on such comprehension skills as getting the main idea, detecting the sequence, and recalling facts. *Schoolhouse Comprehension Patterns.* SRA (see above address).	Mecham, Berko, Berko, and Palmer (1966)
	195 activity cards at 3rd–6th grade levels, designed to increase interpretive skills and sentence comprehension.	Strauss and Lehtinen (1948)
3. The student will develop an effective means of written communication.	3.1 The teacher must determine the preferred approach for teaching writing for the individual: manuscript, cursive, or typewriting. The ability to distinguish between circles, squares, and triangles should precede the introduction to handwriting.	Gardner (1958)
		Campbell (1973)
	Taping paper to the desk with masking tape and providing felt-tip pens may make writing easier.	
	3.2 Cursive writing has been advocated for some brain-injured children because of the smooth flow of connected letters and the ease of left-to-right sequence. The ability to grasp a pencil is necessary. Strauss and Lehtinen suggest a sequence of cursive letters to be taught: *M* is taught first because the abductor movements of the arm are easiest. The next easiest are the pointed letters: *i*, *u*, *t*, and *s*. Next come *e* and *l*. The most difficult letters are those requiring 2 movements: *a*, *o*, *d*, *c*, *g*.	Gardner, W. H . 1958. *Left Handed Writing.* The Interstate, Danville, Ill. This manual offers adaptations for left-handed learners: the pencil should be held between the thumb and the first two fingers. The first finger rests on the pencil about one inch from the tip of the lead with the thumb opposite. The upper end of the pencil should be pointed toward the student's left shoulder. The paper should be at a 35° angle with the edge of the desk.
		Exercises are provided to aid the student in learning the sliding movement, developing the slant, forming ovals, and writing letters.

continued

Objectives	Activities	Facilities/Materials/ Equipment/Modifications/Adaptations	References
	3.3 The electric typewriter provides an important substitute for and/or supplement to handwriting. The student should be taught to insert the paper, set the margins, turn the machine on and off, and use the space bar and carriage return. A hunt-and-peck system is recommended, with the student using as many fingers as he wishes. The typing student can practice reading and spelling words as well as develop composition skills.	An electric typewriter is recommended because it requires less strength and accuracy to operate than a manual typewriter. Possible adaptations for the typewriter include: a metal plate guard that fits over the keyboard so that several keys won't be punched at once, and mouth- and headsticks for persons with limited hand function.

A survey of cerebral palsied students using electric typewriters (Meacham et al., 1966) found that students who could use their hands made better progress than those who used mouthsticks, and students who used mouthsticks made better progress than those who used headsticks. | |
| 4. The student will develop spelling skills. | 4.1 Fernald's (1943) multisensory approach to spelling has helped some children by incorporating visual, auditory, kinesthetic, and tactile input. The child traces the letters while he says and sees the whole word. When the child feels he knows the word, he writes it without the visual cue. This approach requires handwriting ability. | *Basic Spelling* (grades 1-6) J. B. Lippincott Company East Washington Square Philadelphia, Penn., 19105. A series of nongraded books with step-by-step sequencing and emphasis on phonetic structures. | Fernald (1943) Johnson and Myklebust (1967) |

	4.2 Johnson and Myklebust (1967) suggest an approach in which spelling words are divided into those that are phonetically regular and those for which there is no direct sound-symbol correspondence.	*Spelling Games* Milton Bradley Springfield, Mass., 01101. Kit of 5 games for reinforcement of spelling skills.	
	For phonetically regular words, the child reads the words, says them as a whole, and then says them one syllable at a time, writing each syllable as he says it. Then he completes exercises in which he listens to the word said by syllables and inserts the missing part. Example: af___ noon. Next he writes the entire word from dictation without any visual cues.	*Spelling Mastery and Diagnostic Reference Kit* (grades 1–6) Special Child Publications 4535 Union Bay Place, N.E. Seattle, Washington, 98105. A vowel-centered approach, based on linguistic principles.	
	Non-phonetic words are written as a whole, and then letters are omitted in various positions throughout the word. Gradually, the student learns to spell the entire word.		
5. The student will acquire skills in arithmetic operations, logical problem-	5.1 Mathematics approaches that stress meaning and relationships are recommended. Rather than drills, activities that help the child to understand the organization of numbers are recommended. The *Stern Structural Arithmetic Program* is a helpful approach.	Strauss and Lehtinen (1948) suggest that students be involved in the development of instructional materials: number wheels, counting boards, "take-away boxes," number cards, and the abacus.	Strauss and Lehtinen (1948) Hammill and Bartel (1975)

continued

Objectives	Activities	Facilities/Materials/ Equipment/Modifications/Adaptations	References
solving, and applied mathematics.	5.2 Hammill and Bartel (1975) offer a sequence of math skills that should be acquired in an elementary mathematics program. This list can be used as a developmental guide for planning the instructional program.	*Stern Structural Arithmetic Kits* (K–3) Houghton Mifflin Company One Beacon Street Boston, Mass., 02107. These kits use blocks and cubes with the properties of numbers. The manipulative objects are helpful for slow learners. Some problems can be solved by manipulating blocks rather than by having to write answers.	
	5.3 Secondary students should have instruction in mathematics for living: money, time, measurement, and consumer education work.	Sources for practical mathematics: *Learning About Measurement* *Learning About Time* *Useful Arithmetic — Vols. I and II* *Math Made Easy* All are workbooks from: Frank E. Richards Publishing Company P.O. Box 66 Phoenix, N.Y., 13135.	

CURRICULUM AREA: COMMUNICATION

Developmental Level: Severely handicapped

Objectives	Activities	Facilities/Materials/ Equipment/Modifications/Adaptations	References
1. The student will attend to the teacher by: a. sitting still b. looking at teacher c. imitating motor responses.	1.1 The teacher places the child in a chair and immediately reinforces him, usually with food, gradually delaying the reinforcer for increasing periods of time. Training is continued until the child can sit for 30 seconds without a reinforcer or physical restraint.		Kent (1974)
	1.2 The teacher places an object on the table and says, "Look at this." If the child looks, he is reinforced. If he does not respond correctly, the teacher can physically assist him (by turning the child's head toward the object) or use a prompt (by moving the object toward the child's face). When the child will look at objects, practice the new command, "Look at me."		
	1.3 The child should learn to imitate the following motor activities (if physically capable) with prompts, physical guidance, and reinforcement: point to an object; point to nose; point to ears; stand up; and sit down.		

continued

Objectives	Activities	Facilities/Materials/ Equipment/Modifications/Adaptations	References
2. The child will increase receptive language skills.	2.1 Pointing to objects should be taught first as behaviors to imitate and then as actions to perform in response to verbal commands. Initial commands could be: Rock the baby. Throw the ball. Ring the bell. Push the car. Put on the hat. Shine the shoe.	Lorton, M. 1972. *Workjobs.* Addison-Wesley, New York. A guide for teacher-made learning materials in language and perception. *GOAL: Language Development-Games Oriented Activities for Learning* Milton Bradley Company Springfield, Mass., 01101.	Kent (1974)
	2.2 Give the child experience in placing objects in prepositional arrangements: Put the _____ in the box. Put the _____ on the chair. Put the _____ under the chair.	*Peabody Language Development Kits* American Guidance Service Circle Pines, Minn., 55014. Kits designed for oral language, problem solving, and concept development on levels K–3.	
	2.3 Have the child sort objects by size. Provide the child with a quantity of big and little objects of the same kind. Give the child two containers for sorting.		
	2.4 Give experience with task demands involving numbers: "Give me one." "Give me three."		

| 3. The child will increase expressive language skills. | 3.1 The child will learn to say body parts first by imitation. The teacher says, "What is this? This is a nose." and then gradually fades the prompt.

3.2 Show the student 6 objects in a box, then turn away and remove one object. Ask the child to name what is missing.

3.3 The child should be helped in developing an ever-increasing speaking vocabulary. Use pictures of common objects to facilitate this development. | Common nouns (pictures should be obtained for these):
Body parts: eyes, ears, hair, hands, nose, teeth, face, feet, knees
Clothing: hat, shoe, coat, socks
Toys: doll, ball, bell, car, block
Food: bread, cookie, water, juice, milk | Kent (1974) |

CURRICULUM AREA: _____ AFFECTIVE EDUCATION

Developmental Level: _____ Elementary

Objectives	Activities	Facilities/Materials/Equipment/Modifications/Adaptations	References
1. The student will see himself as a separate person by providing accurate autobiographical information.	1.1 Give each student an "About Me" sheet and ask students to complete it. Have students assist each other in measuring height and weight.	"About Me" sheet includes blanks to be filled in: name address telephone number height weight color of eyes color of hair boy or girl grade name of teacher name of school three words that best describe me	Dupont, Gardner, and Brody (1974) Canfield and Wells (1976)
	1.2 Give each student a copy of "Interest Review." Ask students to recall things they liked and were interested in when they were younger and to fill in the blanks. Discuss completed forms as a group.	"Interest Review" sheet includes the blanks: I liked these things when I was: 5 years old, 7 years old, now. I wanted these things when I was: 5 years old, 7 years old, now. When I grow up, I want to be _____ Sample sheets can be found in the *Toward Affective Development* kit (Dupont, Gardner, and Brody, 1974)	

	1.3 Help students develop a personal time line. Encourage students to recall significant events that influenced or affected their lives. Then have students record events on both sides of a horizontal line. Possible events: learning to talk, starting school, travel, and so on.	Draw a horizontal line in the center of a legal-sized sheet of paper (or any other long paper) in pencil or ink.	Dupont et al. (1974) Canfield and Wells (1976)
2. The student will develop a positive self-image by describing himself with an emphasis on positive characteristics and sharing successful experiences.	2.1 Ask students, "If you had to describe yourself to someone over the telephone, what would you say?" Ask students to write a paragraph answer. 2.2 Say, "Today you are going to pretend you are writing to an educational magazine in response to the following advertisement: 'WANTED: Students to sail around the world on a ship called the U.S.S. ADVENTURE. Please furnish a complete description including two strong points.'" Collect letters and read them aloud. 2.3 In small groups, ask the students to share a success, an accomplishment, or an achievement they had before they were 5 years old; next ask them to share a success they had between the ages of 5 and 10.	Pencils, paper, chalkboard	

continued

Objectives	Activities	Facilities/Materials/ Equipment/Modifications/Adaptations	References
3. The student will recognize his own strengths and weaknesses.	3.1 Give each student a copy of a "Descriptive Words" sheet. Have students cut out each word on the dotted lines. Instruct students to put into one stack all the words they feel describe themselves. Ask students to select words that others would use to describe them: mother, father, best friend.	"Descriptive Words" sheet from *Toward Affective Development* kit (Dupont et al., 1974). Words include these: brave, bold, courteous, confident, cautious, cowardly, cheerful, cooperative, disobedient, energetic, fair, friendly, helpful, insecure, kind, lucky, lazy, neat, optimistic, pessimistic, popular, proud, pouty, suspicious, smart, selfish, creative, intelligent.	Dupont et al. (1974) Canfield and Wells (1976)
	3.2 Using the first lists as a guide, have students write: 3 things I like about myself 3 things I wish I could change		
	3.3 Have students complete a personal evaluation sheet. Discuss.	Personal Evaluation Sheet: Today I feel very _____ I'm unhappy when _____ I wish my teachers _____ My classmates think I _____ School is _____ I enjoy reading about _____ I wish grown-ups would _____ I like myself best when _____ I wish _____	
	3.4 Strength bombardment: A small group activity focusing on one person at a time. The group bombards him with all the strengths they see in him. One member of the group should serve as a recorder and give the list of strengths to the person.		

		Dupont et al. (1974)
4. The student will recognize, label, and accept the feelings of others.	4.1 Show 10 pictures that depict these facial expressions: excited, happy, surprised, discouraged, disgusted, angry, embarrassed, envious, scared, and bored. Have students identify the feelings expressed.	*Toward Affective Development* kit Illustrations 1–10 Discussion pictures 28–37 Sample role-playing situation: Edward is a good student and usually does what the teacher tells him to do. After recess one day Edward and his friends were a little noisy and were giggling and laughing a lot. When they reached the classroom door, the teacher looked at Edward sternly and told him to sit down and be quiet. Discuss: How does Edward feel? Role-play: What did Edward do?
	4.2 Discuss each picture with these questions: What is happening in this picture? How does each of these students feel? What do you think will happen next?	
	4.3 Form small discussion groups. Divide the illustrations evenly among the groups. Ask each group to discuss what could have happened to cause the person in each picture to feel as he or she does.	
	4.4 Role-play situations to sensitize students to feelings in various types of situations.	
5. The student will know how to make and keep friends.	5.1 Have students write an essay "My Best Friend." In a group discussion, list the qualities of best friends that are in the essays.	SRA Guidance Booklets: "How to Get Along with Others" "Making and Keeping Friends"

continued

Objectives	Activities	Facilities/Materials/ Equipment/Modifications/Adaptations	References
	5.2 Have students discuss how they would react if their friend: — felt sick in class — forgot his homework — got a chance to go to Disney World — asked you to her birthday party	Science Research Associates, Inc. 259 East Erie Street Chicago, Ill., 60611.	
	5.3 Read the SRA guidance booklets and list ideas for making and keeping friends.		
	5.4 Tell students to choose a friend in the classroom and come up with a plan for free time on Friday afternoon — something they would like to do with a friend.		
6. The student will accept own physical appearance.	6.1 Give each student a copy of the "My Measurements" sheet, have students choose partners, and give each set of partners a tape measure. Tell them to assist each other in completing the forms.	"My Measurements" sheet from *Toward Affective Development*. Mobile students could be assigned to do the measuring; non-mobile students could type responses on sheet.	Dupont et al. (1974) Canfield and Wells (1976)

Wright (1960)

6.2 Using completed "My Measurements" sheet, have students reread completed form. Ask for a volunteer to give his or her first measurement, length from top of head to shoulder, and write figure on the chalkboard. Then ask if anyone else has the same measurement. Keep a frequency count of these figures:

9" | |
8" | | | |
7" | |

Repeat the frequency count for the remaining measurements. Call attention to the span of differences. It is important to stress acceptance of individual differences throughout.

6.3 Have students discuss which things about their physical appearance it is possible to change and which things it is necessary to accept. Where did they get their idea of good looks?

6.4 Have students bring in their baby pictures and current pictures of themselves. Have the class try to guess the identity of each person in the picture. Reinforce ideas that everyone has distinct features and unique characteristics and talk about change and growth.

Baby pictures and current pictures of students

continued

CURRICULUM AREA: _____ AFFECTIVE EDUCATION

Developmental Level: _____ Elementary/Secondary

Objectives	Activities	Facilities/Materials/ Equipment/Modifications/Adaptations	References
	6.5 Bring a full-length mirror to class. Start by having one student at a time look in the mirror and tell what he sees. Instruct each child: "Close your eyes. Open them, look quickly into the mirror, and tell what you see first." "As you look into the mirror, tell what you like best." "If the mirror could talk to you, what do you think it would say?" "What doesn't the mirror know about you?"	Full-length mirror	
	6.6 Have students react in writing to the statement: "Everyone wishes he could change something about his physical appearance." Discuss.	Pencil and paper	
7. The student will identify special problems and concerns associated with being a teenager.	7.1 Discuss physical changes leading to maturity and parallel emotional, social, and sex role development in the teen years.	SRA Guidance Booklets: "You're Maturing Now" "Your Problems: How to Handle Them"	

Goal	Activities	Reference
	7.2 Discuss "When does a person become an adult in this society?" Talk about ways in which a teenager is like an adult and ways in which he is like a child.	Science Research Associates, Inc. 259 East Erie Street Chicago, Ill., 60611.
	7.3 Brainstorm areas of special concern to adolescents: sex role development, dating, popularity, independence, loneliness, identity, crisis, and vocational planning. Brainstorm sources of support.	
	7.4 Read "Your Problems: How to Handle Them." Have students discuss the importance of seeking responsible help for problems they can't solve and list individuals and agencies who might help.	
8. The student will identify special concerns of teenagers who are physically handicapped.	8.1 In small groups with teacher, counselor, or OT as guide, discuss the status of adulthood in society (financial independence, marriage, vocational self-sufficiency, etc.) and how being physically handicapped might make it harder to reach full adult status in the eyes of society. How else might adulthood be defined?	Wright (1960) Easter Seals Bibliography (1973) *Recent Books About Handicapped Persons* The National Easter Seal Society for Crippled Children and Adults 2023 West Ogden Avenue Chicago, Ill., 60612.

continued

Objectives	Activities	Facilities/Materials/ Equipment/Modifications/Adaptations	References
	8.2 Have students describe reactions of strangers to their disability and tell how they have coped with curiosity, sympathy, and communication problems.		
	8.3 Discuss the difference between "a physically handicapped person" and "a person with a physical handicap."		
	8.4 Using the Easter Seals bibliography, have students write a report on at least 2 autobiographical accounts of dealing with a disability. What was the worst part of the disability? What coping skills were developed?		
9. The student will explore ways of interacting well with family members.	9.1 Discuss factors affecting parent-child relations and ways to build satisfying communication.	SRA Guidance Booklets: "About Brothers and Sisters" "Getting Along with Parents" (see address above)	
	9.2 List and discuss the responsibilities of various family members toward one another.		

9.3 Have students read "About Brothers and Sisters." Have each student write a letter to a brother or sister, indicating something interesting or special about growing up with that person.

9.4 Write a brief paper, "What My Family Means to Me."

10. The student will state valued activities and beliefs and will compare the relative strength of those values.

10.1 The teacher passes out paper and asks students to write the numbers 1–20 down the middle of the sheet, then says, "Now make a list of 20 things you love to do. They can be big things in life or little things." Students should place stars beside the 5 most important items.

SRA Guidance Booklet: "Exploring Your Values" (see address above)

Paper and pencil

10.2 Give each student a "Values Grid." Then teacher and students name some general issues: pollution, welfare, inflation, population control, ERA, etc. Students list these issues on the left side of paper. Next to each issue, the student is to privately write a few key words that summarize his position or stand on that issue. The 7 numbers heading the column on the righthand side of the paper represent the following 7 questions:

VALUES GRID

ISSUE	1	2	3	4	5	6	7
1.							
2.							
3.							
4.							
etc.							

Simon, Howe, and Kirschenbaum (1972)

Simon and O'Rourke (1967)

continued

Objectives	Activities	Facilities/Materials/ Equipment/Modifications/Adaptations	References
	1. Do you prize or cherish this position?		
	2. Have you publicly affirmed your position?		
	3. Have you chosen your position from alternatives?		
	4. Have you chosen your position after careful consideration of pros and cons?		
	5. Have you chosen your position freely?		
	6. Have you acted or done anything about your beliefs?		
	7. Have you acted with consistency on these issues?		
11. The student will choose beliefs from alternatives and after considering the consequences.	11.1 Rank Order Teacher tells the class that she is going to ask questions that will require them to look deeper into themselves and make a value judgment. Give students three alternatives for responding to each question and ask them to rank-order their choices. Discuss the reasons for their choices.	SRA Guidance Booklet: "Exploring Your Values" SAMPLE RANK ORDER QUESTIONS 1. Where would you rather be on a Saturday afternoon? ____ at the beach ____ in the woods ____ in a discount store	Simon et al. (1972) Simon and O'Rourke (1967)

12. The student will take a stand on a controversial issue and act on that stand.	12.1 Students should select a controversial issue — something people have strong feelings about. Then each student writes a slogan reflecting his view. These slogans are posted around the room and discussed.	Construction paper, marking pens, addresses of congressmen and newspaper editors	Simon and O'Rourke (1967)
	11.2 Values Survey Teacher hands out the value survey sheet and asks students to number the values listed in order of their importance as guiding principles in the student's life. Students should discuss results and see how much similarity or diversity there is.	VALUES SURVEY ___ a comfortable life ___ equality ___ an exciting life ___ family security ___ freedom ___ happiness ___ inner harmony ___ mature love ___ national security ___ pleasure ___ salvation ___ self-respect ___ a sense of accomplishment ___ social recognition ___ true friendship ___ wisdom ___ a world at peace ___ a world of beauty	Simon et al. (1972)
		2. Which would you give the lowest priority today? ___ space ___ poverty ___ defense ___ ecology	

continued

Objectives	Activities	Facilities/Materials/ Equipment/Modifications/Adaptations	References
	12.2 Teacher asks students to make a list of 5 changes they think would improve some aspect of their school or community. Advocacy issues are appropriate here. Teacher passes out the "You Can Do Something About It" worksheet. Teacher asks students to select one of their 5 changes and identify which types of action could be used to work the change they want to effect. Students are asked to try out an action and report back to class.	YOU CAN DO SOMETHING ABOUT IT worksheet Reading, learning, interviewing, discussing, becoming better informed are necessary steps before doing something. WRITE A LETTER — to newspaper — to congressman ATTEND A MEETING OR ORGANIZE ONE — distribute leaflets — picket — organize a petition drive — wear a button — be part of a delegation to see an official SHARE INFORMATION — speak up for your point of view — try to get someone to read a pamphlet or article	

18. The student will establish some life goals and contract with self to move toward those goals.	**13.1 Life Inventory** Teacher forms students into groups of four. One person becomes the focus person and another records the focus person's responses to the Life Inventory questions. Then the focus rotates. The two free members are to ask clarifying questions and to help the process along. Spend 10 minutes with each person. **13.2 Self Contracts** In this activity, the student is asked to make a contract with herself about some change she would like to make in her life. It can involve starting something new, stopping something old, or changing some present aspect of one's life. The students write out contracts and sign them. A week later, the class can share how well they are doing.	**Life Inventory:** sample questions 1. What was the happiest year of your life? 2. What things do you do well? 3. What has been the lowest point in your life? 4. Was there an event in which you demonstrated great courage? 5. Was there a time of heavy grief? 6. What are some things you would like to stop doing? 7. Tell about something you do poorly that you have continued to do anyway. 8. Tell about some past experiences you have had. 9. Tell about one missed opportunity in your life. 10. Are there some values you are struggling to establish? Simon et al. (1972)
14. The elementary student will identify and express feelings on death, dying, and bereavement in response to special needs in the class.	**14.1** Resources are suggested in the next two columns for help in dealing with questions about death and dying. While death education activities are recommended at the secondary level, at the elementary level death education should be responsive to students' needs. The death of a grandparent or friend or pet may prompt questions that these sources will help answer.	Books about death and children: Cook, S. S. 1974. (ed.) *Children and dying.* Health Sciences Publishing Corporation, New York. Grollman, A. 1967. (ed.) *Explaining Death to Children.* Beacon Press, Boston. Jackson, E. N. 1965. *Telling a Child About Death.* Channel Press, New York. Grollman (1967) Grollman (1976)

continued

Objectives	Activities	Facilities/Materials/ Equipment/Modifications/Adaptations	References
15. The secondary student will identify and express feelings on death, dying, and bereavement.	15.1 The students will view and discuss the 5-part film series: "Death and Dying: Closing the Circle." 15.2 Coat of Arms Strategy In medieval times knights wore coats of arms to reflect what they stood for,	Books for children (5–8): Brown, M. W. 1958. *The dead bird.* Young Scott Books, New York. dePaola, T. 1973. *Nana Upstairs and Nana Downstairs.* G. P. Putnam's Sons, New York. Fassler, J. 1971. *My Grandpa Died Today.* Behavioral Publications, Inc., New York. Zolotow, C. 1974. *My Grandson Lew.* Harper, New York. Books for children (8–11): Smith, D. B. *A Taste of Blackberries.* Thomas and Crowell, New York. White, E. B. 1952. *Charlotte's Web.* Harper and Row, New York. Zim, H. S. and Bleeker, S. 1970. *Life and Death.* William Morrow and Company, New York. Filmstrips and cassettes: "Death and Dying: Closing the Circle." Guidance Associates a. "The Meaning of Death" points out the value of confronting our feelings about death and explores emotions of survivors.	

what they valued in life. Students can adapt this custom to represent what in life is meaningful to them.

Using a Coat of Arms Worksheet, have the student draw a picture for each segment of the shield:

a. If you were to die right now, what do you think friends would miss most about you? Draw a picture to show what they might miss.

b. Think of something about which you feel very strongly, something for which you would be willing to give your life. Make a drawing to show what that something is.

c. What was the closest you ever came to losing your life? Draw a picture to represent that event.

d. Think of someone close to you who has died. Draw a picture to show what you miss most about that person.

e. What are you doing now to help you live a long, happy life? Illustrate this on your coat of arms.

f. Imagine that you have 1 year left to live. Draw something to represent what you would do in that year, what kind of activity you would pursue.

b. "A Time to Mourn, A Time to Choose" examines how death rites serve individual and community needs.

c. "Walk in the World for Me" recreates a boy's 5-year struggle against leukemia and the mother's dealing with loss, courage, hope, and finality.

d. "The Critically Ill Patient" features a candid interview with a person with a life-threatening disease.

e. "The Bereaved" involves interviews with persons in mourning and explores positive approaches to dealing with grief.

Simon and Goodman (1976)

Grollman (1976)

continued

Objectives	Activities	Facilities/Materials/ Equipment/Modifications/Adaptations	References
	15.2 Asking the Hard Questions: Have students tackle these thought-provoking questions, either individually or in small groups of their own choosing: a. What burial rites do you believe in? b. Have you ever been to a funeral? How did you feel about it? Why do you think we have funerals? c. Do you believe in life after death? How does your belief affect how you live? d. Have any of your friends or relatives ever died? How did you feel? e. Would you consider donating your body to science when you die? Why or why not?		

CURRICULUM AREA: _____   VOCATIONAL EDUCATION

Developmental Level: _____   Secondary

Objectives	Activities	Facilities/Materials/ Equipment/Modifications/Adaptations	References
1. The student will explore the world of work and develop awareness of career fields.	1.1 Give each student one career folder to study and discuss. Have the student show the career folder, read the related description aloud, and discuss some unique aspects of the occupation.	37 career folders from the *Toward Affective Development* kit	Dupont, Gardner, and Brody (1974)
	1.2 Invite persons from various career fields to visit the classroom so that students can discuss their work with them. Try to have workers representing all levels of skill and all levels of responsibility. Whenever possible, invite physically disabled workers to share experiences.	Workbooks to aid in career education: *I Want a Job* *On the Job* *Jobs from A to Z*	
	1.3 Have students prepare a collage of pictures from newspapers and magazines showing people working in various career fields.	*Preparing for a Job Interview* Frank E. Richards Publishing Company P.O. Box 66 Phoenix, N.Y., 13135.	
2. The student will develop work attitudes that will facilitate job success.	2.1 Through role-playing and discussion, communicate the importance of job attendance, punctuality, enthusiasm, responsibility, productivity, esprit de corps, and positive response to supervision.	*How to Hold a Job* Speck-Vaughn Company P.O. Box 2028 807 Brazos Austin, Texas, 78767.	

continued

Objectives	Activities	Facilities/Materials/Equipment/Modifications/Adaptations	References
3. The student will develop a vocabulary for the world of work and job applications.	3.1 The students should be taught to read all of the "words of work" and understand what they mean. Students should practice filling out job applications.	Wilson, R. J. *Words of Work.* President's Committee on Employment of the Handicapped 1111 20th Street, N.W. Washington, D.C. This list includes the most commonly used words on job applications. Among these are: employer relatives employee applied employment previous present completed phone social security number application year month business rate	
4. The student will be placed in contact with the State Department of Vocational Rehabilitation for evaluation.	4.1 Vocational Rehabilitation counselors can begin working with students before graduation and can help with work evaluations, work adjustment, work skills, vocational training, and on-the-job training programs.	Vocational Rehabilitation counselors	

CURRICULUM AREA: PHYSICAL EDUCATION AND RECREATION

Developmental Level: Elementary/Secondary

Objectives	Activities	Facilities/Materials/ Equipment/Modifications/Adaptations	References
1. The student will get needed equipment and supplies, set up and clean up work area, and do the skills required for one craft activity.	1.1 Administer Crafts/Hobbies Survey to identify areas of interest.	Some severely handicapped students may not be able to get needed equipment and supplies, set up and clean work area, and do all necessary tasks. However, after they are set up and positioned, they should be encouraged to work as independently as possible. If they are not able to do something for themselves, they should know *how* to do an activity and where things are stored so they can direct someone to do it for them.	Howard and Strathairn (1976)
	1.2 Hold a Crafts Fair Day on which various crafts are demonstrated. Have students select crafts they would like to pursue.		
	1.3 Provide instruction in where materials are stored, how to set up work area, how to clean work area.		
	1.4 When student feels ready, he should demonstrate proficiency in getting materials, doing craft, and cleaning up.	Some successful projects for those with muscle weakness: Acrylic water-soluble painting Seed beading Mandala-geometric patterns with needle and thread	
	1.5 After student has demonstrated proficiency, he should be given the opportunity to teach the craft to other students.	Materials: (partial list) Rug yarn kits Gross point needlework kits	
	1.6 When the student knows the activity and has good work habits, he should be allowed to take the activity material home to work there.	Leather kits with "king life eye" needles (Tandy Leather Company) Link belt kits	

continued

Objectives	Activities	Facilities/Materials/Equipment/Modifications/Adaptations	References
		Liquid embroidery material Beads Acrylic paint Copper tooling material Crafts/Hobbies Survey Indicate which activities you have and have not done before, would like to try, and are not interested in: Sewing with a sewing machine Knitting with a knitting machine Crocheting Rug hooking Weaving Decoupage Paint by number Pen pal Music — live concert Music — records Music — radio Papercraft Textile stenciling Leathercraft Woodburning Copper enameling Insect collecting	

2. The student will demonstrate proficiency in one quiet game by explaining the rules to the teacher and playing the game with the teacher.	2.1 Set aside a daily or weekly time period for leisure activities.
	
	2.2 Survey the class regarding card and table games they
	  a. know how to play
	  b. would be able to teach others
	  c. would like to learn to play
	
	2.3 Set up learning centers, with a game and a person who knows how to play it at each center. Directions for the game should also be at the center. Each student selects a center and works on rules, procedures, and game-playing strategies.
	
	2.4 When ready, the student challenges the teacher to a game.
		Painting
		Creative writing
		Model building
		Ceramics
		Wood carving
		Sculpture
		Stamp collecting
		Coin collecting
		Photography
		Gardening
		Aquariums
		Candlemaking
		Pets
		Flower arranging
		
		Materials:
		Decks of cards
		Checker sets
		Chess sets
		Dominoes
		Variety of commercial games, such as *Life, Careers, Monopoly, Yahtzee,* etc.
		
		Directions for card games and quiet games in *Learning Activity Cards for Children:* Crazy Eights, Fish, Dominoes, Tic-Tac-Toe, Chinese Checkers, Old Maid, War.
		
		Some modified game materials for those with limited hand function are available from J. A. Preston Corporation: Peg Chinese Checkers, 3-dimensional Tic-Tac-Toe, Skitles, and Giant Dominoes.
			Howard and Strathairn (1976)
			
			Taylor, Artuso, and Hewett (1974)
			
			Special materials for children. Catalog 225, J. A. Preston Corporation

continued

Objectives	Activities	Facilities/Materials/ Equipment/Modifications/Adaptations	References
3. The student will be involved in individual and team sports for fitness and for fun.	2.5 More complicated games, such as bridge or chess, should be taught over a period of several weeks.		
	3.1 Archery can be taught with light bows and arrows with rubber tips.	Here are sources for adaptive physical education activities:	Sherrill (1976) Vodola (1973)
	3.2 Use plastic "gym bowl" equipment or plastic detergent bottles for bowling. Students may bowl from a chair or sit on the floor. Roll ball through cardboard tube or box.	Cratty, B. J. Developmental Games for Physically Handicapped Children. Palo Alto, Calif.: Peek Publications, 1969.	
	3.3 Hit plastic practice golf balls into old tennis or volleyball nets that are faced with burlap. Putt on an old rug into a can placed on its side. Make a miniature golf course from odds and ends.	Duncan, T. Recreation and Leisure Time Activities for the Developmentally Disabled. Columbia, S.C.: UAF of SC, 1977. Here are some general ideas for adaptations of games and activities:	
	3.4 For table tennis, use larger paddles, make small table-sized hoops, and play as "hoopbird." Attach plywood sides onto the table so the ball will not bounce off as often.	1. Reduce the size of the playing area: change boundary lines, increase the number of players, decrease the height of the net or goal, or use equipment that will reduce the range of play. Net-type games may be played through a hoop instead of a net.	

continued

3.5 For softball games, use plastic bats and wiffleballs, batting tee. Use base runners and 2 sets of bases (one of shorter distances). Throw the ball into the field rather than batting it.

3.6 Explore the possibility of individualized instruction through the school's physical education department or local recreation agencies such as the YMCA.

3.7 Investigate the possibility of student participation in the Special Olympics. The program consists of training and competition in 9 official sports events: track & field, swimming, volleyball, basketball, bowling, floor hockey, gymnastics, diving, and ice skating. Eligi-

2. Use lighter equipment: plastic bats, wiffle-type balls, large plastic beach balls, yarnballs, and styrofoam balls.

3. Slow down moving objects: change the throwing style to underhand, throw the ball with one bounce, or roll the ball.

Directions for making adaptive equipment can be found in:
Cowart, J. F. 1973. *Instructional Aids for Adaptive Physical Education.* Almeda County School Department, ERIC No. ED 106 304, Howard, Calif.

Guides for swimming instruction for the physically handicapped student:
American Red Cross. 1975. *Swimming for the Handicapped — Instructor's Manual.* American Red Cross, Washington, D.C.
United Cerebral Palsy Associations, Inc. *Swimming for the Handicapped.* United Cerebral Palsy Associations, Inc., New York.

For more information about the Special Olympics, write:
Special Olympics, Inc.
1701 K Street N.W., Suite 205
Washington, D.C., 20006.

Objectives	Activities	Facilities/Materials/ Equipment/Modifications/Adaptations	References
4. The student will attend a spectator sport and demonstrate that he is able to follow the game.	bility for participation is based on the diagnosis of mental retardation. Adaptations are made for the physically handicapped mentally retarded students.		Howard and Strathairn (1976)
	4.1 Using old newspapers and sports magazines, have students identify popular spectator sports for each season of the year. Identify local and regional teams.	Newspapers Sports magazines Published notices Videotapes of home teams Sports rule books TV guide	
	4.2 In small groups, work with the basic rule books of major sports: baseball, football, basketball, and soccer. Have groups report to the class: how many players on a team, how points are obtained, how the game is won, length of playing time, segments of play, typical plays, qualities of players, fouls, penalties, and so on.		
	4.3 Have guest speakers, such as coaches and sports columnists, discuss basics of the game and show videotaped illustrations.		

	4.4 Using a newspaper and the telephone, have students determine when a local game will be held and the cost of admission.		
	4.5 Attend a local game as a group. Ask students questions: "Who's ahead?" "How much time is left?" "Describe that play."		
	4.6 Encourage students to attend local games independently or follow certain teams on television and report these activities to the class.		
5. The student will develop one hobby area that can be pursued independently.	5.1 Students will complete the Crafts/Hobbies Survey to identify their areas of interest.	Crafts/Hobbies Survey (see objective 1)	Howard and Strathairn (1976)
	5.2 Guest speakers from the school and community should be invited to discuss their hobbies with the class. Hobbies described should have the potential to be life-long independent activities: i.e., gardening, sewing, coin, and stamp collecting, photography, music, and movies.	Library Volunteer instructors	
	5.3 Have the class make a bulletin board illustrating their hobby choices.		
	5.4 Have each student identify a hobby he wishes to pursue and discuss it with the teacher and occupational therapist.		

continued

Objectives	Activities	Facilities/Materials/ Equipment/Modifications/Adaptations	References
	Students should research the needed equipment, cost and sources of supplies, etc. 5.5 Students should be given instruction in hobbies; they should then develop a display for the class about the hobby and how it can be pursued independently at home. Examples: a. Student could collect gardening hints and ideas from newspapers and magazines and make a display of hints and plants. b. Movie buffs could discuss how newspaper ratings and reviews can be used as a guide for selecting worthwhile pictures. Oscar predictions could be made.		

CURRICULUM AREA: _____   FAMILY LIVING

Developmental Level: _____   Secondary

Objectives	Activities	Facilities/Materials/ Equipment/Modifications/Adaptations	References
1. The student will be introduced to some important aspects of child care.	1.1 Have students who have younger brothers and sisters at home or who have done babysitting discuss what they have observed about the physical, emotional, and safety needs of young children.	*Family Life* (social adjustment textbooks and workbooks) Frank E. Richards Publishing Co. 330 First Street Box 370 Liverpool, N.Y. 13088	
	1.2 Have a competent mother bring her infant to class and discuss the daily care of a baby.		
	1.3 Ask the Red Cross to provide a modified "Caring for an Infant" course.		
	1.4 Using *Family Life* text, discuss parents' financial and nurturing responsibilities toward children. Discuss how parents can determine their childrearing goals and practices.		
2. The student will know the importance of good prenatal	2.1 Using *Prenatal Care* as a guide, discuss the importance of regular medical care, routine health care, and good nutrition during pregnancy.	*Prenatal Care* by Katie Baer New Readers Press (1973)	

continued

Objectives	Activities	Facilities/Materials/Equipment/Modifications/Adaptations	References
care and will be aware of the adjustments the whole family must make when a child is born.	2.2 Have a Lamaze instructor discuss prepared childbirth. Using *Giving Birth* as a guide, discuss hospital and financial arrangements, labor and childbirth, and care of a new infant.	*Giving Birth* by Katie Baer New Readers Press (1973)	
	2.3 Using *The Baby and the Family*, discuss changes in emotions, interpersonal relationships, family finances, employment, and social life when the new baby arrives. (Parental permission for these discussions is advisable.)	*The Baby and the Family* by Maxine Phillips New Readers Press (1973) 1320 Jamesville Avenue Box 131 Syracuse, N.Y., 13210.	
3. The student will be aware of family planning alternatives.	3.1 Discuss these topics: a. React to statement "Every baby has a right to be a wanted baby." b. Review where babies come from. c. What factors would indicate readiness for having a baby?		
	3.2 Read *Planning Your Family* and view "About Conception and Contraception" and discuss both prescription and over-the-counter contraceptives and call attention to pros and cons of other methods of birth control.	*Planning Your Family* by Maxine Phillips (1976) New Readers Press "About Conception and Contraception" (film number 1008, rental $14.00) Perennial Education, Inc. 1825 Willow Road Northfield, Ill., 60093.	

4. The student will identify some factors that indicate readiness for marriage and factors that make marriage last.	4.1 Read together *Be Informed on Marriage* and identify factors that indicate readiness for marriage, planning for marriage, and making a marriage last. 4.2 Using the *Family Life* text as a guide, role-play solutions to these problem areas: a. finding an apartment b. buying furniture c. budgeting d. being out of work e. moving f. finding a new job g. getting along with in-laws h. deciding about having a baby i. planning a vacation j. setting important life goals k. dividing household responsibilities	*Be Informed on Marriage* *Family Life* Frank E. Richards Publishing Co. 330 First Street Box 370 Liverpool, N.Y., 13088.
5. The student will know facts about human sexuality and reproduction.	5.1 It is suggested that this unit be conducted in single sex groups with parent permission (see Cook, 1974, for suggestions about parent involvement). 5.2 It is suggested that Gordon (1976) be used as a starting point for discussing: a. sexual development in males and females b. menstruation c. sexual intercourse d. human reproduction e. personal responsibility	Gordon, S. *Facts about Sex for Today's Youth.* New York: John Day, 1973. *Social and Sexual Development* (1971) Cook (1974) Jones (undated)

continued

Objectives	Activities	Facilities/Materials/Equipment/Modifications/Adaptations	References
	5.3 Special concerns of physically handicapped people regarding sexuality should be discussed generally (Cook, 1974). Individual concerns should be referred to a physician for specific answers.		

CURRICULUM AREA: _____   INDEPENDENT LIVING

Developmental Level: _____   Secondary

Objectives	Activities	Facilities/Materials/ Equipment/Modifications/Adaptations	References
1. The student will meet sanitation standards for food through personal cleanliness.	1.1 Discuss the importance of cleanliness at home, in the school kitchen, and in public restaurants.	Soap and water	Redick (1976c)
	1.2 Demonstrate and practice washing hands — before starting to cook, and after touching face or hair, or going to the toilet. Also discuss hair care in the kitchen.	Sinks should be open underneath so that wheelchair can be rolled up underneath basin. Pipes should be wrapped so student does not get burned. Faucets may need to be put on sides of sink.	
	1.3 Perform a skit of a kitchen group who are very unsanitary during preparation in food lab. Characteristics could include: not wiping up spills and useing the same utensil for 2 different tasks without cleaning it between tasks.		
	1.4 Demonstrate dishwashing procedures. Have students practice these procedures.	Adapt and modify methods of dishwashing. Use plastic dishes. Develop holder to support dishes or silver. Discuss air drying and ease of storage.	

continued

Objectives	Activities	Facilities/Materials/ Equipment/Modifications/Adaptations	References
2. The student will be aware of safety hazards in the kitchen and will demonstrate the use of safety procedures.	2.1 Develop a checklist for safety in the student's home and for the kitchens students will be working in at school. 2.2 Have students discuss different types of accidents that could occur in the kitchen. 2.3 Write safety slogans on posters, such as "A holder for your pot keeps your hands from getting hot." Display slogans around the room. 2.4 Discuss techniques used at home for safety in the kitchen. Include fire extinguishers — use and location, and alternative methods for extinguishing a fire. 2.5 Role-play kitchen safety.	Special safety considerations: Fire safety: lightweight model fire extinguishers located in kitchen and dining areas; smoke and fire alarms — electrical and automatically operated; switch to battery in case of power failure; fire retardant clothing, oven mitts, and utensil and appliance handles. Electrical outlets: cord shortener to hold excess cord to prevent tripping; a student may use the heels of his hands and sides of both palms of hands pressed together around plug if he cannot pull electrical plug out. Automatic timer to turn off electrical appliances. Food preparation: spoon that clips upright to edge of pan; serated knife to grip food; sharp rather than dull knife.	Redick (1976c)

Redick (1976a)

3. The student will identify, use, and care for common kitchen utensils.	3.1 Have students make a display, a mobile, or a bulletin board of basic basic utensils. Identify each piece of equipment.	Kitchen utensils: rolling pin, paring knife, can opener, vegetable peeler, potato masher, tongs, egg beater, measuring cups, measuring spoons, rubber scraper, mixing bowls.

3.1 Have students make a display, a mobile, or a bulletin board of basic basic utensils. Identify each piece of equipment.

Kitchen utensils: rolling pin, paring knife, can opener, vegetable peeler, potato masher, tongs, egg beater, measuring cups, measuring spoons, rubber scraper, mixing bowls.

3.2 Have a "Utensil Hunt" where students find specific equipment in the kitchen. Give a list to the students for the hunt and include a space for students to write why utensils are where they are.

Adaptations: flat-bottomed pans and bowls; longer and better handles, larger knobs; strainer lids; tongs; egg separator; whisk; rack to hold supplies and prevent spills; electrical appliances to save time and energy; minimum care equipment.

3.3 Have students look over kitchen; the teacher then calls out pieces of equipment and waits until all the students have found it. Stress returning utensils to proper places.

Heavier utensils will reduce tremor and loss of control.

When items must be carried, a utility tray that fits onto the wheelchair could be used.

3.4 Teacher prepares snack or simple food to show the proper use of utensils such as a paring knife, a can opener, a vegetable peeler, etc.

3.5 Have students use such equipment as: a potato masher, tongs, an egg beater, measuring cups, a vegetable peeler, and rubber scraper. Use different pieces of equipment with foods to find which is the easiest to use and most convenient for them.

Experiment with substitutions of equipment that may be more convenient for the handicapped student: tongs instead of fork for lifting and turning, reaching, and as a serving tool; for an egg beater, use a wire whisk substitute or an electric mixer with stabilized bowls; for vegetable peeler, use a two-pronged stabilizer to hold vegetable firm, peelers adapted to specific conditions are

continued

Objectives	Activities	Facilities/Materials/ Equipment/Modifications/Adaptations	References
		also available; make sure bowls have handles, flat bottoms, and pouring spouts; use a suction cup device for holding firm; use long-handled and flat-bottomed measuring spoons.	
		Determine utensils that can be eliminated by using convenience foods.	
		Emphasize rinsing promptly and/or soaking to avoid scrubbing.	
	3.6 Teacher demonstrates the care of various utensils — proper types of cleaning, hard to clean areas to watch for, proper ways of sorting.		
4. The student will be able to prepare: a. beverages	4.1 Make cocoa, using syrup, mix, or heating chocolate milk. Point out that milk must be heated slowly.	Large wooden spoons will make stirring easier.	Redick (1976c)
	4.2 Make lemonade from frozen concentrate, drink mix, fresh lemons, lemon juice. Compare these methods.		
	4.3 Divide the class into groups to make different tea and coffee products: perked and instant coffee, and iced tea from bags.		

continued

b.	cereal and grain products	4.4 Discuss the different cereals available, including both cooked and ready to eat. Prepare different kinds of cooked cereal: Cream of Wheat, oatmeal, Cream of Rice, etc. Compare for flavor and nutrition.	Investigate the use of serving-size boxes with perforated openings for easy opening.
		4.5 Brainstorm all the things that can be made with a box of biscuit mix: pizza, donuts, coffee cake, and pancakes.	
		4.6 Have students prepare a variety of quickbreads, such as orange muffins, biscuits, and fruit and nut breads. Have a tasting lab.	Use an elbow-length mitt when removing pans from oven. Wheeled cart near oven may facilitate removing baked products from the oven and taking them to the table.
c.	fruits and vegetables	4.7 Demonstrate preparing fruits, washing, and paring.	Make use of special tools: vegetable brush attached to board, mesh strainer baskets.
		4.8 Show how fruits lose color when exposed to air, and demonstrate color retention by use of an acid such as lemon juice on a banana.	
		4.9 Prepare a fresh fruit cup.	
		4.10 Prepare a relish tray, showing how to add crispness by adding ice and chilling.	Consider alternative forms of fruit if preparation is too difficult — i.e., canned grapefruit and oranges.

Objectives	Activities	Facilities/Materials/Equipment/Modifications/Adaptations	References
	4.11 Demonstrate ways of cooking green and yellow vegetables, stressing retention of nutrients and color. Have a "taste testing" laboratory.		
	4.12 Prepare a variety of baked fruits, such as apples and bananas. Have a tasting laboratory.	Use cutting board with nail to hold vegetables for cleaning.	
	4.13 Prepare a variety of fruit and vegetable salads. Discuss what salad category each one fits into: appetizer, accompaniment, main dish, or dessert.		
d. milk and milk products	4.14 Using a blender, demonstrate how to make various kinds of milk drinks: malts, shakes, milk and fruit combinations. Stress the relationship of incorporation of air to increased quantity (an electric mixer can also be used).	Some students might best use a standard mixer while others could use a portable mixer with stabilized bowls on lapboard.	
	4.15 Prepare soft and baked custards and different kinds of puddings: tapioca, chocolate, and rice.		

e. egg, meat, and casserole dishes	4.16 Demonstrate the preparation of white sauce.	Consider the convenience of canned or packaged white sauce for disabled students.
	4.17 Have groups prepare different cheese products such as rarebit, cheese fondue, cheese souffles.	
	4.18 Demonstrate different ways to fix eggs: eggs in a nest, baked eggs, and scrambled and poached eggs.	Students with the use of one hand may use adaptive devices for separating eggs. Or demonstrate how to break an egg with one hand: hit side of egg sharply against side of bowl. Thumb and index finger are left at the top while the ring and little finger hold down the lower half.
	4.19 Lecture on tender and less tender cuts of meat and different methods of preparation.	
	4.20 Demonstrate frying, broiling, and roasting.	
f. nutritious snacks	4.21 Prepare lists of snacks and kinds of parties at which these might be served. Emphasize nutritious snacks — avoid junk foods and empty calories.	
	4.22 Plan a nutritious snack party. Invite another class or serve refreshments at a meeting.	
	4.23 Prepare foods from different mixes: snacking cake, brownies, muffins, coffeecake, jiffy cake.	

continued

Objectives	Activities	Facilities/Materials/ Equipment/Modifications/Adaptations	References
g. convenience foods	4.24 Discuss the variety of convenience foods available: beverages, canned stews, canned frostings, skillet meals, frozen foods.		Redick (1976a) May (1974)
5. The student will be able to manage laundry needs by: a. sorting by fabric, color, and amount of soil;	5.1 Use actual clothes and linens for sorting. Have students practice reading labels for washing instructions.	A table may be used for sorting laundry so that garments will stay in easy reach.	
b. choose appropriate laundry products;	5.2 Collect boxes or box fronts and bottles. Identify products and discuss values.	Demonstrate the advantage of different sized containers when opening and using with limited hand use. Boxes can be laid on the side opposite the perforated edge, the edge torn, the box put back up, and the capable arm used as leverage when pulling the rest of the tab on the box. Bottles can be held between the limited arm and the body or between the legs or set in a drawer and the drawer closed against it to hold it tight.	
c. demonstrate prewashing techniques;	5.3 Show how to use a small brush to put extra detergent on dirty parts such as a collar. Show and explain how to use the prewash spray treatments that are commercially available.	A lapboard may be used as work surface for prewashing techniques. Possible equipment	

			Redick (1976a)
d. use laundromat and laundry equipment.	5.4 Practice until student has mastered starting the washer and dryer. Prepare an instruction chart similar to those on the wall of a laundromat. Have students study and indicate their understanding.	adaptations include: sinks that are low and open underneath, insulated pipes, and faucets on the side of the sink.	
	5.5 Practice folding and sorting clothes from a dryer load.	Demonstrate folding clothes with one hand and hanging onto hanger with one hand. Teeth may be used to assist in folding.	
	5.6 Students should practice hanging up clothes on a line.	Slacks may be hung in this way: put slacks over the back of a chair and bring hanger up under one side of slacks. Suggested aids may include: one-handed clothes basket, pulley clothes line, and magnets on cover to keep clothespin bag open.	
6. The student will learn to prolong the life of garments by appropriate repair techniques.	6.1 As a class, brainstorm different methods of repair, such as patching, restitching seams, replacing buttons, etc.	Needle and thread, buttons, snaps, hooks and eyes, Velcro	
	6.2 Practice sewing on buttons, snaps, hooks and eyes, and Velcro.	A needle threader or self-threading needle may be used. A person with a limited hand would be helped by having some means of holding the needle — pincushion or upholstered armchair. The use of a lapboard on which to place fabric may be helpful for immobile persons. An embroidery hoop or frame can be used to hold the area of fabric being worked.	

continued

Objectives	Activities	Facilities/Materials/ Equipment/Modifications/Adaptations	References
	6.3 Demonstrate and practice reinforcement of stress and strain areas.	Reinforced areas will depend on handicapping condition, i.e., contact with braces, splints, and crutches. A leather patch could be placed under the arm to prevent wear from crutches and arm bands. The inside of slacks could be reinforced for braces by adding an extra layer of fabric.	
	6.4 Review or learn methods for putting in a hem. Discuss popular lengths.	Alternative hemming methods: iron-on tapes, stitch-witchery, machine hemming Caution about length in relation to sitting position in wheelchair. Skirt should not be taut across knees.	
7. The student will develop a plan for organizing and arranging supplies and equipment in the kitchen.	7.1 Discuss the principles of storage and set up guidelines to help get the most satisfaction from available space: a. store at point of use b. store within easy reach those things that are used most often c. plan storage space to fit the articles to be stored d. put articles in a planned space e. discard unused articles.	Special considerations for the handicapped: cabinet doors — tap catches omit use of storage areas that require climbing use cupboard space from floor up to 18¼ for storage of seldom used articles store heavy articles near place of use.	Redick (1976c)

		The Slow Learning Program in the Elementary and Secondary Schools (1964)

8. The student will know guidelines for preventing and treating common illnesses.

7.2 Review the different kinds of equipment in kitchens and discuss storage possibilities.

7.3 Use a grab bag of stored items. Ask students to discuss whatever they draw out. Where would it be stored? Why? What guidelines are being followed?

Storage ideas:
pull-out trays
pull-out shelves
revolving corner units
tilt-out bins
sliding racks
pull-out cutting board
rolling cart with shelves
lazy susan
pegboard with hangers, brackets, and shelves

8.1 Read and study *Can You Give First Aid?* Discuss what to do before the doctor comes, the first aid box, bleeding, shock, when breathing stops, broken bones, burns, bites, and poisons.

Bontrager, F. M. 1969. *Can You Give First Aid?* New Readers Press, Syracuse.

For ordering information:
New Readers Press
Box 131
Syracuse, N.Y., 13210.

8.2 Have a Red Cross instructor demonstrate first aid and home nursing techniques. If the student is not able to carry out these techniques, have him learn to direct someone else and/or develop an emergency alert system (i.e., telephoning a neighbor if help is needed).

continued

Objectives	Activities	Facilities/Materials/ Equipment/Modifications/Adaptations	References
	8.3 Discuss common illnesses: causes, symptoms, care, and prevention. Discuss the need for vaccinations and immunizations.		
	8.4 Have the class make reports about what to do when ill: bed rest, proper diet, isolation, when to take medications, etc.		
9. The student will know how to make a dental/medical appointment.	9.1 Have the student bring from home the names of family dentist/doctor.		Howard and Strathairn (1976)
	9.2 Look in the yellow pages for phone number and practice calling that number.		
	9.3 Role-play telling the receptionist what is wrong and writing down date and time of appointment and address.		
	9.4 Role-play telling the receptionist who you are, where you live, and time of appointment.		

10. The student will explore alternatives in housing and will be aware of related expenses and responsibilities.	9.5 Practice paying the receptionist for the visit and keeping appointment slip for next appointment.		
	10.1 Tour housing opportunities in the community: mobile homes, apartments, duplexes, single family dwellings, remodeled homes, and condominiums. Discuss the living space and consider what housing needs might be met by each type of housing available. Discuss the cost of living in each type of housing.	*Your Housing Dollar* Explains how to plan housing needs and costs, whether you rent, buy, or build. ($.35) Houshold Finance Corporation Prudential Plaza Chicago, Ill., 60601.	Redick (1976b)
	10.2 Have the class make a list of the architectural barriers encountered on housing tour.	*Into the Mainstream: a Syllabus for a Barrier-Free Environment* (free pamphlet) The American Institute of Architects 1735 New York Avenue N.W. Washington, D.C., 20036.	
	10.3 List the rights and responsibilities of the renter and landlord. List also the rights and responsibilities of a home owner.	*A Guide for Renters* ($1.00 reprint) Reprint Department Consumers Union Orangeburg, N.Y., 10962.	
	10.4 Use newspaper ads to find out the costs of renting and buying. Compare according to responsibilities, cost, and needs.	Newspapers	

continued

Objectives	Activities	Facilities/Materials/ Equipment/Modifications/Adaptations	References
	10.5 Identify legal documents (such as leases, deeds, titles, etc.) included either in renting or buying. Have students fill out a sample copy or lease.		
	10.6 Have representatives from Civil Rights Commission, American Civil Liberties Union or HUD Equal Opportunity in Housing discuss how to handle discrimination against a wheel-chair confined person.		
	10.7 Clarify meaning of utilities. Students list different utilities they might have to pay. Have students ask parents what utilities are included in their housing costs.		
	10.8 Have resource speakers from a bank or savings and loan discuss financing a home.		
	10.9 Discuss types of insurance for renters and homeowners.		

		Redick (1976b)
11. The student will evaluate housing floor plans and traffic patterns.	10.10 Make a chart that depicts total cost of a home, including mortgage, insurance, closing costs, taxes, utilities, etc. 10.11 Consider the possibility of unemployment, welfare, and social security in regard to housing costs and payment. 11.1 Examine floor plans and traffic patterns on transparencies or house plans. 11.2 Select a floor plan of an apartment or house that students feel would meet their needs as a first home away from home. Students explain why the housing they chose meets their needs. 11.3 Determine the dimensions and space requirements for a barrier-free home. Evaluate selected floor plans for wheelchair accessibility. 11.4 Discuss idea that floor plan of any house actually zones the activities of a particular household. Have students find and label the activity areas on their floor plans: working, sleeping, eating, and leisure.	*Family housing handbook* ($2.00) Midwest Plan Service Iowa State University Ames, Iowa, 50010. *Wheelchair Interiors* by Sharon Olson and Diane Meredith ($1.50) National Easter Seal Society for Crippled Children and Adults 2023 West Ogden Avenue Chicago, Ill., 60612.

continued

Objectives	Activities	Facilities/Materials/ Equipment/Modifications/Adaptations	References
12. The student will recognize safety hazards around the home and devise ways to eliminate or decrease them.	12.1 For a bulletin board, have students bring in news articles relating to home accidents. 12.2 Have students look around the room and make a list of all the things they can see that could cause an accident. 12.3 Point out normal conditions that could be hazardous for the handicapped student. Use Safety Hazards Worksheet. 12.4 Make a list of poisons found under the sink, in the medicine cabinet, the garage, etc. Check labels to see what precautions and antidotes are given. Discuss the Poison Control Hotline phone number. 12.5 Take a field trip to an electrical equipment store and get information on making home improvements and adjustments.	Safety Hazards Worksheet: This list is comprised of housing features that would not commonly be hazards for non-handicapped persons but could present unsafe conditions for persons with limited physical abilities. In the left column is the selected housing feature. You are to fill in the adaptations for making the feature safer in the right column. Housing Feature: Adaptations for Safety: Counter Height Sinks — 　water faucets 　drain placement 　pipes under the sink Floor Surfaces — 　waxed, slick 　stairways Windows — 　height 　operation Doors	Redick (1976b)

			Redick (1976b)
	12.6 Have student locate and determine the accessibility of the fuse box, water main, and gas main in his own home. Practice operating main switches while parents supervise.	Stairways — steep circular handrails Accessories Equipment — washing machine ironing board iron Shower/Tub Furnishings — chairs tables Lighting — switch placement lamps Electrical Outlets placement cord length Other	
	12.7 Discuss what to do in case of a fire at home. Have each student develop a fire escape plan for his own home and discuss it with his family. Look at and try out various fire extinguishers.		
	12.8 Make a list of supplies for a home first aid kit.		
	12.9 Prepare cards showing emergency phone numbers for each student to take home. Practice dialing emergency numbers. Investigate automatic dialing devices.		
13. The student will identify and use basic tools needed in doing simple home repairs.	13.1 Have an exhibit of tools for students to see.	Putty knife, sandpaper, screwdriver, hammer, pliers, paintbrush, saw, plastic sealer, adjustable wrench	
	13.2 Set up a tool lab with stations so students rotate and use tools at each station.		

continued

Objectives	Activities	Facilities/Materials/ Equipment/Modifications/Adaptations	References
	13.3 Using the *Simple Home Repairs* booklet, have students practice doing (or directing someone else in) these home repairs: a. patching holes in wallboard or plaster b. repair drawers c. fixing problem drawers d. repairing screens e. fixing floor tile f. filling the crack around shower or tub g. repairing a leaky faucet h. repairing electric plugs i. replacing a broken window	*Simple Home Repairs* Cooperative Extension Service Iowa State University Ames, Iowa, 50010.	
14. The student will be able to use cleaning supplies and equipment for home care and adapt equipment to own needs and resources.	14.1 Give Household Skills Evaluation Rating Scale in the *Life Experience Program.* Focus on areas not yet mastered. 14.2 Practice dusting tabletop with cloth. 14.3 Practice cleaning refrigerator, freezer, and range.	Houshold cleaning supplies	Howard and Strathairn (1976) Redick (1976b)

	14.4 Practice sweeping and cleaning floors. Divide work into sections of reachable distance.	Possible adaptations: extenders to reach middle of large surfaces long-handled faucets long-handled sponges.
	14.5 Clean windows and mirror.	Detergent, rather than soap, should be used in mopping floors — less slippery.
	14.6 Practice bedmaking: bedding should be lightweight and easy to care for: bottom sheet fitted with elasticized corners, top large enough not to pull out. Students should make one half of the bed and then go to the other side.	Students may need a squeegee or mop with long handle.
	14.7 Practice using a vacuum cleaner; talk about the variety of cleaning jobs that can be done with vacuum cleaner.	Tank type has switch which can be operated with foot, cane, or crutch.	Howard and Strathairn (1976)
15. The student will develop independence in managing transportation needs.	15.1 Using the task analyses found in the *Life Experience Program*, evaluate students' independence in calling a taxi, riding a bus, and taking a trip by car. Provide instruction on the tasks not yet mastered.	Howard, R., and Strathairn, F. 1976. *Life Experience Program.* Santa Clara County Schools, San Jose, Calif.	Gubbins (1977)
	15.2 Provide instruction in crossing streets and in transferring from wheelchair to car.	For quadriplegic students, helpers may be needed. Wheelchair is brought to side of open car door. One person should hold wheelchair and be prepared to pull it as other(s) pick up student; one at the shoulder and one at the knees. Place student in front seat, watching not to strike head, knees, or feet. Be sure seat belt is secure.

LITERATURE CITED

Abeson, A., and Weintraub, F. 1977. Understanding the individualized education program. In: S. Torres (ed.), A primer on Individualized Education Programs for Handicapped Children. The Foundation for Exceptional Children, Reston, Va.

BCP Method cards — Motor Skills. 1977. Special Education Information Management System, Santa Cruz, Calif.

BCP Method Cards — Self-Help Skills. 1977. Special Education Information Management System, Santa Cruz, Calif.

Bigge, J., and O'Donnell, P. 1977. Teaching Individuals with Physical and Multiple Disabilities. Charles E. Merrill Publishing Company, Columbus, Ohio.

Campbell, D. D. 1973. Typewriting contrasted with handwriting: A circumvention study of learning disabled children. J. Special Educ. 7:155-168.

Canfield, J., and Wells, H. C. 1976. 100 Ways to Enhance Self-Concept in the Classroom. Prentice-Hall, Inc., Englewood Cliffs, N.J.

Cook, R. 1974. Sex education program service model for the multihandicapped adult. Rehabil. Lit. 3:264-268.

Cookman, H., and Zimmerman, M. 1961. Functional Fashions for the Physically Handicapped. Institute of Physical Medicine and Rehabilitation of the NYU Medical Center, New York.

Crickmay, M. C. Speech Therapy and the Bobath Approach to Cerebral Palsy. Charles C Thomas Publisher, Springfield, Ill.

Cruickshank, W. A. 1961. A Teaching Method for Brain-Injured and Hyperactive Children. Syracuse University Press, N.Y.

Duffy, G. G., and Sherman, G. B. 1972. Systematic Reading Instruction. Harper and Row, New York.

Dupont, H., Gardner, O. S., and Brody, D. S. 1974. Toward Affective Development. American Guidance Service, Circle Pines, Minn.

Fernald, G. M. 1943. Remedial Techniques in Basic School Subjects. McGraw-Hill, New York.

Finnie, G. M. 1975. Handling the Young Cerebral Palsied Child at Home. E. P. Dutton and Company, Inc., New York.

Gardner, W. H. 1958. Left Handed Writing. The Interstate Printers and Publishers, Inc., Danville, Ill.

Gettings, R. M. 1976. A summary of selected legislation relating to the handicapped: 1975. Programs for the Handicapped. 2-15.

Gordon, S. 1976. Sex education: Love, sex and marriage for people who have disabilities. Except. Parent.

Grollman, E. A. (ed.). 1967. Explaining Death to Children. Beacon Press, Boston.

Grollman, E. A. 1976. Talking about Death. Beacon Press, Boston.

Gubbins, E. L. 1977. Programming and Instructional Techniques for the Multihandicapped. University of South Carolina and SC Department of Mental Retardation, Columbia, S.C.

Hammill, D. D., and Bartel, N. R. 1975. Teaching Children with Learning and Behavior Problems. Allyn and Bacon, Inc., Boston.

Hedbring, C., and Holmes, C. 1977. Getting it together with 94-142: the IEP in the classroom. Educ. Training Ment. Retard. 12:212-224.

Howard, R., and Strathairn, F. 1976. Life Experience Program. Santa Clara County Schools, Calif.

Jedrysek, E., Klapper, Z., Pope, L., and Wortis, J. 1972. Psychoeducational Evaluation of the Preschool Child. Grune and Stratton, New York.

Johnson, D. J., and Myklebust, H. R. 1967. Learning Disabilities: Educational Principles and Practices. Grune and Stratton, New York.

Johnson, J. L. 1978. Programming for early motor responses within the classroom. AAESPH Rev. 5-14.

Jones, M. How to Tell the Retarded Girl about Menstruation. Kimberly-Clark Corporation, Neenah, Wisc.

Kent, L. R. 1974. Language Acquisition Program for the Severely Retarded. Research Press, Champaign, Ill.

Lerner, J. W. 1976. Children with Learning Disabilities. Houghton Mifflin Company, Boston.

McCartney, P. 1973. Clothes Sense for Handicapped Adults of All Ages. Disabled Living Foundation, London.

Magyar, C. W., Nystrom, J. B., and Johannsen, N. 1977. A follow-up study of former cerebral palsied students at a school for neuro-orthopedically disabled children. Rehabil. Lit. 38:40-42.

May, B., Waggoner, N., and Hottle, E. 1974. Independent Living for the Handicapped and the Elderly. Houghton Mifflin Company, Boston.

Meacham, M. J., Berko, M. J., Berko, F. G., and Palmer, M. I. 1966. Communication Training in Childhood Brain Damage. Charles C Thomas Publisher, Springfield, Ill.

Popovich, D. 1977. A Prescriptive Behavioral Checklist for the Severely and Profoundly Retarded. University Park Press, Baltimore.

Redick, S. S. 1976a. The Physically Handicapped Student in the Regular Home Economics Classroom: A Guide for Teaching Grooming and Clothing. The Interstate Printers and Publishers, Inc., Danville, Ill.

Redick, S. S. 1976b. The Physically Handicapped Student in the Regular Home Economics Classroom: a Guide for Teaching Housing and Home Care. The Interstate Printers and Publishers, Inc., Danville, Ill.

Redick, S. S. 1976c. The Physically Handicapped Student in the Regular Home Economics Classroom: a Guide for Teaching Nutrition and Foods. The Interstate Printers and Publishers, Inc., Danville, Ill.

Reynolds, M. 1978. Staying out of jail. Teaching Except. Child. 10:60-62.

Russell, F., Shoemaker, S., McGuigan, C., and Bevis, D. 1976. IEP: Individual Education Programming. State Department of Public Instruction, Boise, Idaho.

Sherrill, C. 1976. Adapted Physical Education and Recreation. Wm. C. Brown Company, Dubuque, Iowa.

Simon, S. B., and Goodman, J. 1976. A study of death through the celebration of life. Learning 70-74.

Simon, S. B., Howe, L. W., and Kirschenbaum, H. 1972. Values Clarification. Hart Publishing Company, Inc., New York.

Simon, S. B., and O'Rourke, R. D. 1967. Developing Values with Exceptional Children. Prentice-Hall, Inc., Englewood Cliffs, N.J.

Sirvis, B. 1978. Developing IEPs for PH students: A transdisciplinary view. Teaching Except. Child. 10:78-82.

The Slow Learning Program in the Elementary and Secondary Schools. 1964. Cincinnati Public Schools, (Curriculum Bulletin No. 119), Cincinnati, Ohio.

Social and Sexual Development. 1971. Special Education Curriculum Development Center of the University of Iowa, Iowa City, Iowa.

Strauss, A. S., and Lehtinen, L. 1948. Psychopathology and Education of the Brain-Injured Child. Vol. 1. Grune and Stratton, New York.

A Task Analysis Approach to Prevocational and Vocational Training for the Handicapped. 1975. Duquesne University School of Education (ERIC Document No. 114621), Pittsburgh.

Taylor, F. D., Artuso, A. A., and Hewett, F. M. 1974. Learning Activity Cards for Children. Love Publishing Company, Denver.

Vodola, T. M. 1973. Individualized Physical Education Program for the Handicapped Child. Prentice-Hall, Englewood Cliffs, N.J.

Wright, B. A. 1960. Physical Disability: a Psychological Approach. Harper and Row, New York.

Yep, J. 1974. Clothes to Fit Your Needs. Cooperative Extension Service of Iowa State University, Ames, Iowa.

9

WORKING AS PART OF AN INTERDISCIPLINARY TEAM

Figure 9-1. An interdisciplinary team shares ideas, develops a common language, and examines the needs of the whole child.

The word "interdisciplinary" implies a group of people — a team — talking together, sharing ideas, and planning for some future event. The education of physically handicapped children does require a team effort, but one team cannot do it alone.

The teacher of physically handicapped students is a member of many teams, all of which have one common goal — helping the student. Although their goal is the same, however, each team provides this help in its own way, based on the needs of the moment as interpreted by the team members.

Medical personnel, educators, volunteers, government agencies, parents, professionals, interested citizens, and the handicapped students themselves are all team members. All of these people are concerned with finding ways to improve the lives of persons with physical handicaps. Teachers incorporate the efforts of these groups into the plans for physically handicapped students, which are ultimately directed at guiding the students toward independence.

This chapter describes the interdisciplinary process, the teamwork required of teachers as they work with professionals in education and other fields, and the available, helpful services of volunteer, governmental, and professional associations.

THE INTERDISCIPLINARY PROCESS

Because of the often complex nature of the problems faced by handicapped persons and their families, an interdisciplinary approach is essential in special education. The child with cerebral palsy may also be mentally retarded, hard of hearing, or blind. The child with muscular dystrophy may not only need to be taught in a special classroom, but also will need physical and occupational therapy to help him continue to function as independently as possible. His family may need counseling support to endure the trauma of this debilitating disease, as well as genetic advice about childbearing because of its hereditary nature.

The term "interdisciplinary" implies that several disciplines are working together, sharing information, building upon the ideas of others in formulating a diagnosis. In practice, the interdisciplinary team works as a unit, studying and examining the same problem with the tools, knowledge, and skills of the individual members' respective professions, sharing the gathered information with one another, and collectively reaching a decision.

This process is similar to, but not the same as, a multidisciplinary approach, in which the team members examine the problem individually and, without consulting one another, present a final report. The final reports are then gathered together and compiled into one document.

The main difference between the "inter" and the "multi" disciplinary approaches, then, is the interaction and interchange of ideas while forming a diagnosis or during evaluation or treatment. Zweig (1975) points out that persons who serve on an interdisciplinary team become "interdisciplinary generalists," understanding the strengths of, and contributions to be made by, each separate discipline, as well as communicating skillfully with each other.

The interdisciplinary process is concerned with solving problems and making decisions. Diagnosis, treatment/educational planning, and the review and alteration of programming or activities are typical orders of business for this team.

The quality of the work accomplished by an interdisciplinary team is determined not only by the contribution of each professional, but also by the leadership provided to the group as a whole (Johnston and Magrab, 1976). The group leader may assume one of two functions. He may seek to best serve the group by assuming the primary responsibility for the ongoing management of the care of a particular child and his family, in which case he would be called a case manager or coordinator. The second leadership style involves taking action to unite the team and to direct it toward a common action plan (Johnston and Magrab, 1976). This leader facilitates decision-making by providing feedback, ensuring that shared information is relevant, encouraging the more reluctant speakers, and seeking more information when necessary.

The leader must remain alert to symptoms of common problems that can disrupt the interdisciplinary meeting. As with any other group of professionals, opinionated people and conflicts over issues or personalities may lead to arguments or stifle cooperative sharing. Occasionally, members of the team who feel "too busy" or are otherwise preoccupied with unrelated thoughts may not participate. Perhaps the most damaging situation is that in which the team is unable to make a decision, define the next task, and reach a point of closure. The leader's responsibility to the group, the student, and the family is to recognize these and other symptoms of misdirection and to guide the group back to the task at hand without inhibiting creative and profitable interchange.

As stated previously, the teacher of physically handicapped students serves in various ways on many interdisciplinary teams: She is a vital member of the placement committees that focus on determining the least restrictive environment for each student, and she is a member of the school's treatment team, working with physical and occupational therapists, and speech pathologists. She periodically confers with parents and physicians about the current status of a child's health and the effects of medication, and she reaches out to the community and government agencies to find help for her students.

The initial requirements for an effective team member, then, are an understanding of the skills, knowledge, and language of other disciplines, and effective leadership and communication abilities.

WORKING WITH OTHER PROFESSIONALS

It is not unusual for a teacher to work with professionals in fields other than education. The school social worker, nurse, and psychologist frequently collaborate with a teacher to solve a particular dilemma; however, these professionals are, to some extent, oriented toward school because of the training and course work in education that is required for their certification. Occasionally, the teacher of physically handicapped students is required to discuss problems and plan programs with professionals totally outside the field of education. It would not be unexpected, therefore, to encounter a professional with a distorted view of school-related issues, an undesirable situation that can impede student progress. All professionals have some level of familiarity with school systems, however, if only as students in their own early school days; thus, they all possess at least a modicum of information on which to build communication.

Heavy involvement with a number of physicians is an accepted way of life for most physically handicapped children. If the child's problems are severe and/or complex, specialists, as well as the family physician, may be involved. Some of these specialists include:

If the disability is genetic ....geneticist
If delivery was a precarious experience ....obstetrician
If the infant's life was in danger following delivery ....neonatalist
If the infant showed signs of spinal injury,
brain anomaly, or seizures..............neurologist or pediatric neurologist
If the child has muscular or postural problems ....orthopedist
If the child has a heart or circulatory problem . . cardiologist or cardiac surgeon
If the child suffered a traumatic spinal cord injury or
amputation ....doctor of rehabilitation medicine or physiatrist
If the nature of the problem is chronic rather
than acute ....pediatrician or general practitioner

Physician

The physician contributes to the diagnosis, formulates a medical maintenance or treatment program, monitors the student's general health and specific health problems, and maintains records of medications, visits, and changes in the student's health.

In a clinical setting the physician may be a regular member of the interdisciplinary team, meeting with other professionals in round table discussions and contributing to the decision-making process. In the public school setting, the doctor provides information pertinent to the child's programming in school activities, verifies medication dosages, describes symptoms that should be anticipated, and makes a prognosis of the child's disorder.

The doctor-patient relationship is built on trust and the giving and sharing of information. It is facilitated by skillful interviewing techniques (Battle, 1975). The interview should be directed by a life plan, which lists the milestones to be encountered as the child grows. It is concerned with the shelter, nurture, and protection of all family members, and financial and security needs, as well as the special, personal needs and concerns of the family. Such a plan can help ensure comprehensive, coordinated, and continuous medical support (Battle, 1975).

The physician plays a crucial role in the effective planning for a handicapped child. He often has the trust of the family and has gotten to know the child over a period of years. Some of the questions asked of the physician may be somewhat out of his realm — educational, counseling, and vocational questions, for example.

The educator can share information with the physician, ultimately benefitting the patient. The teacher should encourage the physician to engage in comprehensive care. The teacher might also provide the doctor with a form to guide his discussions with the child's family, urging the parents to plan for certain crisis periods. The physician should note on this form the plans the family has already made and the problem areas that are currently being considered and resolved. Educators can also help by maintaining accurate records of the child's behavior in school. These records may influence treatment of hyperactivity or epilepsy and/or indicate changes in the child's health. Behavioral observations are best communicated in writing (providing that parental permission is first obtained).

Pless, Satterwhite, and VanVechten (1976) recommend that one physician assume the role of medical manager for the student with a variety of needs requiring the services of several medical specialists. In cases of chronic disease or disability, the managing physician helps to prevent the fragmentation of medical services.

Dentist

The dental needs of the physically handicapped child differ from those of the non-handicapped child primarily in regard to the approach, rather than in the specific services to be provided. The special services for these children are often related to their medication, e.g., dilantin, which may cause gingival problems, or to structural tooth abnormalities, e.g., tooth problems associated with cleft palate (Johnston and Magrab, 1976).

The teacher may observe poor dental hygiene, improper diet habits, or malocclusion that suggest a need for the child to see a pedodontist (pediatric dentist).

The dentist's examination includes a dental history taken during a conversation with the family. During this interview the dentist usually stresses to the parents the need for good preventive dental care and diets that do not stimulate the development of plaque. He may also suggest variations on normal toothbrushing techniques as required by the child's handicapping condition.

The dentist's clinical examination is conducted in such a way as to produce as little anxiety as possible. Social reinforcement and other behavior modification techniques, as well as gentle, unrushed persuasion are incorporated into the preliminary clinical examination. During the examination, the dentist explains what he will be doing inside the child's mouth, what he *is* doing, and tells the child what sensations to expect. X-rays are a necessary part of the examination to locate extra teeth, teeth that have not yet erupted, and to examine the growth of the jaws and other oral tissues.

Physical Therapist

Physical therapy for physically handicapped children originated in rehabilitative efforts for adults with acquired injuries or damage to nerves, muscles, or bones. The habilitative efforts of physical therapists are directed toward individuals with injuries to an immature and rapidly changing nervous system (Johnston and Magrab, 1976).

The physical therapist is concerned primarily with posture and locomotion. Posture refers not only to standing and sitting, but also to the positions of the limbs and trunk in isolation, as well as in relationship to other body parts. The physical therapist is trained to evaluate the physical ability and development of the patient: her education covers muscular and locomotion development and related disorders. Tone, movement, strength, balance, and coordination all depend on muscle efficiency, and can be impaired by delays in development or neurological interference.

A licensed physical therapist practices under the direction of a physician. In cases involving developmental disorders, she may be one of the first team members to become involved with the child.

This therapist contributes much of value to the interdisciplinary team. The proper functioning of one body part may be related to the proper positioning of another. For example, freedom of movement of the hands promotes eye-hand coordination, and the correct positioning of the chest, neck, and head to control respiration facilitates speech production.

The physical therapy techniques in Figures 9-2, 9-3, 9-4, and 9-5 are adapted from the work of Finnie (1975).

Occupational Therapist

The occupational therapist (OT) and physical therapist (PT), both of whom are concerned with efficient muscular movement, usually work closely together. Some rather arbitrary distinctions have been made in the past; for example, PTs are "big muscle people" and OTs are "small muscle people," or PTs work with lower extremities and gait training, while OTs work with upper extremities and hand functioning. Currently, this role differentiation is not quite so distinct, and PTs and OTs may share responsibilities or delineate them according to the needs of clients.

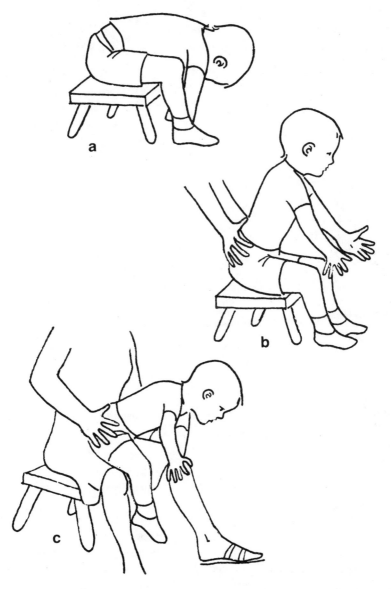

Figure 9-2a. A *floppy* child, when sitting, is unable to raise his head and straighten his back. *b*. Placing both hands firmly (pushing down) over the lumbar area (lower back) with thumbs at either side of the spine gives the child a point of fixation and helps him to raise his head and straighten his spine. *c*. This can also be done with the child sitting on your lap. Finnie (1975), reprinted with permission of E. P. Dutton and Wm. Heineman Publishers.

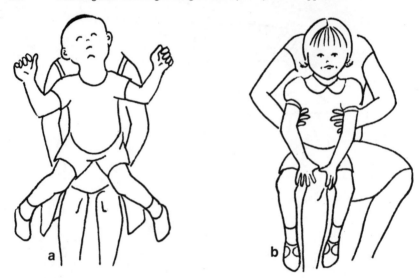

Figure 9-3a. Many cerebral palsied children have a tendency to straighten their hips and turn their legs in, even when sitting. Parents are advised in such cases to sit the child astride their laps. One should realize, however, that this may provide too broad a base on which the child can sit. The sketch shows the exaggerated position of a child trying to sit on too broad a base. Note the effect this has on the rest of his posture. b. The narrower base keeps the legs apart and the hips turned out. The arms and head are controlled from the shoulders, which are lifted and turned in. Finnie (1975), reprinted with permission of E. P. Dutton and Wm. Heineman Publishers.

Three special responsibilities that an OT usually assumes in programs for physically handicapped children are:

1. OTs guide the development of skills in activities of daily living. Feeding, dressing, and toileting are among their areas of concern.
2. OTs develop adaptive equipment (such as splints or special spoons) that facilitate these activities.
3. OTs are trained to provide sensorimotor integration therapy. They evaluate the way in which the handicapped child receives and synthesizes information from his environment and provide exercises to help the child increase his efficiency in perceptual tasks.

As the educational and societal turnabout from the "caretaker" philosophy results in the incorporation of more moderate-to-severely handicapped children into public schools, physical and occupational therapy services will be required (Anderson, Greer, and McFadden, 1976). Physical and occupational therapists, who are licensed by their own professional organizations, generally consider themselves adequately certified to deal with children. Schools, however, demand that professionals who work directly with

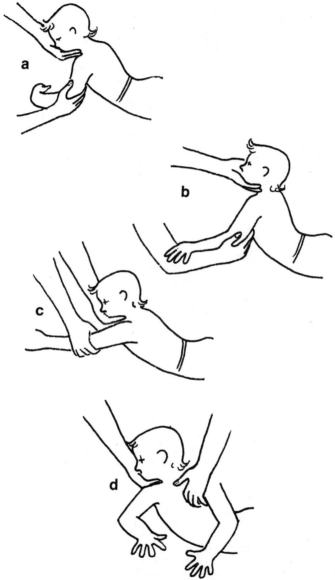

Figure 9-4a. The correct way to control the child so you can put him flat on his tummy. At the same time as you lift, turn the head and start to bring the arm forward. *b*. Turn the shoulder out as you lift and straighten the arm — your point of control is over the elbow joint. *c*. Holding the head up, keep the arm straight and in the air (as illustrated) until it no longer feels heavy and does not press down at the shoulder, and then place the arm on the floor. Follow the same procedure with the other arm. Do not let the head bend forward. *d*. If the arms are not too stiff, lifting the shoulder up and out with rotation of the trunk may be sufficient to bring the arm forward. Finnie (1975), reprinted with permission of E. P. Dutton and Wm. Heineman Publishers.

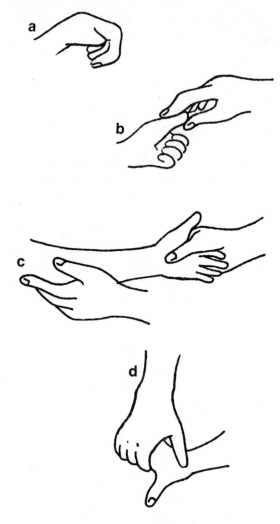

Figure 9-5a. A typical hand of a spastic child; the hand is clenched with the wrist bent and the thumb held across the palm of the hand. b. The incorrect way to straighten the wrist and fingers — by pulling on the thumb in this way, the wrist and fingers bend more; there is also the danger of damaging the thumb joint. c. By first straightening and turning out the arm, it is then much easier to straighten the fingers and the thumb. d. The correct grasp to hold the fingers and wrist straight. Finnie (1975), reprinted with permission of E. P. Dutton and Wm. Heineman Publishers.

children be state certified teachers. This is an issue that must be resolved (Anderson, Greer, and McFadden, 1976).

Speech Clinician

Speech clinicians and speech pathologists provide therapy to children who demonstrate disorders of speech and/or language. The role of the speech clinician is firmly established in public schools; she provides itinerant services to children who have been evaluated and, after a due-process procedure, enrolled in a regularly scheduled treatment program.

The primary role of the speech clinician is to determine that a disorder of speech or language actually does exist. The therapist identifies those factors that will interfere with remediation once the disorder has been verified. Interferents include poor motor control, the need for corrective dental work, or hearing problems.

Remediation programs for articulation problems are individualized according to the disorders of the student. Articulation therapy is a major concern of the speech therapist and constitutes the majority of the workload of the speech clinician in public schools. However, the student with an expressive or receptive language problem presents a greater challenge to the speech clinician because these problems are potentially far more detrimental to future learning (Johnston and Magrab, 1976). Special problems within the physically handicapped population include language delay, dysarthria (interference with motor production), aphasia (difficulty in interpreting or expressing language), and voice disorders.

The correction of speech and language problems is accomplished more quickly when those who deal with the child on a regular basis provide consistent models and reinforcement of appropriate sounds and language usage, and encourage the child to express his ideas verbally.

Interaction with Therapists

Interaction among professionals improves the quality of programming. The student with a speech disorder, for example, may need to improve his control of the breath stream. Working together, the speech clinician, occupational therapist, and teacher can outline a series of school-related activities to reinforce the prescribed therapy. Many cerebral palsied children demonstrate inadequate vegetative functions (i.e., sucking, blowing, chewing, and swallowing). Such children generally have articulation problems and require the services of a speech clinician. Because there is a one-to-one correspondence between articulation and the vegetative functions (Kamalshile, 1973), as one problem improves, so does the other. Classroom activities that incorporate the techniques of both the speech and occupational therapists enhance learning. In case of delay in the development of vegetative functions, for instance, art activities (blowing paint across paper) or competitive games (blowing a ping-pong ball across a table top marked with masking tape to represent a tennis court) can supplement the therapy.

Each therapy discipline, be it speech, occupational, or physical therapy, tends to focus on (and occasionally isolate) the avenue of development that is particularly relevant to its own specialized techniques (Levitt and Miller, 1973). Students benefit when their therapies act upon one another. Because each therapist is concerned with the coordination of movement and perceptual development, it follows that their individual efforts will often overlap. The speech therapist should not only treat speech defects, but also handle the child in a way that facilitates the correction of motor defects. The physical therapist should broaden her approach and be aware of her responsibility to stimulate speech and language, as well as to treat the physical handicap (Levitt and Miller, 1973).

The special educator and the occupational and physical therapists can examine the demands of the scholastic environment and make appropriate joint decisions concerning the preparation of either the student or, in cases involving more debilitating handicapping conditions, the classroom for maximum independent learning.

Social reinforcement (Coffman, 1973) and behavior modification (Johnston and Magrab, 1976) are techniques employed in the therapist-client relationship to promote motivation. The teacher can provide the therapists with school-related activities and information about the content of subject areas being stressed in the class and those areas of classwork in which the student shows strength. This information can then be used to plan therapy tasks, incorporated into conversations during therapy, and reinforced by therapists. In this way the teacher and therapists utilize a team approach to therapeutic education.

Punwar (1976) asserts that motor evaluation could be improved by greater communication among professionals with similar interests. Lewko's (1976) data, compiled from responses to a questionnaire distributed to occupational and physical therapists and special and physical educators, indicates a need for these four major fields to define an interdisciplinary body of knowledge pertaining to motor evaluation as well as to help formulate guidelines for the construction of more appropriate tests than were available at the time of his study for the measurement of motor development.

Concerned therapists and educators, through an understanding of the talents and skills of each other's respective professions and cooperative and joint education and therapy, become skilled collaborators. The leadership among these collaborators shifts according to the issue under discussion at any given time. For example, the teacher should have the most to say when the teaching of reading is being considered; the PT should be the leader in discussions of seating posture — but all members should listen, contribute, share ideas, and make final decisions together.

Parents

It is fitting to include the parents of a handicapped child as valuable member of the interdisciplinary team. If a professional is one who has expertise in a given field, then the parents, with their intimate knowledge of their child, certainly qualify.

Some professionals may be reluctant to include parents in staff meetings because of the emotional and, perhaps, less objective point of view inherent in the ego-involved relationship of parent and child. However, professionals can help parents regain a lost sense of integrity and competence. Early in the process of evaluating a child, parents must be given a chance to have some control, and to learn that they are capable and, given the right support, can deal with the situation (Editorial. *Exceptional Parent*, 1978).

The parent can contribute valuable information to interdisciplinary meetings at the time of the initiation of evaluation (when questions are being listed for which answers will later be sought) and at the summary meeting (when those answers are given). The parents' understanding of the evaluation is essential. A parent suggests that the professional must "put it on the line because otherwise the parents will fantasize. Without facts your false hopes take over" (Editorial. *Exceptional Parent*, 1978).

Too often, programs for handicapped children are designed from the vantage point of clinical assessment and educational expectation, with scant regard for the child's family circumstances. In professionals' diligence to help the child, not only are the rights, feelings, and appreciation of parents neglected, but the enormous task that confronts all parents, — coping with the needs of the total family — is frequently ignored. Emphasis is concentrated on the isolated handicapped child, rather than on the handicapped child as one member of a family unit, all of whom have equal rights and diverse needs (Hewitt, 1977).

TEAMWORK IN THE SCHOOLS

The interdisciplinary process works approximately the same way in the public school as in the clinical setting. Instead of being representatives of many different professions, the school team is comprised of educators, all of whom have different expectations, points of view, and special interests. The interdisciplinary school team parallels the clinical team with regard to the roles assumed by the team members. Dembo (1964) addresses the communication problems inherent with different points of view, and states that the role played by each participant influences his or her perspective of a problem — and seldom do any two people look at an issue in the same way. For example, the special education teacher's perspective of the student's schooling differs from that of the regular classroom teacher, the school psychologist, or the district supervisor. Therefore, to ensure that interdisciplinary discussions will be fruitful, it is essential that all team members be aware that different points of view are represented, recognize the objective insights and individual strengths of others because of these different vantage points, and agree that student benefit is the goal of any discussion.

Teamwork in the school is obviously vital to provide the student with the greatest possible number of experiences and opportunities and to expand his capabilities and to enrich his school life. Because of the frequently diverse needs of a physically handicapped child, more than one educator generally works with a student and more than one point of view is usually expressed in regard to the various issues that arise: compromise and harmony of purpose among the district faculty members is therefore essential.

Student planning sessions include the classroom teacher, the special education and physical education teachers, the itinerant teacher of the hearing or visually impaired, the speech therapist or clinician, the social worker, and the school nurse, psychologist, and principal. It is usually worthwhile to include the parents and, in some cases, the student in early program planning.

In group meetings, because various points of view are represented, it is essential to establish a common goal quickly (Sherif and Sherif, 1969; Worchel, Andreoli, and Folger, 1973). When all group members agree on a common goal, information, ideas, and concerns can be shared and examined in reference to this goal and a program of direct, purposeful action can be formulated.

Practical, efficient action is more likely to be planned when the interdisciplinary team approach is incorporated in groups of 2, 3, 4, or 8. Although not all meetings will involve conference tables, copious notetaking, and the preparation of final reports, all sessions, regardless of size, should have some common features:

1. an understanding of the meeting's purpose
2. a leader
3. a decision — a plan of action or point of closure
4. a follow-up — a time and method agreed upon for evaluation of the plan of action

Teacher to Teacher

The special education teacher is often sought by other teachers to offer an opinion, advice, or just to listen helpfully to their frustrations. When a potentially harmful situation arises involving a physically handicapped student, the special educator should be willing to take the initiative and seek a solution; others are often reluctant to do so.

A problem (e.g., scheduling conflicts, lack of suitable teaching materials, inflexible and/or inappropriate class activities) may first be revealed in informal conversation between teachers at lunch, in the hallway, or in the teacher's lounge. These first comments may be vaguely humorous, or slightly sarcastic, or wearily stated. The teacher of the physically handicapped must always be alert to the early symptoms of teacher distress and quickly determine the best method for confronting the surfacing issue.

Sometimes a direct approach is best. Asking the other teacher to explain the particular problem in more detail or agreeing that the issue is indeed a difficult one may be immediate, direct response choices.

Occasionally, the special education teacher may deem it necessary to make note of the comment, mentally explore some helpful suggestions, and, later, drop in on the other teacher for a private discussion of the problem. This approach might be termed the postponed, planned response.

A third way of responding to issues is indirect: the special education teacher decides to relay the information to an individual who is able to respond more appropriately. Not infrequently, an issue may be better resolved by a member of the special services team other than the special educator.

Regardless of the response method deemed appropriate in a given situation, vital components of all conversations with others are:

listening to what is said
understanding what is said
respecting the speaker's point of view (Benjamin, 1969).

Good team members respond to requests for information with pertinent, reliable data and consider suggestions made by others when solving problems and making decisions.

A decision should be the goal of a problem-solving conversation. A decision is not always formalized by being typed, duplicated, and distributed. A decision may more often be a plan of action informally agreed upon by those involved. As the catalyst, the special educator should be certain that everyone concerned clearly understands the plan of action proposed as a culmination of the discussion.

"Then we'll talk about this on Wednesday at the faculty meeting."
"OK, just send him to my room when you're ready to start the test."
"I'll call Amy [the school psychologist] and see when she can
come over to talk with us."

Teacher to Parent

The teacher of physically handicapped students must keep in mind Hewitt's (1977) caution: too often, in the concern for education, the needs and desires of the family are overlooked. Good communication between teacher and parents increases the likelihood that a mutual goal is established and that a working partnership is possible to facilitate the attainment of that goal.

Parents of disabled children, particularly of those children who are mainstreamed into public schools, have additional reasons for concern with regard to their child's social development, because social adjustment and academic progress often go hand in hand (Freund and Elardo, 1978). It is not uncommon for the physically handicapped student to have trouble getting along with his classmates and great difficulty in interacting effectively with his peers. Manifestations of social immaturity (Freund and Elardo, 1978) should be discussed with the parents, and a plan of action should be recommended for both home and school to reduce behavior that inhibits growth.

The teacher might suggest a behavior modification approach in the home. For example, rewarding a chore done correctly (or, if not done well, at least done conscientiously) increases the possibility of the task being done well the next time. The child should also be shown the consequences of immature behavior and given suggestions for alternative ways of behaving under similar circumstances (Freund and Elardo, 1978).

Parents can be given suggestions for techniques to use in resolving conflicts with their children. Robin et al. (1976) suggest that parents should be given the following steps to follow in a conflict situation: 1) define the problem, 2) list alternative solutions, 3) evaluate the listed solutions, and 4) plan a way in which to implement the best of the possible solutions.

When parents come to the school to discuss child-related problems and/or the child's progress, the teacher should do a little preplanning, incorporating the suggestions of Losen and Diament (1978): The number of staff members involved in the meeting should be a bare minimum so as not to overwhelm the parents, and the topics to be discussed should be delineated so the parents' time is not wasted discussing issues not related to their child. It is possible that during these meetings the parents may feel that the educators are insensitive to their needs and/or problems. Dembo (1964) addresses this problem and suggests that the roles played by parents and professionals do indeed involve different points of view:

> It is one thing to know that *another person* has a handicapped child and quite another thing to be a *parent* of a handicapped child. Characteristically, the professional is in the position of an outsider, and as an outsider he looks at the relationship of the parent to the handicapped children from a distance.

This problem is not unique to parents of the handicapped; it is a problem that exists in all professional-client relationships (Dembo, 1964).

Sharing relevant information about the child's educational progress is effectively handled through the use of instructional objectives found in the IEP of the student and the daily lesson plans of the teacher. Markel and

Greenbaum (1974) suggest the use of objectives in all conversations reporting student progress. It is also suggested that the teacher consider giving the parent home-related objectives that are relevant to the changes desired in the home or in the classroom and that can be achieved through the use of homework and practice in skill areas. Objectives are a useful guide in the home for the child who needs language stimulation (Jelinek, 1975) or sensorimotor stimulation (Tyler and Kahn, 1976) and in any other phase of home-school coordinated efforts. Objectives also provide structure and security to the parents, who may be feeling a bit apprehensive about the new techniques they are using, and can assure the teacher that the parents are making skill-building efforts at home that are similar to hers at school.

The teacher need not feel alone in working with parents: much support and assistance are readily available from other agencies and associations outside the school. As an advocate for the child and the family, the teacher of the physically handicapped should be aware of the national, state, and local resources available in the team approach to improved education.

VOLUNTEER AGENCIES AND ORGANIZATIONS

The teacher can obtain new information regarding available services, resources to facilitate sharing this information, and guidance in various aspects of the therapeutic educational program by contacting advocacy organizations. The majority of organizations that are briefly described in this section have local or state units as well as national headquarters. The teacher can contact the national office for the address of a nearby unit.

The teacher might wish to compile a resource book containing the addresses and service descriptions of volunteer, community, and government agencies for quick reference for classroom and family needs.

According to the American Medical Association (1975), volunteer health agencies share the following common features:

1. They are non-profit.
2. They are organized on a national and state (and often local) level.
3. They are composed of lay and professional people.
4. They are dedicated to the prevention, alleviation, and cure of a particular disease, disability, or group of diseases and disabilities.
5. They are supported by voluntary contributions.
6. Their expenditures are for education, research, and service programs relevant to the disease in focus.

The Alexander Graham Bell Association for the Deaf, Inc.

The Alexander Graham Bell Association for the Deaf, Inc., has three separate divisions to provide specialized information and service for its members.

The American Organization for the Education of the Hearing Impaired (AOEHI) is comprised of qualified educators who are concerned with improving auditory-oral teaching for all learning impaired children. The International Parents' Organization (IPO) is comprised of thousands of parents of hearing impaired children, working singly or in local groups to expand the educational, social, and vocational options available to their children. Members of the Oral Deaf Adults Section (ODAS) are hearing impaired adults who regularly use speech, speechreading, and residual hearing in their social and business contacts.

The Alexander Graham Bell Association collects and disseminates information to parents, educators, students, and the general public. The Volta Bureau Library is one of the world's largest collections on deafness. This association advocates maximum opportunities for all hearing impaired children to learn to speak, to use their residual hearing, and to be integrated into the educational and vocational mainstream.

Asthma and Allergy Foundation of America

The Asthma and Allergy Foundation of America was established to unite the public, the medical profession, research scientists, and public health workers in a campaign to increase our present knowledge of the causes of, and the best treatment for, asthma and the allergic diseases. This foundation provides research and scholarship grants, both to medical students to encourage specialization in the allergy field, and to non-allergist physicians to enable them to obtain a basic understanding of allergies. It provides information and educational materials to the public through booklets, audio-visual materials, the community activities of local subsidiary chapters, and response to inquiries.

National Society for the Prevention of Blindness, Inc.

The National Society for the Prevention of Blindness, Inc. is committed to the eradication of preventable blindness. The society provides the public with sound information about vision and visual disorders and eye health, injuries, disease, and protection. Brochures and films are available at minimal or no cost.

The National Easter Seal Society for Crippled Children and Adults

This society is recognized as the pioneer organization in identifying the needs of physically handicapped persons and in providing rehabilitative services. As an advocate on behalf of equal rights for persons with disabilities, the Easter Seal Society contacts federal agencies and provides legislators with information on the needs and problems of the handicapped. The Easter Seal Research Foundation sponsors grants to finance investigation into those fields that directly relate to enhancing the physical, psychological, and social well-being of persons with handicaps. Scholarships are offered to

HI! I'M CLAIRE HUCKEL

SEVEN-YEAR-OLD PHILADELPHIA MISS IS 1979 NATIONAL EASTER SEAL CHILD

How do you describe Claire Huckel, 7, of suburban Philadelphia, the National Easter Seal Child for 1979? Pretty and cute? Sugar and spice and everything nice? Handicapped? Claire is partially handicapped due to cerebral palsy. She is still pretty and nice, able to enjoy childhood to the fullest, and is a living testimonial of the value of early diagnosis and treatment of a disabling condition. At age two, Claire was enrolled in the Bucks County Easter Seal Center, Levittown, Pennsylvania, to begin a program of therapy and speech and language stimulation. After attending the Easter Seal preschool for three years, she attended regular kindergarten. Today, she is a first-grader in the Pen Ryn School, Cornwells Heights. As the National Easter Seal Child, Claire is representative of the many thousands of children and adults helped by the nationwide Easter Seal rehabilitation network.

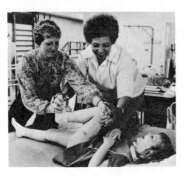

Claire is a happy child, doing most of the things a seven-year-old likes to do. She helps her mother with meal preparations and helps care for brother Charles, 5. She is learning to swim and shares the family interest in sports. She loves to act and sing and has performed in school plays. Claire has been taking dancing lessons and has appeared in recitals with her class.

Claire's mother has played an important role in the youngster's therapy program. While Easter Seal therapists work with Claire at the treatment center, Mrs. Charles Huckel, under their guidance, works at home to keep her daughter's coordination and muscular strength as efficient as possible.

1979 EASTER SEAL CAMPAIGN
MARCH 1 - APRIL 15

THE NATIONAL EASTER SEAL SOCIETY
FOR CRIPPLED CHILDREN AND ADULTS
2023 W. Ogden Ave., Chicago, Il 60612

Figure 9-6. The Easter Seals Poster Child helps inform the public about physical disability.

doctors, physical, occupational, and speech therapists, educators, and others for the advancement of professional training.

Epilepsy Foundation of America

The Epilepsy Foundation of America, a national agency for people with epilepsy, sponsors a wide variety of programs and activities. This foundation provides educational materials and information on epilepsy, employment, housing, transportation, and health services, and supports research.

There are many special programs sponsored by this foundation. *School Alert* is designed to improve the school environment of young epileptics by providing materials for students, teachers, and others. The program includes pamphlets, posters, lesson plans, and films. The *Epilepsy Youth Association* is concerned with fund raising through youth events. The Association works with local chapters to disseminate information enabling young people to organize service projects and peer group activities.

National Hemophilia Foundation

The National Hemophilia Foundation seeks solutions to the various problems associated with hemophilia. The foundation maintains the belief that hemophilia itself is not a handicapping condition, providing that the hemophiliac has ready access to a program of comprehensive care, including sufficient dosages of the "clotting factor." Aspects of the foundation's efforts include: helping the hemophiliac and his family; seeking the eventual care and elimination of the disease; and effectively using our national blood resources.

American Lung Association (Christmas Seal People)

The American Lung Association is primarily an educational organization with a twofold approach: 1)Public education to assist the general populace in the prevention of lung disease, in obtaining effective treatment, and in learning to live with disabled breathing. 2) Professional education, directed toward the preparation of knowledgeable medical care teams equipped to provide comprehensive and continuous care for all lung disease populations. Printed materials, films, and resource materials are available on such topics as emphysema, chronic bronchitis, air pollution, smoking and health, tuberculosis, and other lung diseases.

National Multiple Sclerosis Society

The National Multiple Sclerosis Society is the only national voluntary health agency engaged in research efforts to find the cause, prevention, and cure for multiple sclerosis (MS). The society's second major purpose is to help, in any possible way, the estimated 500,000 Americans with MS and their families as well. The assistance provided may include information, counseling and referral services, the loan of medical equipment, the training and placement of volunteers in service to patients, group activities, and recreational programs.

National Paraplegia Foundation

The three objectives of the National Paraplegia Foundation are:

1. to encourage basic scientific research to liberate paraplegics from their wheelchairs

2. to facilitate and support the best medical care and rehabilitation possible for paraplegics
3. to help paraplegic individuals achieve their own personal goals

To achieve these objectives, this foundation sponsors conferences and seminars, makes small incentive grants for research, and promotes and facilitates the sharing of information. The foundation advocates the coordination of efforts of persons who provide rehabilitative services and medical care and treatment for paraplegics. Through personal contacts, the Foundation provides information on self-help devices. In addition, the National Paraplegia Foundation educates the public with regard to the needs of paraplegics and attempts to motivate paraplegics themselves to set high (but realistic) personal goals.

United Cerebral Palsy Associations, Inc.

The goal of the United Cerebral Palsy Associations, Inc. is twofold: to prevent cerebral palsy, and to help disabled people shape their lives by their abilities rather than by their disabilities. This organization sponsors scientific research and professional training, provides direct services to individuals, assumes the role of advocate for disabled persons in matters of civil and legal rights, and seeks to educate the public about cerebral palsy.

The American Heart Association

The purpose of the American Heart Association is to gather and to disseminate information about the causes, diagnosis, prevention, and treatment of diseases and disorders of the heart and circulatory system. Cardiopulmonary resuscitation programs, support of research projects, blood pressure screenings, and diet education for teenagers are among the activities sponsored by affiliated state chapters.

The American Cancer Society

The American Cancer Society's fight against cancer involves many activities in various fields, including research, professional and public education, service, and rehabilitation. The society states proudly that practically every adult and home in the United States is reached by word of mouth, the printed page, radio, and television with life-saving messages on early detection and diagnosis, prompt treatment, and cancer prevention. The Society's long-range goal — the total control of cancer — can be realized only to the extent that research provides the answers. Therefore, to encourage research efforts, the Society gathers scientists (professionals conducting research studies at universities, medical schools, and laboratories in many areas of medicine and science) twice a year to share the results of their research endeavors.

Muscular Dystrophy Association

The Muscular Dystrophy Association is a dedicated partnership between scientists and concerned citizens aimed at conquering the neuromuscular diseases that affect thousands of Americans. The basic philosophy of the Association, that there are no incurable diseases, only diseases for which no treatments have yet been found, extends to the muscle-destroying disorders, which vary in hereditary pattern, age of onset, initial muscles attacked, and rate of progression. For example, myositis, myasthenia gravis, metabolic diseases, and peripheral neuropathies are all concerns of this group. The Association works to combat such diseases through basic and applied scientific investigation, programs of patient services and clinical care, and widespread professional and public education.

The efforts of volunteers and the salaried administrators of the non-profit associations have contributed greatly to the public's growing acceptance of the rights, needs, and feelings of the physically handicapped. Their publications, borrowed or inexpensively rented films and multi-media materials, brochures and posters, and compiled lesson-plan formats for specific programs are valuable aids for the teacher of the physically handicapped.

GOVERNMENTAL AGENCIES

Various programs on both the state and federal levels are available to citizens with crippling and debilitating disorders. The funds allocated for these programs enable families at all economic levels to obtain appropriate care — medical and therapeutic — for chronic problems, which can often be financially devastating. State and county departments of government agencies provide information to teachers to assist them in making students and their families aware of available services as well as the procedures for contacting the appropriate agencies. As an advocate of the physically handicapped, the teacher should be on the mailing list of the local office of every appropriate agency and should maintain a file of pertinent information to share with others. Two very important agencies that teachers should know about are the Crippled Children's Service and Vocational Rehabilitation.

Crippled Children's Section of the State Department of Health

Crippled Children's programs are funded through Title V funds of the Social Security Act and through state appropriations. The purpose of a crippled children's program is to provide diagnostic and treatment services for those crippled children deemed eligible. Eligibility for such services is based upon diagnosis, length and cost of treatment as related to the family's income, medical indebtedness, and the availability of financial resources.

Referrals to the local health department may be made by anyone in the county of the child's residence. Any child from birth to 21 years of age suspected of having a handicapping condition that is within the scope of the Crippled Children's Program qualifies for a diagnostic evaluation without charge. The eligible diagnostic categories include:

diseases of bones and joints
hearing abnormalities and aural pathology
certain congenital abnormalities, (i.e., cleft palate and lip, heart conditions, myelomeningocele, and renal conditions)
epilepsy
burns
rheumatic fever
trauma
central nervous system disorders
cystic fibrosis
diabetes mellitus and certain other metabolic disorders
hemophilia
sickle cell disorders

State Departments of Vocational Rehabilitation

State vocational rehabilitation offices are funded by Public Law 94–230, the Rehabilitation Act Extension of 1976. Anyone may apply directly to a vocational rehabilitation area office for evaluation of himself, a friend, or a relative. Referrals are also made by doctors, hospitals, schools, and other state agencies.

Diagnostic testing determines whether the individual qualifies as handicapped. Counseling services are available to define employment goals for the handicapped. The realization of these goals may necessitate physical restoration and training, aid in obtaining a job, and on-the-job evaluations by a vocational counselor — all at no cost to the handicapped individual.

To be eligible for these services, the individual must have a physical or mental disability that makes him unsuitable for employment. However, there must also be a reasonable likelihood that he can be prepared for employment. The diagnostic evaluation can also determine whether a person with a speech impairment or dyslexia is eligible for these services.

PROFESSIONAL ASSOCIATIONS

Two influential professional associations that provide a variety of services for the physically handicapped, their families, and their teachers are The American Association for the Education of the Severely/Profoundly Handicapped (AAESPH) and the Council for Exceptional Children (CEC). These associations were formed to facilitate communication among professionals, to establish standards for education, treatment, and care of the handicapped, to function as advocate groups, and to develop and disseminate training packets for educators and parents.

AAESPH's orientation is toward those concerns arising from the needs of the severely/profoundly handicapped. CEC deals with all handicapping conditions: divisions of CEC are oriented according to the specific handicapping conditions. The division of the CEC that is of particular interest here is the Division of the Physically Handicapped, Hospitalized, and Homebound (DOPHHH). Through seminars, regional and national meetings, and publications, these professional associations communicate recent noteworthy programs, research and activities, and in this way contribute greatly to the improved education of handicapped children and adults.

SUMMARY

The interdisciplinary approach is recommended in the educational planning for physically handicapped students. Special education teachers interact with physicians, dentists, physical and occupational therapists, speech and language therapists, parents, and other teachers and educators with special interests. The advocacy role of the teacher is demonstrated through the gathering and sharing with others of information about services provided by volunteer health organizations and government agencies. For the teacher to be an effective communicator and to share helpful information, she must first have an understanding of the special skills and knowledge of other professionals and be a capable, willing, and effective leader when necessary.

LITERATURE CITED

American Medical Association (AMA) 1975. Cited in American Cancer Society — A Factbook For The Medical and Related Professions. The American Cancer Society, New York.

Anderson, R. M., Greer, J. G., and McFadden, S. C. 1976. Providing for the severely handicapped: A case for competency-based preparation of occupational therapists. Am. J. Occup. Ther. 30:10, 640–645.

Battle, C. U. 1975. Symposium on behavioral pediatrics: Chronic physical disease. Pediatr. Clin. North Am. 22:525–531.

Benjamin, A. 1969. The Helping Interview. 2nd Ed. Houghton-Mifflin, Boston.

Coffman, D. A. 1973. Effects of social reinforcement in physical therapy. Doctoral dissertation, University of Missouri-Columbia. Dissert. Abstr. Internat. 2298-B.

Dembo, T. 1964. Sensitivity of one person to another. Rehabil. Lit. 25:8, 231–235.

Editorial. 1978. Parent-professional communication: Practical suggestions. Except. Parent 8:2, 15–18.

Finnie, N. R. 1975. Handling the Young Cerebral Palsied Child at Home. B. P. Dutton, New York.

Freund, J., and Elardo, R. 1978. Developing parenting skills. Except. Parent 8:3, 8-9.

Hewitt, H. A. 1977. Early intervention: A guidance program for parents of handicapped children. Except. Child 24:1, 12-17.

Jelinek, J. 1975. The role of the parent in a language development program. J. Research Dev. Educ. 8:2, 14-23.

Johnston, R. B., and Magrab, P. R. (eds.). 1976. Developmental Disorders: Assessment, Treatment, Education. University Park Press, Baltimore.

Kamalshile, J. 1973. Speech problems in cerebral palsied children. Paper prepared for the Vth. Annual All India Speech and Hearing Conference, 1973.

Levitt, S., and Miller, C. 1973. The inter-relationship of speech therapy and physiotherapy in children with neurodevelopmental disorders. Dev. Med. Child Neurol. 15:188-193.

Lewko, J. H. 1976. Current practices in evaluating motor behavior of disabled children. Am. J. Occup. Ther. 30:413-419.

Losen, S. M., and Diament, B. 1978. Parent involvement in school planning. Except. Parent 8:4, 19-22.

Markel, G., and Greenbaum, J. 1974. How teachers, parents and administrators can use objectives and feedback in programs for special students. Paper presented at the Annual International Convention of the Council for Exceptional Children (ERIC Reproduction Service No. ED 133 977.) April, New York.

Pless, I. B., Satterwhite, B., and VanVechten, D. 1976. Chronic illness in childhood: A regional survey of care. Pediatrics 58:37-46.

Punwar, A. 1976. A commentary on Dr. Lewko's article. Am. J. Occup. Ther. 30:420-421.

Robin, A. L., Kent, R., O'Leary, E. D., Foster, S., and Prinz, R. 1976. An approach to teaching parents and adolescents problem solving communication skills. Paper presented at the Annual Meeting of the Eastern Psychological Association. (ERIC Reproduction Service No. ED 128 679.) April, New York.

Sherif, M., and Sherif, C. 1969. Social Psychology, 3rd. Ed. Harper and Row, New York.

Tyler, N. B., and Kahn, N. 1976. A home-treatment program. Am. J. Occup. Ther. 30:7, 437-440.

Worchel, S., Andreoli, V. A., and Folger, R. 1973. The effect of types of previous interaction and success of combined effort on intergroup hostility. Canada Council of National Science Foundation (ERIC Reproduction Service No. 116 086.) Ottawa, Canada.

Zweig, H. H. 1975. Interdisciplinary team functioning: A case team approach to habilitation in a residential facility for the mentally retarded. Willowbrook Development Center, June (ERIC Reproduction Service No. 112 615.) Staten Island, N.Y.

10

ISSUES IN
ADVOCACY

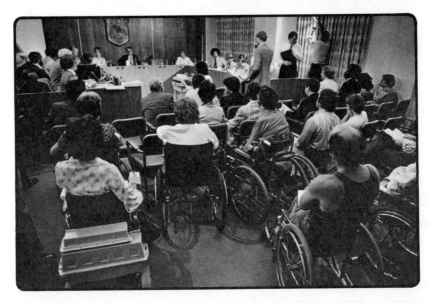

Figure 10-1. Physically handicapped citizens confront the Charlotte, N.C., city council about the accessibility of government services. Photo courtesy of the *Charlotte Observer*.

Teachers of physically handicapped children and young people have a special responsibility to prepare their students for the future and to enable them to participate freely in age-appropriate independent life experiences. Not only must persons with physical handicaps face and overcome those problems associated with their physical limitations; they must also deal with man-made environmental barriers and public prejudices that shut the doors to full participation in the mainstream of life. The teacher, then, must undertake the responsibility of looking beyond the classroom and working with handicapped people and their families to eliminate these obstacles. When the teacher accepts and acts on this responsibility, she is acting as an advocate for the physically handicapped.

This chapter defines the role of the advocate and discusses several major issues in advocacy: access; travel and transportation; alternative living arrangements; and love, sex, and marriage. (For a discussion of the additional advocacy issues of employment and recreation, see Chapter 4.) At the end of this chapter are some suggestions for ways in which teachers and other concerned persons can help to effect much needed change.

The aim of advocacy is to ensure that every physically handicapped person has the best possible chance to experience this credo:

Each disabled person deserves:
- Love, honor and freedom from stigma;
- The celebration of being special;
- A life-sharing family, home, and nurturing support;
- A community of concern and friendship;
- Economic security, health, and the full benefits of modern technology with a varied continuum of services;
- Freedom from the threat of injury due to pollution of food, air, water, and the earth on which we dwell;
- The opportunity to grow, to learn, to choose, to work, to rest, to play, to be nourished, and to experience well-being;
- Solitude when needed;
- Space, comfort, and beauty to discover himself/herself;
- The power to improve his/her environment;
- Justice
- The dignity of risk, joy, and the growth of spirit;
- A valued social future.

(From *Way to Go,* 1978,
reprinted with permission)

ADVOCACY DEFINED

The protection of human rights is an issue of world-wide concern. In recent years the American public, the courts, and the legislative bodies have demonstrated an increasing awareness that the phrase "the human rights of persons" does indeed include persons with handicaps as well as the non-handicapped population. That this increasing awareness is needed becomes apparent when one considers that handicapped persons have, in the past, been kept out of school because they were hard to teach. Handicapped persons who have difficulty walking are still denied access to many buildings, sidewalks, or systems of public transportation. Some persons with handicaps have been discouraged from marrying or having children; others have not been hired for jobs for which they are qualified because of prejudice or fear.

Many of these abuses of human rights still occur; however, they are increasingly considered illegal as well as immoral, and the weight of the law and the precedents of public custom are working together to make change possible. A powerful series of court decisions and new laws has resulted in this shift. Among the rights of the handicapped (as stated by law) are these:

1. Persons with developmental disabilities have the right to treatment, services, and habilitation plans (P.L. 94-103).
2. Handicapped persons have the right to be considered for jobs for which

they are qualified even if reasonable special accommodations must be made by an employer (Vocational Rehabilitation Act of 1973).

3. All handicapped children have the right to an appropriate education in the least restrictive environment (P.L. 94-142).

These important changes have not been realized easily or automatically. Indeed, these major federal laws, and others like them, are the result of countless smaller steps achieved through lobbying, litigation, and public education by both the disabled themselves and other people who care about them. As Ursin (1976) points out, in social systems that are faced with the problems of allocating scarce resources to a number of competing concerns, it is the vocal, sometimes disruptive elements who are not afraid to make demands that are successful. These, then, are the people we call advocates.

An advocate is someone who speaks for the rights of others. An independent movement of disabled people, their families, and their allies has worked and is working to ensure the rights of handicapped people. These people are advocates for the physically handicapped. Advocacy can be described as having six primary elements (*Way to Go,* 1978):

1. *client:* a person (or group) who needs someone to speak up on his behalf
2. *issue:* a specific problem that needs to be solved
3. *target:* a source that can provide the remedy to the problem
4. *outcome:* the desired solution to the issue
5. *advocate:* a person (or group) who can and will act in the client's best interests
6. *action:* a strategy that an advocate can use to achieve the desired outcome

Advocacy — speaking for the rights of others — is defined by Biklen (1976) as a revolutionary way of "helping people." The handicapped have sometimes been burdened by an "expert knows best" approach, in which they have had no options, in either the sphere of human services or the broader realm of our society (Kriegel, 1969). People with handicaps have also been helped through the charitable model. Charitable organizations have done, and still do, a superior job in providing human services that have been absent in the public sector, but this approach has its own limitations. Charity can have the effect of romanticizing children with special needs, presenting them as "holy angels" rather than as what they are: real, complex people. In addition, charity permits public irresponsibility to continue.

Advocacy, as a way of helping people with disabilities, is defined by these principles:

- Advocates attempt to help handicapped people be more self-reliant and free from dependence on charity.

- Advocates try to understand the client's feelings, experiences, and needs through the client's own words and accounts.
- Advocates do not express pity, but rather anger about the conditions and attitudes in society that dehumanize persons who have disabilities.
- Advocates are active in their pursuit of positive change and are willing to handle criticism and resistance (Biklen, 1976).

Who Are Advocates for the Physically Handicapped?

In an article entitled "Tiny Tim is Dead!," Remmes (1974) speaks of an emerging national coalition of consumers of rehabilitation services. The "customers" of programs and agencies for the physically handicapped are speaking out for themselves. The American Coalition of Citizens with Disabilities, founded in 1975, directs its efforts to increasing public awareness and influencing government to remove the obstacles that prevent disabled persons from enjoying a healthy, normal life (*Disabled Americans*, 1977). It is important to point out that this consumer activism should affect public school services for physically handicapped students. Consumers ask not only that services be provided, but that they be appropriate, effective, and of high quality. Teachers, as providers of services, are increasingly held accountable for the quality of those services. Teachers should encourage young persons with physical handicaps to contact this advocacy group by writing to:

> American Coalition of Citizens with Disabilities, Inc.
> 1346 Connecticut Avenue, N.W., Room 308
> Washington, D.C., 20036.

In addition to the strong voice of disabled persons themselves, other advocates include parent organizations, professional organizations (e.g., the Council for Exceptional Children), and voluntary citizens groups (e.g., the President's Committee on the Employment of the Handicapped).

Advocacy is commonly thought of as a legal process. Legal advocacy can take the form of an attorney representing a client in litigation, in legal proceedings, or in other legal matters. Although this chapter does touch lightly on legal advocacy through legislation and litigation, advocacy here refers to the broader coalition of concerned persons, working at many levels and in many ways, to eliminate the barriers to full participation in life. As President Carter said at the May 1977 White House Conference on Handicapped Individuals, "the time for discrimination against the handicapped in the United States is over."

ACCESS

High curbs and steps, heavy doors, narrow toilet stalls, and inaccessible elevator buttons and drinking fountains all complicate the lives of some handicapped people. Just as school buildings can present tremendous obstacles to physically handicapped children (see Chapter 5), so does the rest of the world present numerous architectural barriers. If handicapped people cannot enter and use public buildings, they cannot easily vote, obtain government services, or become independent and self-supporting. Efforts to enhance talents and to market job skills are meaningless if places of employment are inaccessible (Comptroller General of the U.S., 1975). The National Center for Health Statistics indicates that at least 67,900,000 Americans suffer from limiting physical conditions and would benefit from a more accessible environment (Aino and Loversidge. 1977).

A frequency count of the number of barriers faced on a daily basis by a person in a wheelchair illustrates the kinds of obstacles that make daily living difficult:

Activity	Average Daily Count
• passing through doors, openings, or archways at home and/or work	30–40
• climbing curbs or steps, or making detours to ramps	15–20
• going to bathroom	7–10
• getting in and out of bed/sofa/easy chair	4–6
• getting in and out of car	4–6

(*Personal Licensed Vehicles*, 1976)

Government attention to the problem of inaccessible environments has increased in recent years. In 1961, the President's Committee on the Employment of the Handicapped, together with the National Easter Seal Society for Crippled Children and Adults, undertook the development of standards for making buildings accessible to the disabled. The resulting document was *The American National Standard Specification for Making Buildings and Facilities Accessible and Usable by the Physically Handicapped* (Cohen, 1977). The International Symbol for Access (Figure 10-2.) was developed to designate those buildings that meet these standards. The development of these standards is particularly relevant when one considers that more buildings will be built between 1960 and 2000 than have been built since Columbus discovered America (Aino and Loversidge, 1977).

The development of standards for accessibility did not, of course, magically transform old buildings or automatically influence the construction of new ones. Later legislation increased the use of these standards. *The Architectural Barriers Act of 1968* required public buildings using government funds to be accessible. Section 504 of the *Rehabilitation Act of 1973* states that "no otherwise handicapped individual. . .shall, solely by reason of his handicap, be excluded from the participation in, be denied the benefits of, or be subjected to discrimination under any program or activity

Figure 10-2. International symbol of access.

receiving Federal assistance." These regulations pertain to program and architectural accessibility in preschool, elementary, secondary, and post-secondary educational facilities, as well as to health, welfare, and social service agencies. All newly constructed facilities must be accessible to, and usable by, disabled persons. Structural changes in existing buildings must also be made if there is no other way to ensure accessibility (Aino and Loversidge, 1977).

Advocates for the physically handicapped should encourage compliance with these regulations not only in public buildings, but also in private construction (e.g., churches) as well (Russ, 1978). Less than 1% of new construction costs is needed to make buildings barrier-free, and the renovation of existing structures can also be accomplished at modest cost (Russ, 1978). The addition of ramps and handrails, the widening of doors, and the smoothing of curbs can open a whole new world to those who have been "detoured out of the mainstream of American life, unable to secure their rightful place as full and independent citizens" (Califano, 1977).

A consumer's guide to dealing with issues in access, including guidelines for telephone shopping, how to use government services, and how to complain effectively, has been developed by Bruce (1978). *Access: The Guide to a Better Life for Disabled Americans* can be ordered from:

Consumer Reports Books,
Dept. A088, Consumers Union,
Orangeburg, N.Y. 10902

TRANSPORTATION AND TRAVEL

Even if all public and private buildings were barrier-free, physically handicapped people would find it difficult to make use of them because of problems with transportation. Indeed, recent investigations have shown that one of the most serious barriers to the employment of handicapped persons is inaccessible transportation (Garrett, 1976).

Public Transportation

Public transportation, because of obstacles in the form of equipment design and in attitudes, is difficult if not impossible for many physically handicapped people to use independently. Buses, for example, present a great barrier in their narrow, steep boarding steps. Further, narrow aisles and crowded seating greatly restrict mobility with a wheelchair, crutches or a cane. Prototype models of accessible buses (Figure 10-3.), featuring wider aisles, lowered floor levels, wheelchair lifts, and less steep boarding steps have been constructed, but their manufacture for public use is not being planned at this time (Aino and Loversidge, 1977).

Aircraft present similar structural problems in aisle width, seating clearance, restroom accessibility, and in space for wheelchairs (Aino and Loversidge, 1977). The lack of definitive regulations about what services airlines must provide for the disabled presents additional obstacles (Cohen, 1977). In December, 1962, the Air Traffic Conference of America approved a resolution on the carriage of the physically handicapped: "Persons who cannot take care of their personal needs should not be transported unless, by previous arrangement, a suitable attendant accompanies them" (Schleichkorn, 1972). This resolution claimed the right of each airline to reject disabled passengers on any flight if, in the opinion of airline personnel, the number of disabled persons applying for that particular flight would constitute a health hazard. Handicapped people, reports Cohen (1977), express great dismay over the unpredictability of airline service: questions about the requirement of an additional ticket for an attendant or the accep-

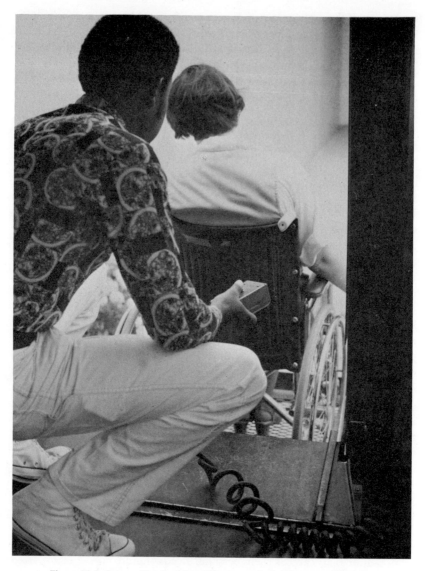

Figure 10-3. Buses with wheelchair lifts are not in public use at this time.

tance of a handicapped passenger on a particular flight are not handled in a consistent manner. New regulations are currently being developed.

Private Transportation: Personal Licensed Vehicles

Although no vehicles are currently available that have been designed especially for handicapped people, such vehicles do exist in the experimental stage (Peizer, 1976). Adaptations of commercially available automotive vehicles are presently in use. For the most part, they consist of rods and fasteners to adapt levers mounted to the accelerator and brake pedals for manual operation.

Because electric wheelchairs are not readily foldable, many severely handicapped people make use of vans equipped with elevator systems. Vans make it relatively easy for severely handicapped people to get in and out of the vehicle (Staros, 1976).

Government agencies concerned with the transportation needs of physically handicapped persons include the Department of Transportation, the Rehabilitation Services Administration, and the Veterans Administration (*Personal Licensed Vehicles,* 1976). Requests for government support in designing, building, and evaluating transportation devices include:

powered carts with special control switches
automobiles that have been modified to accommodate drivers who wish to
   remain in their wheelchairs while driving
wheelchairs that will climb and descend stairs (Laster, 1976).

There is a well-defined need for private industry, perhaps with government incentives, to develop, to produce, to market, and to distribute innovative and safe vehicles to broaden the independence capabilities of handicapped individuals (Garrett, 1976). Ross (1976) makes a strong case for involving handicapped people in the design of special equipment. As a consumer, he points out that equipment developed by the non-disabled often misses the mark in meeting the needs of the handicapped.

Because the availability of transportation can greatly increase the potential for employment, a full social and recreational life, personal freedom, and independence for physically handicapped persons, the teacher as advocate has a responsibility to explore driver education possibilities at the secondary level. Reynolds (1967) offers suggestions on adapting driver education courses for physically handicapped students. This is one instance in which the teacher of physically handicapped students and another faculty member (the driver education teacher) can work together as a team to meet special needs.

Travel

A comprehensive information service is available to physically handicapped people throughout the world who wish to explore travel contacts and exchange possibilities and receive information about international accessibility. This organization, Mobility International, is a non-governmental agency that not only responds to specific requests, but also provides a platform for the lobbying of national and international bodies concerned with travel (Lumley, 1978). Advocates interested in being placed on the mailing list should write to:

> Mobility International
> 2 Colombo Street
> London SE 1 8DP
> England

ALTERNATIVE LIVING ARRANGEMENTS

Most young people, as they reach adulthood, expect to leave their parents' home and establish an independent residence. Independent living is generally anticipated, not only by these young adults, but by their parents as well. For many physically handicapped persons and their families, however, this natural progression toward independence is not considered possible. Instead of independent living, continued dependency at home or institutionalization have traditionally been the only options for those with severe physical handicaps.

A 1972 Illinois investigation of the needs of adults with cerebral palsy found that a significant number were dissatisfied with their current living arrangements and needed alternatives immediately or within five years (Norton, 1976). A New York study (Fenton and Ayers, 1972) revealed similar critical needs. When asked why living at home was no longer possible, adults reported most frequently that their aging families were physically unable to continue fulfilling their needs and providing adequate care. Descriptions were given detailing the deterioration of many families as a result of the constant 24-hour, year-in, year-out demands of caring for severely disabled persons at home. Another frequently given response concerned the reported lack of needed supportive services. Recreation, therapy, rehabilitation, and education services are frequently unavailable to the postschool-age handicapped person living at home.

Institutions were also described as inadequate. Mentally alert physically disabled persons in institutions in the New York study were most often living in geriatric nursing homes. They expressed discomfort and displeasure at being placed in facilities designed for aged (sometimes senile) patients, and reported a lack of adequate rehabilitation services, recreation, and homelike atmosphere. These reports of the unsuitability of nursing home care are especially significant in view of the reported estimate that 16.5 per 1,000 cerebral palsied persons are in nursing homes. This figure is 20 times higher than the rate of cerebral palsy in the general population (National Center for Health Statistics, 1973).

An alternative to remaining with parents or living in a nursing home is an independent living situation, which gives a disabled person the opportunity to live in a house or apartment that is integrated into the community. (Support services, such as attendant care, rent subsidy, and transportation and homemaking services, may be needed to make independent living possible for some severely handicapped persons.)

The kinds of living arrangements that are possible and the extent to which supportive services are needed vary with the severity of the individual handicap. Lurie (1977) provides guidelines for choosing the best living arrangements for a handicapped individual from among the available alternatives. The 2565 mentally alert physically handicapped adults in the Fenton and Ayers (1972) study were categorized this way:

1. Ten percent of those studied were *functionally independent* — these individuals had a permanent physical disability, but were capable of managing their basic daily needs with only minor architectural modifications and assistive devices.
2. Sixty percent of the subjects were *partially dependent* — they could generally handle some of their simpler needs (like eating) and some bathing and dressing, and had limited locomotion. They needed some assistance in the activities of daily living but did not need full-time nursing or attendant care. Some kinds of employment were possible for these individuals.
3. Thirty percent of those studied were *completely dependent* — their physical disabilities were severe enough to prevent them from handling the majority of their daily needs. They required assistance from another person on a daily basis, as well as periodic nursing care.

In 1976, Norton conducted a survey of nine alternative living arrangements for the severely physically handicapped. The settings ranged from single houses and apartments, to group homes, to skilled nursing facilities. Funding for these homes was almost always provided by a combination of federal, state, local, and private funds. A significant source of federal support is the Department of Housing and Urban Development Act of 1974, providing subsidized rents for low-income tenants. The survey concluded that while a wide range of living arrangements is necessary to meet the differing needs of the physically disabled adult population, those handicapped adults who are mentally alert generally find that small supervised apartments and independent living offer the greatest potential for personal development. Only the extremely severely physically disabled required full-time personal care.

Interviews with the residents of these alternative living situations indicated that these adults had always wanted to live this way but had not thought that it would ever be possible.

While the availability of appropriate independent living arrangements for the physically handicapped is increasing, the need cannot be filled by the current possibilities. Barriers to independent living exist both in the housing market and within the repertoire of personal skills and attitudes of disabled persons. Among these barriers are:

1. structural barriers that make existing housing inaccessible
2. a lack of income to make housing payments (Medicaid will pay for nursing home care; no such support exists for independent living)
3. a lack of emotional commitment (Because many severely physically handicapped adults missed out on opportunities to interact with different people and to make decisions about personal living when they were younger, they may not have the emotional commitment to try a different living arrangement.)
4. deficient independent living skills (Because of inadequate educational programs or exclusion from school, some adults missed out on educational opportunities to acquire the necessary living skills.)

Teachers of physically handicapped children and young people must help disabled persons and their families explore the availability of independent living opportunities in their community, lobby for more opportunities, and help handicapped students develop the skills and emotional readiness to live as independently as possible.

LOVE, SEX, AND MARRIAGE

The advocacy issues that have been discussed above, although they have had a great impact on personal growth and freedom for handicapped people, are somewhat impersonal in nature. The solutions to the problems of access, transportation, and housing require environmental planning and government intervention. The solution to this next issue requires instead personal commitment, attitudinal changes, information, and education.

"Everyone is entitled to love, to the opportunity for sexual expression, and to be considered marriageable" (Gordon, 1976). This sweeping statement might seem really radical to many handicapped people and to those who care for them because of the existing internal and external barriers that make warm, close, personal relationships difficult among handicapped persons.

Barriers

The barriers to love, sex, and marriage for persons with physical handicaps include:

1. society (including the families of handicapped persons and the agencies that serve those with disabilities), which has difficulty dealing with the sexuality of disabled people
2. physical disabilities, which can interfere with sexual functioning
3. negative self-image; handicapped people may feel unlovable as well as unloved

Societal Attitudes

As a society we are not quite comfortable with our sexuality. Johnson (1976) gives these examples of our discomfort: the genital organs of children frequently are improperly labeled or not named at all; sexual discussions are often prohibited in the home; many commonly used sexual words have insulting connotations; and some people think that education related to sexuality leads to moral decadence, particularly among the young. If we as a society are unsure of what it means to be sexual beings, it is understandable that we have trouble defining what it means to be a *handicapped* sexual being. As a result of our own insecurity, then, Maddock (1974) suggests that we prefer to think of handicapped people as asexual because they are "different," and may seem vulnerable and open to exploitation.

This desire to view handicapped people as asexual beings is sometimes most apparent in their own families. When Cook (1974) began sex education classes for adults enrolled in United Cerebral Palsy programs, parents expressed great concern. The kinds of questions raised were these: How much sex information is really necessary for handicapped people? Will my "child" cause embarrassment to himself or the family by what he might say or do? Will sex information be overly stimulating to him?

The agencies and professionals who work with handicapped persons often reflect the perspective that sexual concerns should be secondary to other issues. Agencies may be more concerned with job placement or independent living than with personal growth issues, and professionals, whether physicians, psychologists, social workers, or teachers, may consider sexual counseling outside the legitimate scope of their concern (Diamond, 1974).

There seems, then, to be a conspiracy of silence that limits the chances of handicapped people to obtain sexual information and to be regarded as sexual people.

Physical Problems

A physical disability does not remove sexual desire or feeling, nor does it make sexual performance impossible (Johnson, 1976). However, physical disabilities can cause some problems that may make sexual functioning difficult. Bardach (1977) lists these specific problems with which some disabled people must cope: bladder incontinence as a result of spinal cord injury; involuntary muscle contractions as a result of spasticity; limited sensation and arousal capabilities because of spinal cord dysfunction; clumsiness due to paralysis and weakness; and balance problems.

Feelings of Being Unloved

Being handicapped wins no points in our society; therefore, many people with disabilities feel inferior (Gordon, 1976). Because of physical limitations and distorted social experiences, some handicapped persons have had few opportunities to view themselves or be viewed by others as total human beings with real feelings, emotions, and needs (Cook, 1974).

What Can Disabled Persons Do?

1. Gordon (1976) suggests that the disabled should operate on the assumption that the general public is uncomfortable in the presence of severely handicapped people. If the handicapped person lets it be known, therefore, that one does not have to feel guilty about being uncomfortable in his presence, then the general public will not have to respond by withdrawing or feeling pity. Removing interpersonal barriers is a shared responsibility.

2. Disabled people should request sex education programs and should seek out (and share information about) counselors who can help them increase their communication skills, decrease their guilt about sexual thoughts and behavior, and assist them in coping openly and creatively with personal sexual issues (Diamond, 1974). In addition, Bardach (1977) suggests that for persons with acquired physical handicaps, sexual counseling should be available to both the individual person and his or her partner very early in the rehabilitation program to explore attitudes, means of communication, and how each couple and individual can best handle their own unique situations.

3. Handicapped persons should write for *Options,* a free monthly newsletter published by the Association for Sexual Adjustment in Disability. It is printed and mailed through the courtesy of the Easter Seal Society, P.O. Box 3579, Downey, CA 90242.

STRATEGIES FOR ADVOCATES

Being alert to the special needs of persons with physical handicaps is the beginning of advocacy. Developing competence and strategies to facilitate change is the logical next step. The following are some general guidelines for teachers who wish to be effective advocates for the physically handicapped:

1. Be aware of, and understand, the existing federal laws relating to handicaps. One source of this information is the National Center for Law and the Handicapped, Inc. (Bigge and O'Donnell, 1977). To be placed on their mailing list, write:

    > National Center for Law and the Handicapped, Inc.
    > 1235 North Eddy Street
    > South Bend, Indiana

2. Contact the State Department of Education for a statement of guidelines and regulations for programs for physically handicapped students.

3. Commit yourself to public education. Ideally, advocates should work toward building a caring environment for all people (Levin, 1976). Passivity, stereotyping, fear, and avoidance of handicapped people are the enemies; the best way to combat this kind of public prejudice is through education and contact.

Public education programs, through the media, in-service workshops, and community public service activities, should focus on highlighting the competence of disabled people. One resource for such a program is *The Able Disabled Kit* (Pieper, 1975), a collection of photographs and cartoons of handicapped people emphasizing ability.

Ignoring The Handicapped

The Washington Post

WASHINGTON — The first time I met Robert was right after a meeting I had attended. He was waiting for me outside the building — a tall, bearded man with a weird look in his eye. He walked alongside me, telling me about himself — walking awkwardly like a man drunk or on drugs — and what he said after a while was that he was a handicapped person. "I could drop dead at any moment," he said.

This is the way it began. He wanted me to write something about handicapped people. He wanted something in print about how handicapped people are pushed aside, about how people can't deal with them, about how they find them threatening or something. That's my word — threatening. Robert doesn't find the handicapped threatening.

We walked down the street and I walked faster than he did, and he was trying to keep up. But he was slow. He is a big man, well over six feet tall, and he says, he used to be a whiz at tennis. But he was walking slowly and I wanted to get back to the office and I was impatient. I kept walking ahead and then waiting for him to catch up. He had trouble with the curbs. He never seemed able to gauge their height.

He did most of the talking. He told me is an adult hydrocephalic, meaning he has water on the brain. There is a tube that runs from his brain to his kidney, which is called a shunt,

Richard Cohen

and it drains the fluid. Robert has a very rare case of the disease. He got it as an adult, when he was 19. Most people get it when they are children. Most die from it. Robert nearly did and for six months once he was in a coma. He was flown home to die. Instead, he simply came out of it.

The idea of writing about the handicapped appealed to me. Robert did not. The idea is that you would write about how terrible it is to hide them, to refuse to deal with them, to build your world, your streets and your public buildings as if they didn't exist — to do worse than that. To treat them as if their handicap was their fault — their fault that they are what they are, and then when they scream a bit or act pushy or cry out in some way for attention, we get angry.

I am against all this. He raised his voice and said something about how I didn't have to write anything if I didn't want to, but I said I did, I did, and I would, I would. We were still walking and I either told him, or when I thought about, how obsessed I was with the handicapped about the time my child was born.

I thought a lot about it, you know, about all the things that could go wrong and I thought, too, how it was wrong to want a child because you wanted something cute, something to enhance your life-style — like a piece of furniture or a summer home. So I said nothing about it and then in the delivery room when I thought I had this fear under control, the doctor caught me staring at the new-born baby and counting toes. I felt like ... you know what I felt like.

So I told Robert I would write about the handicapped. I took his phone number but I never called. The subject appealed to me but not the people. So when he called I told

him how busy I was and how this was coming up and that was scheduled and how my life was coming apart and I had no time. So he started to call me at home, which I resented. He would call me early in the morning. He was at work and I was still at home and still in my bathrobe and still fighting the cobwebs of sleep and I was mad that he was calling me and I was ashamed that I was still at home.

Anyway, he kept calling and I kept putting him off and after a while I started to really dislike him — to feel righteously irate and think he was pushy and that he was taking advantage of being handicapped. I put him off once a month but then he called again, saying that a White House conference on the handicapped was coming up and that we had to talk.

Finally, we met for lunch. He told me about his double vision and how his memory is not so good and how he is sometimes slow — slow to talk and slow to walk and slow to pick up on a remark. He forgets what he is saying and sometimes he has trouble getting his words out, but, if you wait just a bit, he'll catch up.

I wanted the waiter to serve quickly and I was thinking all the time of a column I had to write and I was trying hard to be courteous but really I was just going through the motions. But Robert talked on and on and he turned out to be a very nice guy. After a while I was in no great rush.

He told me how people didn't seem to have the time for him, how they were always in a rush, and he, well — sometimes you had to wait for him. That hit home and then I asked a dumb question about what people could do for the handicapped or about the handicapped. I expected him to say something like give to this charity or write your congressman, but instead he just looked at me and said, "Make contact."

"Make contact with them. This hasn't been so bad, has it? I didn't embarrass you or anything, did I?"

A little while later we left and I went back to the office to write about Robert and to write also that there's no handicap like a closed mind.

Contact is probably the most effective way to weaken and to eliminate public prejudice. As Richard Cohen (1978) points out, contact is a more valuable way to help the handicapped than charity or political action. Once the abstract concept of "the handicapped" becomes a real person, it is difficult to continue thinking in the same old stereotypical way, with the "handicap of a closed mind."

The teacher of physically handicapped students has many opportunities to facilitate contact through the involvement of her students in school activities and by encouraging involvement in the community.

4. Learn the political strategies of advocacy (Biklen, 1976): demonstrations, demands, letter writing, factfinding, communications, symbolic acts, negotiations, boycotts, lobbying, model programs, legal advocacy, and demystifying.

5. Develop a creative problem-solving state of mind: The advocate for the physically handicapped will encounter unique situations for which no solution has yet been found. These challenges must be approached with a willingness to brainstorm, take risks, and try something no one has ever done before.

SUMMARY

The responsibilities of the teacher of physically handicapped students extend beyond the classroom: First, the teacher has a responsibility to provide her students with the skills and attitudes that are essential for a full and independent life. Second, the teacher has a responsibility to be part of the human rights movement that is trying to eliminate the manmade environmental and attitudinal barriers to full life participation. Creative problem-solving skills and informed commitment to change are needed for these tasks.

LITERATURE CITED

Aino, E. A., and Loversidge, R. D. 1977. Access for All. The Ohio Governor's Committee on Employment of the Handicapped and Schooley Cornelius Associates, Architects/Engineers/Planners, Columbus, Ohio.

Bardach, J. L. 1977. A problem oriented approach to sexual functioning in the physically disabled. Paper presented at the 85th Annual Convention of the American Psychological Association, August, San Francisco.

Bigge, J., and O'Donnell, P. A. 1977. Teaching Individuals with Physical and Multiple Disabilities. Charles E. Merrill Publishing Company, Columbus, Ohio.

Biklen, D. 1976. Advocacy comes of age. Except. Child. 42:308-313.

Bruce, L. 1978. Access: The Guide to a Better Life for Disabled Americans. Random House, New York.

Califano, J. A. 1977. Speech delivered at the White House Conference on Handicapped Individuals, May, Washington, D.C. Cited in: E. Russ. 1978. Does the church handicap the disabled? Presbyter. Survey 68:25.

Carter, J. A. 1977. Speech delivered at the White House Conference on Handicapped Individuals, May, Washington, D.C. Cited in: E. Russ. 1978. Does the church handicap the disabled? Presbyter. Survey 68:25.

Cohen, R. 1978. Ignoring the handicapped. Charlotte Observer. May 12, 19A.

Cohen, S. 1977. Special People. Prentice-Hall, Englewood Cliffs, N.J.

Comptroller General of the United States. 1975. Report to the Congress: Further Action Needed to Make All Public Buildings Accessible to the Physically Handicapped. United States General Accounting Office, Washington, D.C.

Cook, R. 1974. Sex education program service model for the multihandicapped adult. Rehabil. Lit. 35:34-40.

Diamond, D. 1974. Sexuality and the Handicapped. Rehabil. Lit. 35:34-40.

Disabled Americans: A History. 1977. Performance January, 27:7, 63-71.

Fenton, J., and Ayers, R. 1972. Residential Needs of Severely Physically Handicapped Non-Retarded Children and Young Adults in New York State. Institute of Rehabilitation Medicine of the New York University Medical Center, New York.

Garrett, J. 1976. Handicapped mobility concerns of the Rehabilitation Services Administration. In: Personal Licensed Vehicles for the Disabled. Rehabilitation Engineering Center of the Moss Rehabilitation Hospital, Philadelphia.

Gordon, S. 1976. Sex education: Love, sex and marriage for people who have disabilities. Except. Parent

Johnson, A. D. 1976. Assessment of values for management of sexual problems of the physically and mentally impaired. Paper presented at Winthrop College, August, Rock Hill, S.C.

Kriegel, L. 1969. Uncle Tom and Tiny Tim: Some reflections on the cripple as negro. Am. Scholar 38:412-430.

Laster, I. 1976. Efforts of the Department of Transportation to improve transportation for the handicapped. In: Personal Licensed Vehicles for the Disabled. Rehabilitation Engineering Center of the Moss Rehabilitation Hospital, Philadelphia.

Levin, L. S. 1976. Developmental disabilities: educating the public. Birth Def. XII: 171-179.

Lumley, A. 1978. Mobility International — What is it? Mobility International, London.

Lurie, G. 1977. Housing and Home Services for the Disabled. Medical Department, Harper and Row Publishers, Hagerstown, Maryland.

Maddock, J. 1974. Sex education for the exceptional person: a rationale. Except. Child. 40:273-278.

National Center for Health Statistics. 1973. Prevalence of selected impairment-United States 1963-1965. Series 10, Number 99. U.S. Department of Health, Education, and Welfare, Washington, D.C.

Norton, M. 1976. Moving Ahead. United Cerebral Palsy of Illinois, Inc., Ill.

Peizer, S. 1976. Automotive vehicles for the handicapped. In: Personal Licensed Vehicles for the Disabled. Rehabilitation Engineering Center of the Moss Rehabilitation Hospital, Philadelphia.

Personal Licensed Vehicles for the Disabled. 1976. Rehabilitation Engineering Center of the Moss Rehabilitation Hospital, Philadelphia.

Pieper, B. 1975. Some curricular experiences for children. In: S. Cohen (ed.), Fostering Positive Attitudes toward the Handicapped. City University of New York, Special Education Development Center, New York.

Remmes, H. 1974. Consumer feedback: Tiny Tim is dead! Rehabil. Lit. 35: 298-300.

Reynolds, J. 1967. The physically handicapped and driver education, Safety 8-11.

Ross, L. 1976. Some problems of the consumers. In: Personal Licensed Vehicles for the Disabled. Rehabilitation Engineering Center of the Moss Rehabilitation Hospital, Philadelphia.

Russ, E. 1978. Does the church handicap the disabled? Presbyter. Survey 68:25, 43.

Schleichkorn, J. S. 1972. Carriage of the Physically Handicapped on Domestic and International Airlines. United Cerebral Palsy Associations of New York State, Inc., New York.

Staros, A. 1976. Problems in providing self-reliance in transportation for drivers with physical handicaps. In: Personal Licensed Vehicles for the Disabled. Rehabilitation Engineering Center of the Moss Rehabilitation Hospital, Philadelphia.

Ursin, K. G. 1976. Influence of litigation on the lives of the developmentally disabled: a preliminary report. Birth Def. 137-138.

Way to Go. 1978. University Park Press, Baltimore.

APPENDICES

A

AGENCIES FOR SHARING TEACHING IDEAS

Dissemination of information regarding researched techniques and practices for the education and treatment of physically handicapped students is necessary to avoid unnecessary duplication of effort and to share helpful solutions. The following addresses are provided to enable teachers and inventors to request and to share the information necessary to solve the problems that confront physically handicapped students:

Division for the Blind and Physically Handicapped
    Library of Congress
    Washington, D.C. 20542
The Council for Exceptional Children Publications
    1920 Association Drive
    Reston, Va. 22091
Department of Health, Education and Welfare
    Rehabilitation Services Administration
    Office of Human Development
    330 Independence Ave., S.W.
    Washington, D.C. 20201
Deputy Commissioner for Education of the Handicapped
    Office of Education
    Bureau of Education for the Handicapped
    400 Maryland Ave., S.W.
    Washington, D.C. 20201
The Governor's Committee on Employment of the Handicapped
    Your local Governor's office
The American Association for the Education of the Severely/Profoundly Handicapped (AAESPH)
    P.O. Box 15287
    Seattle, Wash. 98115
Blissymbolics Communication Foundation
    862 Eglinton Ave. East
    Toronto, Ontario
    Canada M4G 2L1

NICSEM (National Information Center for Special Education Materials)
   University Park
   Los Angeles, Calif. 90007   (213) 741-5899
NIMIS (National Instructional Materials Information System)
   Center of Educational Media and National Materials for the Handi-
   capped
   The Ohio State University
   Columbus, Ohio. 43210   (614) 422-7596
FAIR (Federation of American Industries for Rehabilitation)
   c/o Maddak, Inc.
   Industrial Road
   Pequannock, N.J. 07440

GUIDELINES FOR BARRIER-FREE SCHOOL FACILITIES

Name of Building_____ Phone Number _____

Street Address _____City _____State _____

Person Interviewed _____ Title _____

Circle Yes or No
(Complete answer
in space provided
when necessary)

1. OFFSTREET PARKING
   a. Is an offstreet parking area available adja-
      cent to building?............................ Yes   No
   b. If adjacent offstreet parking is not available,
      identify and give location of nearest and
      most convenient parking area

   _____

   _____

   c. Are parking area and building separated by
      a street?.................................... Yes   No
   d. Is the surface of the parking area smooth
      and hard (no sand, gravel, etc.)?.............. Yes   No
2. PASSENGER LOADING ZONE
   a. Is there a passenger loading zone?............. Yes   No
   b. If yes, where is it located in relation to
      selected entrance? _____
3. APPROACH TO SELECTED ENTRANCE
   a. Which entrance was selected as most accessible?_____
   b. Is the approach to the entrance door at
      ground level? .... Yes   No
   c. Is there a ramp in the approach to or at the
      entrance door? .... Yes   No
   d. If there are any steps in the approach to or at
      the entrance door, give total number of steps ..... _____

e.   If there are steps, is there a sturdy handrail
     on at least one side or in the center?. . . . .   Yes   No

4.   **ENTRANCE DOOR**
a.   What is the width of the entrance doorway
     (with door open)? . . . .   _____
b.   Is the door automatic? . . . .   Yes   No
c.   Are there steps between entrance and main
     areas or corridor? . . . .   Yes   No
d.   If yes, what is the total number of steps? . . . .   _____
e.   If there are steps, is there a sturdy handrail
     in the center or on at least one side?. . . . .   Yes   No

5.   **ELEVATOR**
a.   Is there a passenger elevator?. . . . .   Yes   No
b.   Does it serve all essential areas? . . . .   Yes   No

6.   **ACCESS FROM ENTRY TO ESSENTIAL AREAS**

	(1)	(2)	(3)
a. Is the usable width of corridors and aisles at least 32"?.	Yes No	Yes No	Yes No
b. Is the narrowest clear doorway with door open 28" or more? . .	Yes No	Yes No	Yes No
c. If not, what is the width?	_____	_____	_____

7.   **INTERIOR OF ESSENTIAL AREAS**

	(1)	(2)	(3)
a. Are there any steps between essential areas not served by elevator?	Yes No	Yes No	Yes No
b. Does each flight of steps have a sturdy handrail on at least one side or in the center?.	Yes No	Yes No	Yes No

8.   **PUBLIC TOILET ROOMS**
a.   Where are toilet rooms located?
     Men _____
     Women _____

	Men	Women
b. Would one need to go up or down steps to get to toilet room?	Yes No	Yes No
c. If so, how many?.	_____	_____

    d. If there are steps, does each flight of steps have a sturdy handrail on at least one side or in the center? . . . . .   Yes   No   Yes   No

    e. What is the width of toilet room entrance doorway (with door open)? . . _____ _____

    f. Is there free space in the room to permit a wheelchair to turn? . . . . . .   Yes   No   Yes   No

    g. What is the width of widest toilet stall door? . . . . _____ _____

    h. Does this stall have handrails or grab bars? . . . .   Yes   No   Yes   No

9. PUBLIC TELEPHONE

    a. Where is the most accessible phone located? _____

    b. What type (booth, wall, desk)? _____

    c. If phone is in a booth, what is width of booth door (with door open)? . . . . _____

    d. Is the handset 48″ or less from the floor? . . . .   Yes   No

    e. Does the phone have amplifying controls for the hard of hearing? . . . .   Yes   No

10. ASSISTANCE AND AIDS AVAILABLE

    a. Is there an attendant who will take cars? . . . .   Yes   No

    b. Is there help available for those needing assistance in entering? . . . .   Yes   No

    c. If not, is help available for those needing assistance if arranged for in advance? . . . .   Yes   No

    d. Who to call in advance for assistance _____

    e. Telephone number _____

    f. Are wheelchairs available? . . . .   Yes   No

Surveyor _____ Date _____

Address_____ Phone _____

ADDITIONAL COMMENTS

From *Barrier-free School Facilities*, 1977. Published by the National Easter Seal Society for Crippled Children and Adults.

C

MEDIA FOR IN-SERVICE EDUCATION

Films

Title	Description	Length	Distributor
Children Are Not Problems; They Are People	Demonstrates an integrated preschool model for normal and severely handicapped children.	27 min.	Media Resource Center Meyer Children's Rehabilitation Institute 4445 44th Street Omaha, Nebraska 68105
Devices for Self-Help Task Performance	Illustrates problems of persons with multiple physical handicaps and demonstrates supportive devices and techniques for task performance.	27 min.	National Audiovisual Center National Archives and Records Service General Services Adm. Washington, D.C. 20409
Elaine Dart: Not Like Other People	About a cerebral palsy victim who is able to control only her feet. In spite of this severe handicap, she writes, knits, etc. A great example of overcoming trials and achieving success.	14 min.	Media Marketing W-STAD Brigham Young Univ. Provo, Utah 84602
Feeling Free	A series of six films designed to help students know a few disabled individuals well. Featured is a 12-year-old boy with cerebral palsy. Teaching guide available.	30 min. (ea.)	Scholastic Feeling Free 904 Sylvan Avenue Englewood Cliffs, N.J. 07632

I Am Not What You See: Sondra Diamond Overcomes Cerebral Palsy	Sondra is severely disabled and is studying psychology. She describes what it feels like to be disabled in our society.	28 min.	Filmakers Library, Inc. 290 West End Avenue New York N.Y. 10023
Like Other People	A British film about spastic adults. Central characters make a plea for humanity to understand that they are real people.	37 min.	Perennial Ed. 1825 Willow Road Northfield, Ill. 60093
Multi-level Teaching for Normal and Handicapped Children	Demonstrates a classroom where normal and handicapped children receive ongoing, individualized instruction from a single teacher.	21 min.	Media Resource Center Meyer Children's Rehabilitation Institute (see above)
Nicky: One of My Best Friends	Ten-year-old Nicky goes to school, works and plays with other 5th graders in spite of blindness and cerebral palsy.	15 min.	CEM McGraw-Hill Films 110 Fifteenth Street Del Mar, Calif. 92014
One More Time	A couple tells what it was like to be told their child had cerebral palsy.	13 min.	Media Resource Center Meyer Children's Rehabilitation Institute (see above)

continued

Title	Description	Length	Distributor
Out of the Shadows	Demonstrates an intensive training program for severely handicapped children.	17 min.	Media Resource Center Meyer Children's Rehabilitation Institute (see above)
People You Never See	About the special problems accompanying cerebral palsy.	28 min.	Filmakers Library, Inc. 290 West End Avenue New York, N.Y. 10023
Wheels	About multiply handicapped children who require special care and the purpose of the modified wheelchair.	13 min.	Media Resource Center Meyer Children's Rehabilitation Institute (see above)
Where to Begin	Helps teachers choose among alternatives and select courses of action when they encounter a nonverbal child in the classroom.	17 min.	Media Resource Center Meyer Children's Rehabilitation Institute (see above)
Audio Tapes Realities of the Physically Handicapped	A series of 12 presentations covering such topics as types of disability, prejudices against the handicapped, activities of daily living, and the need to communicate.	6 cassettes	Affective House P.O. Box 35321 Tulsa, Okla. 74135

TESTS FOR PSYCHOLOGICAL AND EDUCATIONAL ASSESSMENT

Tests of General Intelligence

Terman, L., and Merrill, M. 1973. *Stanford-Binet Intelligence Scale.* Houghton Mifflin Company, Boston.

This scale, the result of pioneering work in the development of mental tests, is of such historical significance that new scales almost always attempt to show a high correlation with the Stanford-Binet. The scale consists of 6 subtests and one alternative, administered at half-year intervals when the client is 2-5 years of age, at yearly intervals between 5-14 years of age, and 4 times during the client's adult years. The content varies considerably from age to age; some tasks are highly verbal and abstract, others require precise fine motor skills. Speed of responding sometimes affects scores. IQ scores are derived from mental age scores. This test should be administered only by a licensed psychologist.

McCarthy, D. 1972. *McCarthy Scales of Children's Abilities.* The Psychological Corporation, New York.

This instrument is designed to determine the general intellectual level and the learning strengths and weaknesses of young children from 2½ to 8½ years old. Indexes provided include verbal, perceptual-performance, quantitative, general cognitive, memory, and motor scales. The test should be administered only by a licensed psychologist.

Wechsler, D. 1974. *Wechsler Intelligence Scale for Children — Revised.* Psychological Corporation, New York.

This test of general intelligence yields a full-scale IQ score, as well as a verbal IQ and performance IQ. The verbal scale is made up of five subtests: information, similarities, arithmetic, vocabulary, and comprehension. The performance scale consists of: picture completion, picture arrangement, block design, object assembly, and coding. Speed of responding influences the score on several of the subtests. Fine motor precision is needed on most performance subtests, and verbal responses are needed on the verbal scale. The test is appropriate for persons in the age range 6½-16½ years, and should be administered only by a licensed psychologist.

Performance Tests

Burgemeister, B., Hollander, L., and Lorge, I. 1959. *Columbia Mental Maturity Scale.* Harcourt Brace Jovanovich, Inc., New York.

The *CMMS* was designed to yield an estimate of intellectual ability in children with a mental age of 3 to 10 years. Only minimal motor or verbal responses are required. The scale includes 100 items, each of which has a series of 3 to 5 drawings printed on 6"×19" cards. The task involves the selection of the card in the series that is different from the other cards in the series.

Raven, J. C. 1965. *Progressive Matrices.* Grieve, Great Britain.

The *Raven Progressive Matrices* measures intellectual functioning individually or in groups. The *Standard Progressive Matrices* was the original test, intended for use by children 6 and older. *Colored Progressive Matrices* is a revision designed for the 5–11 age group. Each of the tests is comprised of a series of designs from which one section has been removed. The task is to find the missing part of the design from 6 to 8 choices.

Language Tests

Dunn, L. M. 1965. *Peabody Picture Vocabulary Test.* American Guidance Service, Circle Pines, MN.

This is a quick, individually administered test of verbal receptive ability. The examiner names a word, and the child points to the one of four pictures that best relates to th   rd named. Norms are available for ages 2½ to 16¼ years.

Kirk, S. A., McCarthy, J. J., and Kirk, W. D. 1968. The *Illinois Test of Psycholinguistic Abilities.* Revised Edition. University of Illinois Press, Urbana.

Based on a clinical model of information processing, this test was developed with support from the Easter Seal Research Foundation. It is designed to identify a child's relative strengths and weaknesses in receiving, processing, and expressing information. The subtests evaluate auditory reception, visual reception, auditory association, visual association, verbal expression, manual expression, grammatic closure, auditory sequential memory, visual closure, and visual sequential memory. Several of the tests require only a point or yes-no response. The age range for this test is 2½ to 9½ years.

Adaptations of IQ Tests

Dubose, R. 1974. *Peabody Intellectual Performance Scale.* George Peabody College for Teachers, Nashville, Tenn.

The *PIPS* is based on items appearing in published scales, adapted to be high in stimulus value for the sensory impaired child. The administration of the scale is free from dependency on verbal language. The child needs some usable vision to complete the test, but no hearing is necessary. The test consists of 31 items that tap behaviors in 10 sequential developmental levels in the 6- to 53-month mental age range.

Dubose, R. F., and Landley, M. B. 1977. *Developmental Activities Screening Inventory.* Teaching Resources Corporation, Boston.

This test, designed for children in the age range 6–60 months, measures cognitive abilities and does not penalize sensorily handicapped children. Stimuli are presented in the form of picture, symbol, or number cards, manipulative objects (such as blocks, cups, and geometric shapes), and simple toys. Directions are given by demonstration, gesture, or a few simple words. Studies with 200 multiply handicapped children indicate that the *DASI* can be used successfully to screen for possible developmental delays.

French, J. L. 1964. *Pictorial Test of Intelligence.* Houghton Mifflin Company, Boston.

This individual, nonverbal test of intelligence is designed to assess the cognitive abilities of normal and handicapped children between the ages of 3 and 8 years. The test requires few verbal or manipulative responses; thus, it is particularly appropriate for the assessment of the physically handicapped. The subtests are: 1) picture vocabulary, 2) form discrimination, 3) information and comprehension, 4) similarities, 5) size and number, and 6) immediate recall.

Stanford-Binet Modified. Reported in: Sattler, J. M. 1970. Intelligence test modifications on handicapped and nonhandicapped children. Progress Report of the San Diego State College (Grant No. 15–P–5527719–02) September 30, 1970. Department of Health, Education, and Welfare; Social and Rehabilitation Service.

The *Stanford-Binet Modified* is an experimental modification consisting of tests located at year levels II through V of the *Stanford-Binet, L-M.* All tests in the modified form are nonverbal, requiring a minimal response, such as a point or some indication of yes or no.

Adaptive Behavior

Balthazar, E. E. 1971. *Balthazar Scales of Adaptive Behavior.* Research Press Company, Champaign, Ill.

This measure was designed for severely and profoundly mentally retarded adults, and younger, less severely retarded persons. The Scales of Functional Independence involve ratings for eating, dressing, and toileting skills. Scales of Social Adaptation have ratings in the areas of unadaptive self-directed behavior, unadaptive interpersonal behavior, adaptive interpersonal behavior, verbal communication, play activities, responses to instruction, and a checklist of personal care behaviors.

Doll, E. A. 1953. *Vineland Social Maturity Scale.* American Guidance Service, Circle Pines, Minn.

Items are arranged in order of increasing difficulty and represent progressive maturation in self-help skills, self-direction, locomotion, occupation, communications, and social relations. Scores are based on information obtained in an interview with someone intimately familiar with the person, or the person himself. The Vineland assesses progress toward social maturity, competence, and independence from birth to adulthood.

Lambert, N., Windmiller, M., Cole, L., and Figueroa, R. 1975. *AAMD Adaptive Behavior Scale — Public School Version.* American Association on Mental Deficiency, Washington, D.C.

Adaptive behavior has been defined as the effectiveness with which an individual copes with the natural and social demands of his environment. This measure of adaptive behavior consists of two parts: Part I is organized along developmental lines and evaluates an individual's skills and habits in 10 behavior domains related to daily living (independent functioning, physical development, economic activity, language development, numbers and time, domestic activity, vocational activity, self-direction, responsibility, and socialization). Part II provides measures of maladaptive behavior related to personality and behavior disorders (violent and destructive behavior, withdrawal, inappropriate interpersonal manners, or hyperactivity). The scale can be administered by someone who has direct knowledge of the child and who rates the child on each item or through an interview in which the responses of someone who knows the child well (such as a parent) are recorded by the interviewer.

Self-Concept

Muller, D. G., and Leonetti, R. 1974. *Primary Self-Concept Inventory.* Learning Concepts, Austin, Texas.

The inventory is composed of 20 picture items, each depicting at least one child in a positive role and at least one child in a negative role. The child is asked to mark (or point to) the child that is "most like you." Aspects of self-concept that are measured are physical size, emotional state, helpfulness, success, peer acceptance, and intellectual self-esteem. There are separate male-female forms and directions in English and in Spanish. This instrument is appropriate for children in kindergarten through grade 6.

Wright, G. N., and Reemer, H. H. 1960. *Purdue Handicap Problems Inventory.* Purdue Research Foundation, Lafayette, Ind.

This is a measure of self-perceived social, family, vocational, and personal problems for handicapped adults. The inventory requires a yes-no response to 280 items and a 5th grade reading level. It can be administered in 20–35 minutes.

Academic Achievement

Dunn, L. M., and Markwardt, F. C. 1970. *Peabody Individual Achievement Test (PIAT)*. American Guidance Service, Circle Pines, Minn.

This test provides a wide-range screening measure of achievement in the areas of math, reading recognition, reading comprehension, spelling, and general information. The untimed test generally requires 30-40 minutes to administer and score and is normed for a kindergarten through 12th grade population. The math, reading comprehension, and spelling subtests require only a pointing response. The other subtests require verbal responses.

Jastek, J. F., and Bijou, S. 1946. *Wide Range Achievement Test*. Psychological Corporation, New York.

The purpose of the *WRAT* is to study achievement in reading recognition, spelling, and arithmetic computation. The test was revised in 1965, and covers two levels. Level I extends from 5 to 12 years of age, and Level II ranges from age 12 to adulthood. The reading subtest requires verbal responses, while the arithmetic and spelling subtests require a written responses.

Jedrysek, E., Klapper, Z., Pope, L., and Wortis, J. 1972. *Psychoeducational Evaluation of the Preschool Child*. Grune & Stratton, New York.

This test, designed to serve as a guide in evaluating the educational potential of preschool children, is based on work with young, physically handicapped children. Test items explore physical functioning and sensory status, perceptual functioning, competence in short-term retention, language competence, and cognitive functioning. Probes allow the teacher to pinpoint the child's learning style. Required motor responses are minimal; some verbal responses are required.

Assessment/Curriculum Guides for the Severely Handicapped

Behavioral Characteristics Progression (BCP). 1973. Vort Corporation, Palo Alto, Calif.

The *BCP* is a nonstandardized continuum of behaviors in chart form. It contains 2400 observable traits, organized in 59 strands (such as health, toileting, oral hygiene, self-identification, and homemaking skills). Of special interest to teachers of the physically handicapped are strands in mobility, wheelchair use, and ambulation. Curriculum guides are available to establish an educational plan.

Sanford, A. R. (ed.). 1974. *Learning Accomplishment Profile (LAP)*. Chapel Hill Training-Outreach Project, Chapel Hill, N.C.

This is an assessment tool that uses normed evidence for the sequential ordering of development of gross and fine motor, language, cognition, socialization, and self-help skills. The *LAP* provides a recording system for existing skills, skills not yet performed by the child, and curriculum suggestions for the development of new skills.

Somerton, M. E., and Turner, K. D. 1973. *Pennsylvania Training Model Individual Assessment Guide.* Pennsylvania Department of Education, Division of Special Education, Harrisburg.

This tool is designed for use with severely and profoundly retarded persons. Initial screening is conducted by the teacher, using a curriculum assessment guide, in the areas of sensory and motor development, activities of daily living, communication, perceptual-cognitive development, and social and emotional development. Major areas of interest are then assessed in smaller units with competency checklists. The outcome of this assessment allows the teacher to prepare specific instructional objectives and initiate training. Guidelines are presented for tracking student progress.

Shearer, D., Billingsley, J., Frohman, A., Hilliard, J., Johnson, F., and Shearer, M. 1972. *The Portage Guide to Early Education.* Cooperative Educational Service Agency 12, Portage, Wisc.

This guide is designed for use with children whose mental ages range from 0 to 5 years. It was originally developed for home intervention and consists of two parts: a sequential behavior checklist (in the areas of cognition, self-help, motor, language, and social development) and a set of curriculum cards to match the behaviors on the checklist. The curriculum cards include a specific behavioral description of each item on the checklist, as well as suggested teaching activities.

The *Radea Program.* 1977. Melton Book Company, Dallas, Texas.

This curriculum, designed for students functioning within the developmental ages 0 to 7 years, provides a testing procedure for correct placement, 564 developmentally sequenced task cards, and checkpoints to ensure that the tasks have been learned.

E

ORGANIZATIONS AND AGENCIES SERVING PERSONS WITH PHYSICAL HANDICAPS

Alexander Graham Bell Association for the Deaf, Inc.
  3417 Volta Place, N.W.
  Washington, D.C. 20007   (202) 337-5220
Asthma and Allergy Foundation of America
  801 Second Avenue
  New York, N.Y. 10017
American Printing House for the Blind
  1839 Frankfort Avenue
  P.O. Box 6085
  Louisville, Kentucky. 40206
National Society for the Prevention of Blindness, Inc.
  79 Madison Avenue
  New York N.Y. 10016
National Easter Seal Society for Crippled Children and Adults
  2023 West Ogden Avenue
  Chicago, Ill. 60612   (312) 243-8400
Epilepsy Foundation of America
  1828 L Street N.W., Suite 406
  Washington, D.C. 20036   (202) 293-2930
The American Heart Association
  44 East 23rd Street
  New York, N.Y. 10010
American Association for the Education of the
Severely and Profoundly Handicapped (AAESPH)
  P.O. Box 15287
  Seattle, Wash. 98115

The Council for Exceptional Children
   1920 Association Drive
   Reston, Va. 22091
National Hemophilia Foundation
   25 West 39th Street
   New York, N.Y. 10018   (212) 869-9740
American Lung Association
   1740 Broadway
   New York, N.Y. 10019   (212) 245-8000
National Multiple Sclerosis Society
   205 East 42nd Street
   New York, N.Y. 10017   (212) 532-3060
National Paraplegia Foundation
   369 Eliot Street
   Newtown Upper Falls, Mass. 02164   (617) 964-0521
NPF Research Division
   4440 N.W. 19th Street
   1-1133 Key Palm Willa
   Lauderhill, Fla. 33313   (305) 735-9050
United Cerebral Palsy Associations, Inc.
   66 East 34th Street
   New York, N.Y. 10016
Muscular Dystrophy Association
   810 Seventh Avenue
   New York, N.Y. 10019
American Cancer Society
   777 Third Avenue
   New York, N.Y. 10017
Rehabilitation International
   432 Park Avenue South
   New York, N.Y. 10016

INDEX

definition of, 4
psychological aspects of, 53-68
Duchenne type muscular dystrophy, 41

Education
appropriate, as aid to psychological adjustment of handicapped child, 59-60
see also Appropriate education for physically handicapped
for children, 1-14
for handicapped children, *see* Handicapped child(ren), education for
in-service, media for, 341-344
Education for All Handicapped Children Act (P.L. 94-142), 2-3
evaluation concerns related to, 129-130
individualized education program of, 193-288
see also Individualized education program (IEP)
Educational achievement of physically handicapped child, evaluation of, 187-189
Educational assessment of handicapped child, 127-153
see also Psychological and educational assessment of handicapped child
Educational services
for hospitalized child, 76, 105, 108-110
for severely handicapped, 78-81
Encoding technique for acquisition of communication skills by physically handicapped child, 178, 180
Environment, physical, in facilitating mainstreaming of handicapped, 121-123
Epilepsy, 22-26
functional problems in, 24-26
medications for, functional problems related to, 25-26
physical description of, 22-24
psychosocial problems in, 25
seizures in, characteristics of, 23

Epilepsy Foundation of America, 307-308
Evaluation of appropriate education program for physically handicapped child, 186-190
Experiences as basis of aptitude and intelligence tests for handicapped children, cautions on, 132

Family(ies), with handicapped children
periods of crisis for, 63-66
psychological adjustment of, 61-66
see also Parents
Family living skills, curriculum goals for, for handicapped student, 263-266
Fine motor skills, curriculum goals for, for severely handicapped, 212-213
Furniture, classroom, in appropriate education for physically handicapped child, 159, 160

Governmental agencies aiding handicapped, 310-311
Gower's sign in muscular dystrophy, 41, 42
Grand mal seizures
characteristics of, 23
dealing with, guidelines for, 24
Gross motor skills, curriculum goals for, for severely handicapped, 208-211
Guilt in adjustment of parents to handicapped child, 62

Handicap(s)
definition of, 4
health, 35-41
cystic fibrosis as, 35-37
see also Cystic fibrosis
heart disease as, 37-38
hemophilia as, 38-39
sickle cell anemia as, 39-41
physical
conditions causing, 15-52
classification of, 16-17

A self-contained guide for teachers and students of education...

INDIVIDUALIZING EDUCATIONAL OBJECTIVES AND PROGRAMS
A Modular Approach

By **Peter J. Valletutti, Ed.D.**, Dean, Division of Extension and Experimental Programs, and Professor of Education, Coppin State College; and **Anthony O. Salpino, Ph.D.**, Assistant Professor of Special Education, Coppin State College, Baltimore

This book provides twelve modules as a guide to implementing diagnostic/prescriptive teaching. It is ideally organized for individual use by inservice teachers as well as for use as a classroom text in special education. It clarifies and greatly simplifies the process of individualizing educational programs and objectives by showing how to understand pupils as total human beings and how to develop ways of helping them realize their greatest potential.

The modules in the book stress the critical role of the pupils themselves in the total diagnostic and prescriptive process and emphasize as well the crucial role that parents must play. The modules develop in detail the content of individualized education programs (IEP's) mandated by P.L. 94-142 for handicapped students, and the book shows how the same approach may be modified to serve as a model for optimum education of all pupils.

The modular approach of this book allows readers to proceed at their own pace, judging for themselves the areas to be stressed and developed. The approach stresses self-evaluation and self-instruction within the structure and direction of the program. Each module includes a statement of the modular objective and a pretest that will help the reader determine whether the mastery criteria have been met or whether the activities and experiences in the module need to be completed. A posttest is provided in each module to measure achievement of the modular objectives; each module contains references and suggested readings; and a section of test answers makes the book a totally self-contained guide for teachers and students wishing to master the concept of individualizing instruction.

300 pages   *Illustrated*   *Paperback*   *1979*
ISBN 0-8391-1265-3   CIP

The most complete and detailed reference guide and how-to manual of its kind...

FACILITATING CHILDREN'S DEVELOPMENT

A Systematic Guide for Open Learning

By **John H. Meier, Ph.D.**, Director, Children's Village, U.S.A., Beaumont, California, Adjunct Associate Professor of Psychology and Education at University of California at Los Angeles, University of California at Riverside, University of Redland, and California State College, Dominguez Hills; and **Paula J. Malone, Ph.D.**, Director, Child Development Center, Alfred I. duPont Institute, and Clinical Assistant Professor of Psychiatry and Pediatrics, Temple University Medical School

---

Published as two volumes, this work provides a complete and detailed guide to a systematic program of open learning. It comprises a basic reference and how-to manual covering a complete sequence of learning episodes for infants, toddlers, and older preschool children. It is equally relevant for new students and professionals desiring to update their skills.

The open learning program presented here in plain language deals with remediation disabilities and habilitation procedures for developmentally disabled children. It is based upon a general information-processing model that can be easily adopted by a wide range of disciplines. Each episode contains detailed behavioral objectives or purposes, entry behaviors, materials lists, procedures, suggested variations, and terminal behaviors to aid in its use for an individualized education program.

Volume I covers learning episodes for infants and toddlers. Its introduction covers how to use the learning episodes effectively, suggestions for episodes during daily infant and toddler routines, guides for facilitating parent learning, evaluation of developmental progress, and principles of behavior change. The episodes are grouped into sensory/receptive episodes (hearing, seeing, touching, and sensory integration); cognitive/affective episodes (process—spatial relationships, process—object permanence, process — cause and effect, cognitive content, self-image, creativity, emotional development, role playing, and family identity); and motor/expressive/social episodes.

Volume II covers learning episodes for older preschoolers. Its introduction covers topics similar to those in Volume I, suitably modified. The section on sensory/receptive episodes covers hearing, seeing, tasting, smelling, and touching. The cognitive/affective section includes concept formation episodes involving color, geometric shapes, relative size, number relationships, problem solving, and language. The section on motor/expressive/social episodes moves from gross and fine motor to creative motor integration, expressive language, and creative language integration.

Facilitating Children's Development is an excellent text for introductory courses concerned with developmental or learning disabilities and recommended reading for child care and day care workers and others taking child care courses. It will also prove useful as collateral reading in educational psychology, special education, and early childhood education, as well as nursing and physical and occupational therapy.

Volume I—Infant and Toddler Learning Episodes
336 pages   *in large format (8½" x 11")*   Paperback
Illustrated   1978   *ISBN 0-8391-1261-0   CIP*

Volume II—Learning Episodes for Older Preschoolers
384 pages   *in large format (8½" x 11")*   Paperback
Illustrated   1978   *ISBN 0-8391-1339-0   CIP*

TEACHING THE MODERATELY
Curriculum Objectives, Strategies, and Activities

Volume I   **Behavior, Self-Care, and Motor Skills**
Volume II   **Communication, Socialization, Safety, and Leisure Time Skills**
Volume III   **Functional Academics for the *Mildly* and Moderately Handicapped**

Teaching the Moderately and Severely Handicapped is the authoritative, intensively research curriculum guide and teaching text now required for teachers, administrators, students, parents, therapists, and others who are working to provide comprehensive educational programming for the handicapped. It is the only publication that describes a complete, modern curriculum for moderately and severely handicapped students:

- **General and specific teaching objectives, strategies, and activities**
- **Complete lists of material and equipment**
- **Diagnostic checklists for pre-tests, doubling as student report cards**
- **Assistive devices and activities for non-verbal and non-ambulatory students**
- **Activities for reducing destructive and objectionable behaviors**
- **Leisure time activities for the handicapped, and other unique curricula**

The curriculum guide has been developed for teachers and teacher aides, for resource teachers and students in training, for principals and supervisors, and for the staffs of state and departments of education and local school districts. It also contains information essential for members of state departments of health and mental hygiene, occupational and physical therapists, and child development, recreational, and speech and hearing specialists responsible for planning and implementing therapeutic programs for the moderately and severely handicapped.

The guide is being published in three volumes that can be used independently or in combination to serve a broad range of individual needs. All three volumes are printed in professional workbook format with plastic spiral-comb binding for ease of use.

Volume I
Behavior, Self-Care, and Motor Skills

376 pages   Workbook format with plastic spiral-comb binding
ISBN 0-8391-0868-0   CIP   *1976*

AND SEVERELY HANDICAPPED

By **Michael Bender, Ed.D.,** Director of Special Education, The John F. Kennedy Institute for Habilitation of the Mentally and Physically Handicapped Child; and **Peter J. Valletutti, Ed.D.,** Dean of Extension and Experimental Programs and Chairman of the Department of Special Education, Coppin State College, Baltimore, and **Rosemary Bender, B.Sc.(Ed.)**

Because it covers systematically and with unprecedented thoroughness one the most demanding areas of modern educational practice, **Teaching the Moderately and Severely Handicapped** is essential for everyone in teaching or any area of public service involving the walfare or education of handicapped children, adolescents, or adults. It is particularly recommended as:

The curriculum guide for teaching moderately and severely handicapped students of all ages

Required reading as a basic textbook for undergraduate and graduate courses in educational evaluation, curriculum development for the trainable retarded, and teaching strategies for the severely and profoundly handicapped

Assigned reading for introductory courses on special education, exceptional children, and mental retardation, and for classes studying problems in curriculum development for all types and degrees of handicaps

A valuable guide for parents, foster parents, and other family members, as well as for house parents in group homes

A working reference for institution and ward personnel in residential centers, and for industrial education, physical education, and sheltered workshop teachers

An important source of materials and activities for students in nursery, preschool, Headstart, and kindergarten programs.

Volume II
Communication, Socialization, Safety, and Leisure Time Skills

420 pages   Workbook format with plastic spiral-comb binding
ISBN 0-8391-0869-9   CIP   *1976*

Volume III
Functional Academics for the *Mildly* and Moderately Handicapped

263 pages   Workbook format with plastic spiral-comb binding
ISBN 0-8391-0963-6   CIP   *1976*

A practical educational program for severely impaired and behaviorally disturbed adolescents...

A CURRICULUM MODEL FOR INDIVIDUALS WITH SEVERE LEARNING AND BEHAVIOR DISORDERS

By Linda N. Rumanoff, M.A., Master Teacher and Resource Consultant for Vocational and Residential Programs, Benhaven School/Community for Autistic and Neurologically Impaired Individuals, New Haven, Ct.

This book describes a practical, easily implemented curriculum for an effective educational program for severely impaired and behaviorally disturbed individuals. It is applicable for students within a wide range of learning disorders and differs from other curricula in its emphasis on teaching practical, useful activities in a wide variety of areas of self-care, daily living skills (such as bed making, table setting, food preparation, and vocational activities), and the related functional academics. It concentrates on achieving competence in specific skills, rather than teaching developmental or readiness skills, so as to foster appropriate work behaviors and increase the individual's level of independence.

Another key difference in this curriculum is its appropriateness to older learning-impaired individuals (ages 12 to 21 +) with severe disabilities, whose educational needs differ greatly from those of younger students. Throughout, its emphasis is on teaching skills in language, reading, numbers, and supplementary skills as they relate to useful activities.

The curriculum is based on behavioral principles and a task-analysis approach. Activities are broken into small teachable components, and each level of an activity is the prerequisite to the next. Objectives are stated in terms of the learner's behavior, and criteria for success are explicit. The particular method for achieving each objective can be adapted to the individual needs of the learner and to the learning situation or environment.

A welcome addition to the book is its outline of a methodology for teaching language to a wide range of language-impaired individuals (verbal and nonverbal) as well as the specific content to be taught. The book also includes an evaluation of the program, sample lesson plans and procedures, examples of data charts, and progress reports.

A Curriculum Model for Individuals with Severe Learning and Behavior Disorders is a highly recommended resource for educators in special education and a primary text for college and graduate courses in vocational training, atypical language development, and special education.